# GEOFFREY BOYCOTT ON CRICKET

EBURY PRESS

LONDON

*My thanks and appreciation to John Callaghan for his help and contribution in the writing of this book.*

GEOFFREY BOYCOTT

First published in Great Britain in 1999

1 3 5 7 9 10 8 6 4 2

Copyright © Partcount Ltd 1999

Ebury Press
Random House, 20 Vauxhall Bridge Road, London SW1V 2SA

Random House Australia Pty Limited
20 Alfred Street, Milsons Point, Sydney, New South Wales 2061, Australia

Random House New Zealand Limited
18 Poland Road, Glenfield, Auckland 10, New Zealand

Random House South Africa (Pty) Limited
Endulini, 5A Jubilee Road, Parktown 2193, South Africa

Random House UK Limited Reg. No. 954009

www.randomhouse.co.uk

Papers used by Ebury Press are natural, recyclable products made from wood grown in sustainable forests.

A CIP catalogue record for this book is available from the British Library.

ISBN 0 09 185376 1

Printed and bound in Great Britain

# CONTENTS

# CHAPTER ONE

# Trueman
# and Co.

T here are some things in life that I simply do not understand, one of them being the complex chemistry of human nature that shapes patterns of behaviour and relationships. I can honestly say that I have never knowingly done anything to hurt anyone, yet a number of people consistently seem to go out of their way to damage me and my reputation. One of my most persistent and vicious critics is Fred Trueman, who for reasons best known to himself began a public and private campaign against me more than twenty-five years ago.

When I forced my way into the Yorkshire side on a regular basis in 1963, Trueman stood unchallenged as the best fast bowler in the world, having just ended the England tour of New Zealand with the wonderful record of 250 wickets in 56 Tests. We were Yorkshire team-mates until his retirement at the end of the 1968 season, sharing in four championship triumphs in six years, and Trueman spearheaded the England attack when I made my Test debut against Australia at Trent Bridge in June 1964. I have always regarded him as a very great cricketer with a great deal to offer the game. I cannot recall a single incident in that successful period in which I crossed him, but he has since chosen to go out of his way to attack me at every opportunity.

He accused me of destroying Yorkshire cricket during my term as captain from 1971 to 1978, and of playing entirely for myself, but not once did he take the trouble to contact me to discuss the situation. If he cared so much about the club he claimed to love, why didn't he give me the benefit of his advice man to man in the days when, he argues, things were going badly wrong, and why did he turn his back on the young players? When I was captain I asked him on a number of occasions to help the emerging seamers – Arnie Sidebottom, Arthur Robinson, Howard Cooper, Graham Stevenson – and Trueman is happy to create the impression that a whole generation of bowlers, including Darren Gough, benefited from his coaching, but nothing could be further from the truth. He promised a lot, but delivered nothing. He turned up only at the Roses match, and then merely to do his newspaper report.

Once, as an aside, he made a comment to Steve Oldham about his action. 'When did you see me bowl, then, Fred?' Oldham retorted.

'I've seen thee enough,' responded Trueman.

'Well, it must have been from behind a tree, because we've never seen thee,' Oldham snapped back.

Even when serving on the committee, Trueman contributed very little, preferring to save his energies for anti-Boycott outbursts.

The only explanation that makes any sort of sense is that he became jealous of my popularity with the Yorkshire supporters. But to me that is stupid. Trueman's performances guarantee him a place in the history of world cricket for all time, but gradually I came to realise that he resented both my success and the way in which the public responded to it. It is hardly surprising that the rumour of a feud between us grew to the extent that it became generally regarded as a fact, although the bitterness and resentment have been totally one-sided. Up to now, I have never once publicly criticised the man or his cricketing abilities.

Undoubtedly matters were brought to a head in Yorkshire at a special general meeting in January 1984, when the committee, of which Trueman was by then an influential member, was defeated over the issue of my sacking at the end of the previous summer and instructed by an overwhelming majority of the members to reinstate me. At the same time, the administration was forced to seek re-election after failing to gain support for a vote of confidence. As the district representative for Craven, and as such a massive figure in terms of achievement on the field, Trueman no doubt expected to be swept back into office. He must have found it impossible to believe that cricket lovers in Yorkshire, and particularly in his own area, would reject him, but he suffered the humiliation of losing to Peter Fretwell, who owned a small print and design business and was completely unknown in cricket circles. Fretwell received 128 votes against 65 for Trueman, whose response to the democratic process revealed the terrible depth of his bitterness, as animosity turned into naked hatred: 'The Yorkshire members chose to vote me out of the club and replace me with someone with a deaf aid from Keighley,' he snarled. That constituted an uncalled-for personal attack on a man Trueman did not know who happened to suffer from a hearing problem. As a matter of record, I did not know Peter Fretwell either when he opposed Trueman, but he did tell me later that he acted in the belief that Yorkshire could not afford to dispense with my skill as a batsman: 'To me it was common sense to keep you as a player, and most members thought the same.'

Fred's memory seems to have soon dimmed as he never ceases to tell people that he resigned from the club 'soured by the aftermath of the Boycott war' and by a number of imaginary 'snubs, rebuffs and disappointments over the years'. What he conveniently forgets to say is that the reason he was not elected by his district members was because he told everyone publicly that when he was re-elected he still wouldn't vote for me to have another contract to play for Yorkshire – that is, he would totally disregard the wishes of the membership. He shouldn't have been surprised by their answer.

Obviously the biggest elections in Yorkshire CCC's history prompted a good deal of campaigning, some of it quite heated, and Trueman subsequently wrote: 'I and my family were inundated with dirty, filthy hate mail. The writers vilified me for daring to criticise the man from

Woolley. Most of the postmarks were from places like Rotherham, Barnsley and Wakefield. Veronica told me that she tore up the really offensive ones.' Veronica, a lovely lady, is Trueman's second wife, and in happier times I met her and found her to be charming. On reading his comments, I wrote to her, assuming that he would consign anything from me to the dustbin. In my letter I wrote:

> *I had no idea that sort of thing happened – and if I had known I don't know what I could have done to stop it. I deplore that sort of behaviour. If it was done by supposed supporters of mine in an effort to help me, then I could not condone it then or now as it never would help me in any shape or form. I am so sorry it happened. As a family, Fred said it affected you all, and that you personally had to handle some of the correspondence. I wanted you to know how I feel. With sadness and warmest regards.*

Sadly, I received no reply, so another attempt to build bridges fell on stony ground, despite my best intentions.

Trueman also persists in spreading the myth that I somehow controlled the whole club after the January elections of 1984, claiming: 'The majority of the so-called Reform Group have all apologised to me for being hoodwinked by Boycott.' That is demonstrably rubbish, and it would be interesting to see the list of names of those who allegedly said they were sorry. After Yorkshire had sacked me in 1983, a number of meetings took place at the Ossett Post House, with literally hundreds of members attending, and it would have been impossible for me as one individual to persuade so many to give up their leisure time on Sunday evenings. I did not take any part in these meetings because I wanted to stay clear of the politics, although obviously I recognised my good fortune in having a lot of decent people on my side. Unfortunately, the ex-players lined up against me, with Trueman at their head, acting as spokesman for the official viewpoint. This was a shrewd move on the part of the committee, for Trueman's opinions counted for something and could not easily be dismissed. But those in charge underestimated the members, who actually constitute the club, patronising them by indicating that the committee knew best. In my case, the ordinary man in the street decided they were wrong.

From the moment the result of the ballot was announced at the annual meeting in Harrogate on Saturday, 21 January 1984, Trueman turned his back on Yorkshire, proclaiming: 'I'll never have anything to do with them so long as that so and so from Woolley is there.' (It is interesting to note that he continued to stay away after 1993, when I lost out to Huddersfield's Bob Platt in the committee election for the West district.) After the decision at Harrogate, Trueman also flatly refused to speak to me. Even when publicising a book about the Yorkshire Dales as recently as December 1998, he said: 'I never bothered with Boycott for years. I'll say hello if I see him, but finding anyone who's got a good word for him will be difficult.' That was another convenient lapse of memory, as I shall explain.

A remarkable change in his attitude occurred at Headingley in August 1994 during the second Test between England and South Africa. Trueman's loathing of me was so well-known that his fellow commentators on *Test Match Special* had slipped into the habit of dropping my name into the exchanges now and again to get him going, and he usually rose to the bait, pouring forth the invective in such a torrent that at times he became nearly incoherent. It came as a huge surprise, therefore, when he approached me as I sat in the Yorkshire president's lounge sipping a cup of coffee before doing the first-day pitch report for television. 'Just the man I want to see,' he said. As I reeled from the shock, he continued: 'Let's shake hands. I'll never forgive thee, but let's put the past behind us.' Although I found it impossible to work out what there might be to forgive, for I had done nothing to him, I shook his hand and told him: 'Look, the situation was not of my making. I have always been ready to shake your hand.' Trueman then got down to business, and in a fleeting second, all became clear. 'Now what about these lunches?' he asked, adding, 'We could make thirty or forty grand each. Let's get in touch with Mike Newlin and get cracking.'

Mike Newlin is the head of MBN Promotions, a company which runs luncheons at around twenty-five venues throughout the country, and he had previously contacted me with the aim of getting me to speak at some for him. I understand that Trueman still does a fair bit of public speaking and is very good, but he is not paid as much as I am, nor was he then, and I realised at Headingley that he knew I operated on a fifty-fifty basis. Having shared the 'bill' with Michael Parkinson and others, I reckon that this is the fair way to go about it. Trueman had clearly raised the possibility with Mike Newlin, who had, in turn, approached me.

I was very doubtful. How could I speak at any function alongside a man who detested me and could not bear to hear my name mentioned? With this in mind, I realised that Trueman's motives were not straightforward and that his intention was to bury the hatchet in a substantial pile of money. All he could see were the pound signs. In the circumstances, I backed away from the project. I had no intention of sacrificing my principles for money, although Mike Newlin continued to act as liaison man, and as recently as July 1997 faxed me to say: 'FS has suggested we have lunch at home with him in Flasby next week. We have to get together if the Boycott–Trueman lunches are to go ahead. Freddie was very sincere in wanting us all to have lunch together and make a decision.' Mike clearly appreciated the commercial value of such a partnership, but I remained sceptical.

In 1994 Trueman had another matter to raise with me, and he made his second approach at the back of the Leeds rugby stand as we met on the way to our respective radio and television commentary points. He opened the discussion by attacking the committee. 'This lot are useless,' he said. 'We should get together and take over the club.' Such an outrageous proposal took my breath away, but I tried to placate him. After all, we had just shaken hands the day before and I didn't want to start another row. I'll meet anyone halfway, so I told him: 'Go and see the president [Sir Lawrence Byford], and if you have anything to put forward I'll help where I can.' Sir Lawrence has always been absolutely straight with me and I thought that this was the best way to proceed. I trust the president and the chief executive, Chris Hassell, far more than I did the members of the old committee, and I still enjoy a very good relationship with them both. But while ready to help, I did not want to interfere.

The next act in the drama involved Ted Corbett, a freelance journalist who 'ghosted' Trueman's column in the *People* newspaper. He came up to me on the Saturday morning, just as I was going on air, to ask: 'Are you doing this with Fred?' 'Doing what?' I queried, not knowing what he was talking about and not wanting to be held up. Corbett, despite stressing the need for urgency, agreed to come back later in the morning after my first stint of commentary. When we met again at 11.30 he did not waste any time, saying: 'You are taking over Yorkshire, you and FS.' In the face of my stunned silence, it did not take long for him to fill in the details, leaving me open-mouthed. Corbett revealed that Trueman had told the *People* office that he and I had agreed to take control of the club; the newspaper was allocating the whole of the back page and a spread inside to the story. Everything was ready for publication, the only thing missing a few quotes from me. Echoing the famous words of tennis ace John McEnroe, I said: 'You cannot be serious.' Corbett refused to believe my vehement denials for some considerable time. Finally, he accepted the inevitable. 'The office,' he complained, 'will be livid. It's all set up for a huge exclusive and now FS has done it again. It's kite flying.'

It was all a product of Fred's imagination and desire to make money. Whatever anyone might say, I am known for telling the truth – often, it seems, to my own detriment – so I hurried to see Hassell and the president to put the record straight as I could not be sure how much, if anything, of this silly business had leaked out. To my great relief, Sir Lawrence expressed no concern. 'Don't worry,' he insisted. 'I know where you are coming from and that Trueman is causing trouble.' His forthright attitude impressed me and I wish Sir Lawrence had been president in my time as a player, because I do not think I would have had any problems. He would have been strong enough to stand up to the ex-players who resented my position and would have sorted out the difficulties which arose from weak management. Having seen him in action, I recognise that if he had thought I was in the wrong he would have taken me to one side for a word of friendly advice or a stern lecture, and, because of my respect for him, I would have listened. It is not hard to co-operate with an individual who is absolutely straight, even if you don't always like what he says.

Predictably, Trueman reverted to type. On turning down the luncheon circuit offer, I found myself reinstated as public enemy number one in his eyes. Behind the scenes, one or two of Trueman's old cronies pushed him forward to stand for president in 1997, when Sir Lawrence indicated he might retire because of illness. That horrendous prospect inspired a group of committee men to persuade Sir Lawrence to stay on, although he handed over the chairmanship to Keith Moss.

Theories abound to account for Yorkshire's decline, which accelerated through the 1970s and continued for more than thirty years. A group of outstanding players departed as the last team to record a hat-trick of championships broke up – Raymond Illingworth, Ken Taylor and Trueman in 1968, Jimmy Binks in 1969, Brian Close in 1970 and Doug Padgett in 1971 – but a lack of harmony within the club proved equally destructive, and while Trueman sowed the seeds of discord in a wide area of social contact, Richard Hutton, a senior player at Yorkshire, flourished as a disruptive element inside the dressing room.

It was in his nature to be humorous, but his humour always came at someone else's expense and he adopted a supercilious attitude towards the rest of the players, talking down to them. He bristled, however, when an irrepressible character like David Bairstow faced up to him. Hutton adopted the practice of calling people by their surname, which might have been acceptable in the public school environment, but which rankled among the others in the side. 'I say, Bairstow,' he would shout across the dressing room as the prelude to a supposedly smart remark. To his credit, David invariably replied in kind. 'Yes, Hutton?' he would answer in a loud voice, indicating his intention to give as good as he got.

I must admit that I never managed even an uneasy truce with Hutton, who gained pleasure from being awkward and uncooperative when I became captain, using my regular absences on England duty to confuse the younger players. Neither Hutton nor Trueman appreciated that in chipping away at me they also damaged the fabric of Yorkshire cricket. I can only guess at Hutton's motivation, but I am convinced that his background shaped his thinking. Being the son of Sir Leonard Hutton, one of the greatest batsmen of all time, enabled him to live a charmed life. His name opened important doors and opportunity came to him quickly and easily. When he arrived at Yorkshire, committee men who were his father's age and had either played with Leonard or watched him from a respectful distance, actually fawned over Hutton junior and paid him homage on the strength of his father's great deeds.

Richard Hutton, however, reached the county side with a limited playing pedigree and failed to come even close to adding lustre to the family's reputation. He was an ordinary county cricketer – a decent seam bowler, a useful middle-order batsman and a reliable catcher, nothing more. He simply could not live up to the unrealistic expectations of so many of Leonard's admirers. He could take wickets and do a good job on uncovered pitches, but, as he trundled along at no more than medium pace, good batsmen regarded him as cannon fodder on flat tracks. When able to get on the front foot in favourable conditions, he made a few runs, but the better bowlers soon worked him out and forced him to play back. Comparisons with his father must have been particularly irksome to Richard, gnawing away at his well-developed self-esteem. Leonard dominated the stage throughout his career, featuring in 79 Tests to score 6,971 runs for an average of 56.67. Richard, in picking up five England caps, accumulated 219 runs for an average of 36.50, although he captured nine wickets at 28.55 against his father's three at 77.33. Similarly, for Yorkshire Leonard made 24,807 runs (53.34) and took 154 wickets (27.40) against Richard's 4,986 runs (20.18) and 468 wickets (21.19).

I suspect that this comparative lack of success haunted Richard Hutton to the extent that in his heart of hearts he became obsessed with doing something that his father had never managed. The solution to his inner turmoil took the shape of the Yorkshire captaincy, even though it represented half an answer as Leonard had played in the days when amateurs held sway and no professional could expect to lead Yorkshire. Indeed, Leonard played alongside one of the few top-class cricketers among the county's amateurs, Norman Yardley, the two men retiring in the same year, 1955. Richard Hutton made his Yorkshire debut in 1962 under Vic Wilson, the first professional captain of Yorkshire in modern times. Brian Close replaced Wilson in 1963, but his appointment did not receive approval among a minority who yearned to revive an amateur tradition stretching back to the 1880s and Lord Hawke. Wilson's promotion owed everything to the absence of a suitable amateur alternative with acceptable credentials, as a player and as a tactically sound leader. Subsequently, to some, Richard Hutton appeared as the answer to a prayer, for not only did he possess a very famous name, he had also attended Repton and Cambridge, where he earned a cricket blue. Socially and as a cricketer he had the right qualifications.

The championship triumphs in the 1960s ensured that no challenge to Close emerged, but the minute Yorkshire's fortunes suffered a reverse the move for a change gathered momentum, and the only man standing in Hutton's way was me. My very position as the leading batsman of the day clearly irritated him, the more so as I did not accord him any preferential treatment. Indeed, his sarcastic manner left me feeling nothing but contempt. Overall, he set a very poor example to his less sophisticated team-mates who were not sure whether to follow his lead or go their own way.

Hutton showed himself up badly with a display of open hostility at Harrogate in 1971, when I became the first English batsman to average more than a hundred per innings in a season. Northants were dismissed for 61 in their first innings of that final match of the season at St

George's Road. I contributed 124 not out to a reply which reached 266 for 2 before the declaration. As those familiar with the compact Harrogate ground know, the dressing room windows open out on to the members' seating area, and Hutton amused himself throughout the Yorkshire innings by loudly advising me to hit out and by encouraging Northants to remove me. After the game he refused to take part in the celebration of Yorkshire's much-needed victory by an innings, drinking my champagne in sullen silence, beside himself with anger and frustration.

For all his disloyalty to me and, by extension, to Yorkshire, Hutton remained popular with the ex-players, and by 1973 Ronnie Burnet and Trueman were clamouring for him to be made captain. The value of their opinions, though, can be gauged by the fact that a year later, as I survived a captaincy crisis by one vote, Yorkshire sacked Hutton on the recommendation of the cricket sub-committee. He put this turn of events down to me, complaining that I had stabbed him in the back, but I could not have got rid of him even if I had tried. As the narrow captaincy vote demonstrated, I held no sway over the committee; I only hung on by my fingertips myself. Like Trueman, Hutton refuses to speak to me, or, at best, mumbles to himself as he turns away, and to my certain knowledge he has upset private dinner parties by causing a scene at the slightest mention of my name. For all the poison he puts out about me, privately and publicly, I would love to ask him: 'What did I actually do to you?'

They say that power corrupts, and in later years Hutton used his position as editor of the *Cricketer* magazine to attack me, dragging into an editorial column details of the French court case brought against me as the result of an incident with a woman called Margaret Moore. His comments had nothing to do with cricket and his opinions could hardly have concerned his readers, but he could not resist twisting the knife. Hutton also cruelly scarred the memory of David Bairstow, whose suicide in January 1998 left me shattered, writing that the former Yorkshire wicketkeeper died with a pile of debts at his door. This wicked rubbish upset David's widow, Janet, when she was at her most vulnerable. Hutton's version of events was not true, but experience has taught me that it is very difficult to undo the damage caused by wild and inaccurate reporting, and it was virtually impossible for Janet to correct the awful impression created by the article. Eventually, Hutton went too far. He was dismissed from his position as editor by his father-in-law Ben Brocklehurst, the magazine's chairman and former Somerset captain, in the wake of a tasteless comment at the expense of the blind Secretary of State for Education, David Blunkett. In challenging a perceived threat to college cricket, Hutton used the phrase 'Blind Man's Blunkett', illustrating the depths to which he is prepared to sink in order to score a point.

In this instance, he created a family rift between his wife, Charmaine, and her father. I like Charmaine immensely, having been friendly with her since Ray Illingworth's 1970–71 tour to Australia, during which she acted as personal assistant to manager David Clark. Unfortunately, we were unable to maintain any sort of friendly contact because of Richard's antagonism, but I hope that eventually the split between Charmaine and her father is healed.

My association with both Trueman and Hutton has always been strained, but at least I know where I stand with them. My relationship with popular radio and television pundit Henry Blofeld is a different case altogether. When the default judgement against me in the Margaret Moore case came out on 20 January 1998, Henry left a message on my answerphone, expressing his concern and wishing me well. He added that he looked forward to seeing me in the West Indies, where England were touring that winter, and the tone of the recording confirmed the friendship I thought existed between us. Although he obviously knew I had been found guilty of assault in my absence, he gave no indication of any misgivings about me as a person, sounding, on the contrary, very supportive. Others were less generous. A few radio and television companies refused to employ me, but I went to the West Indies to cover the Test series for the *Sun*, who were at that time still standing by me and, briefly, their word.

Part of the case against me rested on Ms Moore's insistence in court that I was known in England for violence, so my French lawyer asked me to get a series of sworn statements with which to challenge this assertion. I was not asking for a character reference, as some of the media wrongly printed in the press, and I wasn't looking for people to say I was a good batsman or a good commentator. I had secured from New Scotland Yard, under the Data Protection Act, written evidence that no information about me was held by any police force, and all I wanted in addition was for people to say how long they had known me and whether they believed me to be honest or whether they thought me violent.

I outlined my position to a variety of friends and acquaintances, covering a cross-section of players and social contacts, and during the mid-March Barbados Test I invited Henry to join the list of those prepared to give me an affidavit. He agreed without hesitation, but explained that he would have to do it later as he was hurrying to fulfil his broadcasting commitments. A number of other press personalities complied with my request and twice, without prompting, Henry repeated, as he rushed backwards and forwards about the ground, that he wanted to help and had not forgotten his promise to make a statement. I certainly did not put him under any pressure at any stage as, in the final analysis, the decision to testify on my behalf was up to him.

We got to Antigua for the fifth Test starting on 20 March and, guarding against the possibility that Henry might be going home after the Test finished, I broached the matter again when we bumped into each other behind the press box. His furious response rocked me back on my heels. He tore into me with a volley of verbal abuse which I could not have anticipated even from Trueman or Hutton. 'I will not do a statement for you,' he shouted. 'My brother says I must not do it and I will not. You are so rude!' This from the man who a week or so earlier in Barbados had assured me three times of his willingness to act on my behalf, and who, back in January, had telephoned to boost my morale following the original guilty verdict in France.

Henry also appeared to have forgotten that when he was unemployed, having fallen out with Sky television, BBC radio, TWI and World Tel, I kept in touch and did my best to advertise his availability and expertise as a broadcaster. He had worked for BBC radio a number of years ago before moving on to Sky when David Hill offered him a two-year deal for a lot more money in 1991 and 1992. The merger between BSB and Sky resulted in Henry and I teaming up to top and tail the Test match highlights with a kind of 'Mad Hatter's tea party' which provided something different – informed yet entertaining off-the-cuff comment. Much to Henry's disappointment, Sky declined to extend his contract, so he found himself out of work before TWI rescued him with some exposure overseas, but that association did not last long. Around this time he lost a lot of money in the Lloyd's insurance disaster, so he was pretty desperate when World Tel took him on, giving a guarantee of employment which enabled him to pay off some of his debts. A dispute over money ended his links with World Tel, but I did my best to help him, speaking to Peter Baxter at BBC radio many times, hoping that others were doing the same. I felt that radio was his forte and kept plugging away, admittedly along with other friends of his, and we continued to meet socially without any mention of my apparent shortcomings.

I have outlined this to illustrate the nature of our relationship and to make the point that I had no reason to suspect any lurking resentment on Henry's part. More in sorrow than in anger, I wrote to him after his Antigua outburst:

*A true friend would have privately pointed out my failings at the time and not berated me at my most vulnerable period without fully hearing my request. I did not require a character reference regarding what an upstanding person I am. My manners, morals, batting ability or professional skills as a commentator are of no interest to*

*the French court. I simply required people who knew me or worked*
*with me to state whether they knew me to be honest and not a*
*physically violent man. Nothing more. I do have faults, I accept that,*
*and it was your right to decline. A simple no would have been*
*sufficient rather than the blast I received without hearing me out or*
*letting me explain.*

I have never received a reply.

As he sought to advertise a book published later in 1998, Henry, with
whom I had spent a lot of time in Pakistan the previous year, wrote of
me: 'He was going around almost cajoling everyone to write letters
saying he was not a violent person. He came up to me in Antigua, and I
said, "I'm sorry, I can't do it. You were so violent with your tongue to
those poor Pakistani waiters that I really can't do this. I think there's a
narrow line between verbal and physical violence."' I wonder what
Henry would think if I told him there is also a fine line between the
eccentric and the buffoon, between the character and the caricature.

In adopting such a trenchant line, Henry claims 'It is time to put the
record straight.' Well, when you get into trouble you discover who your
friends are, and his timing is amazing. The only part of his book which
attracted any serious newspaper attention involved the attack on me.
How convenient.

More hurtful than all the insults was the fact that Henry bragged
about his tirade against me in the press box, as Viv Richards later told
me. And the great West Indian run-maker's entry into this sorry tale
spotlighted the lengths to which some people were prepared to go to
undermine my credibility. On 5 April 1998, under the headline
BOYCOTT'S COURT OUT, David Norrie wrote in the *News of the World*:
'Mike Atherton has sensationally snubbed Geoff Boycott's desperate bid
to overturn a French court conviction for attacking his former girlfriend.
Boycott has spent the past month of England's West Indies tour
collecting evidence to support his claim that he is not a violent person,
and Athers is not alone. West Indies legend Viv Richards and

commentator Henry Blofeld both refused to sign during the final Test in Antigua.' Well, one out of three might add up to a good average for Norrie.

I spent a few weeks on holiday in the Leeward Islands over Easter that year with Richard Knaggs, a solicitor friend, and bumped into Richards on the flight home. Norrie's highly imaginative article had been drawn to my attention and I showed a copy to Viv. He assured me that he had not spoken to Norrie, who had misrepresented him on previous occasions. During a couple of brief meetings in the West Indies, Viv and I had talked about what he was doing and never mentioned the court case. Nor had I asked Atherton; my only approach to him was in relation to the signing of some miniature bats. No one can front up to me and say I asked Atherton to make a statement on my behalf, naming the time and place. It did not happen, nor did I make a request to Richards. Too many people invent half-truths or embellish snippets of half-understood information.

Henry Blofeld went even further by recounting a fanciful tale to a reporter from the *Daily Mail*. He alleged that, as a guest of Javed Zaman, Imran Khan's cousin, in Pakistan, I abused our host and a driver sent to collect us. I then 'became involved in an argument with a member of the Pakistan board' and resorted to extremely bad language, causing a terrible scene. Like Norrie, Henry got very little right.

Javed Zaman is a friend of mine. I first met him when I went on Mike Brearley's 1977–78 tour to Pakistan. It was Christmas time, but I was eager to practise. Javed Zaman, who was captain of a side that had a fixture on Christmas Eve, invited me to play. Initially, I reluctantly declined because I had to attend the England squad's celebrations, but Zaman insisted that his team could bat first and I would not be expected to field. A lot of people wanted to see me bat, he said, and I must admit that I felt as though all my Christmases had come at once. I got a hundred, had a cup of tea with them and went back to the hotel, so everyone was happy. I actually played for Zaman twice over that Christmas holiday and got a century each time. He was delighted, and presented me with copies of the scorecards, which I still have in my boxes of memorabilia.

On the evening in 1997 to which Henry referred, I did visit Zaman's home, but nothing untoward happened between us and we remain good friends. I admit I lost my patience with one guest, but only under extreme provocation. He was talking about ball tampering, which is a touchy subject in Pakistan, and mention was made of Atherton having had dirt in his pocket when he fiddled with the ball in 1994. In the course of this conversation, the Pakistani gentleman condemned, without exception, all English cricketers as cheats. I refused to let such a slander pass unchallenged and the exchanges developed along heated lines. Perhaps I did express myself too strongly, but it obviously suited Henry's purpose not to want to hear the full story, as how otherwise would he have been able to justify his turnabout attitude and his deliberate attempt at mischief-making in his book? I was one of the few leading figures to stand up for the Pakistanis throughout the ball-tampering controversies, and I certainly don't regret standing my corner for all honest English sportsmen.

I nurse no grudge against Henry, but rather feel an overwhelming sadness at the death of a friendship. Until recently, Henry used to refer to me as the 'greatest living Yorkshireman' with a touch of warmth and humour. Now, with his eyes on the pound-note signs with regard to his book sales and newspaper serialisation, it seems to have been more profitable to use the saying sarcastically. As a friend he seems to have been only too eager to latch on to me in his hour of need, but when I was in trouble, instead of helping me he appears to have relished exploiting my vulnerability. He has never accused me before of being rude, and if he didn't regard my behaviour as being appropriate on the many occasions we dined together, why didn't he just say so?

Life is too short to waste time in petty squabbles, and I wish those people who use up so much energy lashing out at me would simply meet me to sort out their differences man to man. It is ironic that it took an elderly lady who is a complete stranger to sum me up. She wrote a touching letter of support after the French court case, saying: 'You rely on verbal forthrightness and frankness as a substitute for physical aggression.' I thought she got it in one. Perhaps I should have sent that on to Henry.

# CHAPTER TWO

# Close
# Encounters

There is a saying in Yorkshire that a person cannot do right for doing wrong, which basically means that sometimes, with the best of intentions, an individual innocently takes a course of action which leads to trouble. In my case, forces outside my control in July 1996 propelled me reluctantly into the centre of the legal dispute between Imran Khan, on one side, and Ian Botham and Allan Lamb on the other. Botham and Lamb were suing Imran in the High Court in London over what they saw as an 'offensive personal attack' on them in the *India Today* magazine. Alleged ball tampering by the Pakistan team stood at the core of the argument, with Botham and Lamb claiming that Imran had labelled them 'racist, uneducated and lacking in class and upbringing', a claim they failed, in the end, to make stick.

From the start, I was concerned at the possibility of being called as a witness, not because I had any fears about standing up to say what I believed, but entirely because I knew that whichever side used me to support their case the other would claim that I had let them down. It was such a high-profile event, attracting vast media coverage and involving substantial sums of money, that there could be no halfway house for me. Whatever I said I could see myself being cast at exactly the same time as hero and villain by the two parties. Imran and his solicitor contacted me because they recalled my appearance on a Channel 4 television programme called *Devil's Advocate*. In fact Imran featured as the main figure in that show, having just published a book in which mention had been made of the use of bottle tops to alter the condition of the ball. As an invited member of the audience, I was asked for my views, and I emphasised that there were degrees of offence:

*Look, it's like driving a car. The speed limit is seventy miles an hour, but is anyone telling me that we all don't do that little bit more, seventy-five, eighty, eighty-five? People do exceed the limit while keeping an eye out for a police car. We are not talking about doing eighty in a thirty-mile zone and knocking down pedestrians. Strictly as motorists, most of us break the law marginally, but that does not make us criminals alongside bank robbers and murderers. Similarly, in cricket most players have picked the seam on the ball or scuffed the surface on one side. I have done it in the nets to trick a colleague. I have never used a bottle top or any artificial substance, but bowlers do try to swing the advantage their way a little.*

Michael Atherton said much the same in another context, and so did the England coach, David Lloyd.

Imran wanted me in court, but I tried to keep out of the dispute because I did not understand all the background to the case. One day, however, the intercom on my drive gates buzzed. When I answered all I could hear was a voice saying 'Hello, hello'. I thought autograph hunters were trying to get in and I went to investigate. I discovered a small man outside. He hesitantly asked: 'Are you Geoffrey Boycott?' I replied: 'Yes.' He persisted: '*The* Geoffrey Boycott?' I wondered for a second if the *Candid Camera* people were waiting to pounce. 'Yes,' I confirmed, and he handed me a subpoena. I had to go to court. In giving my evidence and referring to ball tampering, I repeated the honest opinion I had given on *Devil's Advocate*, adding: 'You could say there is a controversy because those that won't accept that ball tampering has gone on in whatever form keep trying to pretend that it doesn't go on, and it's gone on for as long as I can remember. It's done privately, surreptitiously.' I regarded my evidence as providing information for the court about what actually happened in my experience in first-class cricket.

I was very annoyed at the time by the comments of Brian Close, who had given evidence earlier. After being shown a video of the television programme, Close had been asked by George Carman QC, counsel for Imran, if I was a friend of his. He had replied: 'He was a colleague in the same team. I don't agree with him. I know it's been done but certainly not in teams I have led.' In cross-examination, Close clearly implied that I had lied on television, an accusation which made front-page headlines. The significant exchange was as follows:

Carman (referring to me): 'You would say he is an honest man, wouldn't you?'

Close: 'I wouldn't like to answer that.'

Carman: 'Were you surprised by what Mr Boycott was saying?'

Close: 'Knowing his personality, I am not surprised. He was full of bravado, making assumptions that were wrong.'

Without doubt, it was Close in the wrong. I made no assumptions on the television programme, but merely said what I knew to be the case from first-hand experience. Close also told the court: 'I was brought up to play the game properly, where the game came first, the team second and the individual last. We would never abuse the moral code of conduct that the game had' – a convenient attack of selective amnesia that allowed Close to forget the instructions he had once handed out as a captain to his batsmen, demanding that we use boots with big spikes to rough up the surface of the pitch. He would instruct us to go down the pitch frequently to prod the surface, then to turn heavily on the heel of the foot to damage the pitch. When I had asked him what we should do if we did not want to pat down the playing surface, he merely told me to obey his orders. I had brought a cricket boot with me, intending to use it to bring this practice to the attention of the court, but the technicalities of legal procedure silenced me.

All I wanted to do was put the record straight. I had no argument with Close for sticking up for Botham, with whom he enjoyed a friendly relationship, but his attack on my honesty and selectivity with the truth really angered me, although it appeared that the court believed my evidence and Imran won the case. Botham reacted childishly and exactly as I feared he would if he lost. Although happy to shake my hand publicly before the verdict, he has refused to speak to me since that day, even turning his head away from a polite 'Good morning' when our paths have crossed at cricket matches; and I am saddened by his reaction to the outcome.

I find it difficult to understand Close, who played an important part in my development. Our working relationship could have blossomed into a mutual understanding, if not warm friendship, but things changed after he retired from first-class cricket and returned to Yorkshire as a committee man. In many ways Close is the ideal Yorkshire cricketer: talented, tough, knowledgeable and ready to stand his corner. Powerfully built and impervious to pain, Close has always been larger than life, blessed with a physique and ball sense which allowed him to accomplish with almost casual indifference feats far beyond the powers of his contemporaries. However, since becoming the youngest player to appear for England in a Test match at the age of 18 years and 149 days against New Zealand at Old Trafford in 1949, he has tended to live in a fantasy world, accepting no sensible restraints.

He used to boast endlessly that he would welcome a fight with Muhammad Ali, or Cassius Clay as he then was, claiming he could survive any punches from the great heavyweight boxing champion. 'He can dance about all he likes, but he can't hurt me, and if I hit him once it would be all over,' he would insist, to much amusement from the assembled audience. Although a useful boxer in the Army, Close didn't realise that people were laughing at him rather than with him. Once, when staying at Worcester, he swam across the River Diglis late at night just to prove that he could do it, while on another occasion left-arm seamer Mike Cowan conned him into a race around the hotel lawn.

Close, straining every muscle and sinew, won comfortably, because Cowan pulled up after a few yards to enjoy the spectacle.

The driving force for Brian appeared to be his constant need to prove himself better than the next man. When Yorkshire struggled, it was always someone else's fault. When we did well, he put it down to his superb captaincy. He insisted that as a team we were nothing without him, and from time to time he would lose his temper. I found myself on the receiving end at Swansea in 1965 when, on a turning pitch, Yorkshire dropped a succession of catches to let Glamorgan off the hook. Unfortunately my dropped catch had been off his bowling. Close himself spilled three of them, a fact I foolishly pointed out when he launched into me during the luncheon interval, making a huge song and dance about my one error. White with rage, Close lifted my trembling body clear off the ground with one hand and drew back a clenched fist. I closed my eyes. Only the intervention of Trueman and Ray Illingworth saved me from injury, and I often wonder just how he would have justified his extreme man-management technique had I been carried off to hospital. Still, in those days you got what you saw, and Brian was invariably up-front in the dressing room, speaking his mind without fear or favour.

In fact, in terms of method of leadership, Ray Illingworth resembled Close in many respects, although perhaps not with such an underlying threat of violence. Drawing from my experience of his term in sole charge of the management side of things at Yorkshire, which lasted five years from 1979 to 1983, Illingworth's interest was purely in operating as a dictator, brooking no interference from anyone. Unfortunately for him, he found it impossible to pull all the strings on the field – as he was wont to do during his playing days – from his seat in the pavilion, and frustration set in as he watched inferior minds at work.

This led Illingworth and Yorkshire down the road to confusion as the political side of his nature came to the fore. It became his habit, often off the record, to blame his captain when things went wrong, claiming that his instructions were being ignored or misunderstood. At best, players were damned with faint praise, while Illingworth claimed full credit for what little success Yorkshire achieved. As with Close, victory reflected his shrewd thinking, defeat merely underlined the errors of others. In that way Illingworth covered himself, but stories relating to his activities drifted back to players in the dressing room, turning Yorkshire cricket into a hotbed of gossip. Morale plummeted as rumour added to a general air of suspicion. By seeking to insulate himself from poor results, Illingworth lost the trust of the players he disparaged.

Almost as an act of deliberate defiance in the face of growing internal hostility, he further alienated his senior squad in 1981 by heavily favouring Neil Hartley, a very moderate all-rounder, for the captaincy. He handed Hartley the distinction of becoming the first uncapped professional to captain the county, albeit on a match-by-match basis, and went further by capping him in the same year in which Hartley managed a mere 654 first-class runs for an average of 25.15 and captured nine wickets at 53.22. These figures indicate that Illingworth's decision did not make much sense from a cricket point of view, while the fact that Hartley was mixing socially with the manager's eldest daughter did not escape the players' notice. It caused massive resentment, and any remaining shreds of credibility disappeared.

In no way, again like Close, did Illingworth's man-management survive close scrutiny, and he once almost came to blows with all-rounder Arnie Sidebottom at Nottingham, where Yorkshire lost a typically hectic Sunday League scramble in the rain. Illingworth claimed that Sidebottom had let down the side and, more seriously, implied that he had not tried. That was the last criticism that could be levelled against a player who had learned the disciplines of professional sport at Old Trafford, where he spent some time on the Manchester United books. Whatever else, Arnie never gave less than one hundred per cent, and only the intervention of Alan Ramage and David Bairstow saved Illingworth from a punch in the mouth.

Illingworth's one triumph – leading Yorkshire to the Sunday League title in 1983 – stemmed entirely from his return to active service. This came after the demotion of a stressed-out Chris Old in 1982, allowing Illingworth to do what he did best. At fifty he struggled physically, batting at number eleven, hiding a bit in the field and bowling occasionally to save fingers that had become a touch arthritic, but his skilful manipulation of events emphasised the point that he needed to be out in the middle to be effective. His reappearance transformed Yorkshire as he got people in the right positions and organised his bowling to the best advantage. As part of his overall plan, Illingworth used me as both a batsman and a key bowler in the Sunday League, and I enjoyed myself tremendously. But having turned things around and raised the profile of Yorkshire cricket, he proceeded to sweep away the foundations by plunging the county into another crisis. Winning the Sunday League went to his head, and he persuaded a sufficient number of those on the committee to sack me. Believing himself unassailable, he grasped the opportunity to remove the only man in the club with an equal, if not bigger, standing.

Although our careers were so closely intertwined and, as products of the same hard school, we related closely on cricket matters, I never felt we were close. Raymond never once lowered his guard. He wrapped himself in a protective cloak of wariness and looked after number one, telling you just as much as he thought you needed to know. He never lied, but he kept his cards very close to his chest until he discovered how all the hands had been dealt. He saw Yorkshire's moment of triumph as too good a chance to miss, for with me gone he could rule Yorkshire cricket as autocratically as Lord Hawke had done from 1883 until his death in 1938. He reasoned that, on the back of his playing record, he could talk down any opposition within the committee, but he misread the feelings of the Yorkshire members, failing to realise that many of them, like many of the players, did not trust him. Democracy prevailed, I stayed, and the new committee, elected after the revolution of 1984, dispensed with his services.

It is uncanny how similar Close's post-1984 story is. The transformation in Close once he joined the Yorkshire committee in 1984 brought the two of us into increasing conflict, although, as with Fred Trueman, none of the rows was of my seeking. During his election campaign in the Bradford district, Close said: 'I think the slate should be wiped clean so far as Boycott is concerned. So long as he does what captain David Bairstow and manager Ray Illingworth require, I see no reason why he should not be given a contract for this year and next.' Close remembered Illingworth as his right-hand man in his captaincy days and he felt sure he could handle him and me, so he was furious when the general committee dispensed with Illingworth's services. He put this down to another plot by the Reform Group, labelling them as little men of no real significance and blaming me for their decision. The possibility that committee men were expressing their own view never occurred to him. The illusion that the administration would unfailingly follow his lead on cricket matters was shattered, his dreams of becoming a benevolent dictator in ruins.

Within a few days of 'wiping the slate clean', Close pocketed a substantial fee from the *Sun* for an exclusive and personal attack on 'Boycott, the one-man disaster'. All his bitterness flooded out:

*The time has come to stop Geoff Boycott's fan club from taking over Yorkshire cricket. Boycottshire – all the little nobodies on the so-called Reform Group – have had their rebellion. Now they must be stopped in their tracks. They have won the day on their demand to recall Boycott to a team he has selfishly torn apart over the years. For years Boycott has been the ruination of Yorkshire on the field. We won't get things right until he is off the scene.*

So much for a new start and further contracts!

In that same article, however, I think he inadvertently went some way towards explaining his antagonism towards me, admitting: 'In 1970 I had better reason than Boycott to be bitter about being sacked. I had a team record to be proud of. But I accepted it – and all the mud slinging that went with it – because I accepted the committee's authority.' To be accurate, an Action Group had challenged his dismissal and cricket chairman Brian Sellers had stood down as part of a peace formula, but Close had also had an attractive offer from Somerset up his sleeve. He could afford to shrug his shoulders and journey to the West Country, leaving me the already uneasy inheritance of captain. I am convinced that he subsequently became jealous of the much greater support given to me in 1983 and 1984, believing that in some way it belittled him. If that was the case, then he failed to appreciate that my position was obviously very different as I did not want to go to another county, and in addition the committee had awarded me a testimonial in 1984. This mystified the man in the street, who sensed the double standards and worked out for himself that I would have had great difficulty organising fundraising events from outside the team. I certainly could not have a testimonial in Yorkshire while playing elsewhere, so the county was effectively ending my career.

Next, Close turned his attentions to the contentious business of the dual role I held as player and committee representative for Wakefield. Probably unaware that such a distinguished figure as Lord Hawke had once held office and played for Yorkshire at the same time, he made great play of the unease caused in the dressing room by my presence, at the same time clearly resenting my attendance at committee meetings, imagining that, like a puppet master, I pulled the strings of colleagues. This was ludicrous, and by mid-June he had gone some way towards reality by accepting that 'the lads are not afraid of Boycott any more'. Close and Bob Appleyard tried hard to persuade me to resign from the general committee, asking me to put my trust in the cricket chairman and conveniently ignore all Close's apparent backstabbing. It didn't add up to a worthwhile proposition.

Brian Close's record of failure hardly inspired confidence, either. His cricket career fell short of expectations and a series of bankruptcies and other commercial disasters left him living off hard-luck stories. Finally, the Yorkshire members saw through him and voted him off the committee in 1998, re-electing Tony Vann. The county will not miss

Close. He was a brave and good leader of a very strong team, but his judgement in other areas consistently let him down. He needed Yorkshire far more than the county needed him. A seat on the committee raised his profile and added some authority to his opinions, which would otherwise have been ignored, and it also made him feel important, but I can see little he did while in office that benefited the club. Hidden agendas governed every one of his actions. While announcing my sacking in 1986, Close tried to justify the decision by saying: 'Boycott is standing in the way of a host of good young batsmen and we must give them a chance.' In the ensuing years Yorkshire signed five overseas players – Sachin Tendulkar, Richie Richardson, Michael Bevan, Darren Lehmann and Greg Blewett – all of them batsmen, and added Richard Harden, a moderate performer with Somerset, for good measure. Yorkshire's batting has hardly prospered in my absence. Not one Test-class batsman has emerged in twelve years, so once again Close got it wrong because he refused to drop his vendetta against me. Having missed his way so often, he has turned himself into a sad figure, a man who might have done so much for Yorkshire cricket at a time of crisis had he not let personal feelings get in the way.

This unreasonable, burning resentment seemed to manifest itself again when the question of my honorary life membership arose in 1992. Newly appointed president Sir Lawrence Byford, unaware of the fact that twice before during my absences abroad the same move had been blocked, imagined that a proposal to recognise my achievements would go through without challenge. Tony Vann, as proposer, was ready to say a few words at the January committee meeting which sets the agenda for the annual meeting in March; Sir Lawrence, however, felt that the situation needed no explanation. 'We all know Geoffrey,' he said, preparing to call for a vote, but Bob Appleyard stepped in to object. Together with Close and Brian Walsh he complained about my book *Boycott on Cricket*, in which I criticised some of them. 'Certain individuals have been attacked by Boycott and some did not take legal action to spare the club's good name,' said Walsh, cleverly advocating a twelve-month delay to consider the issue. Walsh added that I had been in trouble with the Test and County Cricket Board, who tried to gag me by writing to Yorkshire about some of my newspaper articles. The mandarins at Lord's also introduced regulations attempting to make each county responsible for the comments of their committee men, but the law of the land simply prevented such draconian legislation. To his credit, Sir Lawrence spoke up for me, particularly as I had been a paying member of the club for twenty years, something few ex-players could claim.

The voting went 11–8 against me; those in favour, for the record, were Vann, Jack Sokell, Bev Stokes, Philip Akroyd, Peter Quinn, Robert Hilliam, Terry Jarvis and Tony Woodhouse. After the meeting, Bev Stokes, a prominent businessman in Sheffield, asked Appleyard why he could not have simply let the life membership go through, adding: 'You want Geoffrey to work with you and then you do this. What is the sense?' I think that Close, Appleyard and Walsh were too interested in settling old scores with me, and that this was not good for Yorkshire cricket.

I was in New Zealand covering England's tour while these events unfolded, and the president both telephoned and sent a letter expressing his regret, saying: 'I sincerely hope that this decision will not affect the constructive and helpful contribution you are making to the club's affairs, and especially since I became chairman.' On the telephone he was adamant that 'it won't happen again next year, Geoffrey', and true to his word, I was made an honorary life member in 1993.

I could not understand what was going on: only the previous November Appleyard and Bob Platt had invited me to work with them on the cricket committee. I felt this was underhand treatment, and it took away a lot of my enthusiasm for serving on such a body, although I did put up the following year. I undertook no canvassing, deciding instead to leave it to fate and see which way the members would vote. The administrative body reduced itself to twelve in 1993, with the top three in each of four districts being elected. I finished fourth in the West, three votes behind Platt; the results were: Akroyd 360, Tony Cawdry 357, Platt 348, Boycott 345. I had sat on the sub-committee in 1992 which drew up the blueprint for a streamlined voting system and had advocated an end to district representation. I favoured creating a twelve-man committee on a first-past-the-post basis, but settled for a divisional compromise in the hope that at some stage further progress would be made. If it isn't, Yorkshire's affairs will continue to be debated against a background of factional infighting.

No matter how many people sit on the committee, the danger is that a majority are likely to go on putting the interests of their own areas first. This is understandable, as they need the votes of the local members to keep them in office, so the present system does Yorkshire cricket no favours. Too much time is spent settling old scores and going over familiar arguments, the centralising of fixtures at Headingley and Scarborough being a case in point. During the winter of 1996–97, Yorkshire decided to stop playing at Sheffield, Harrogate, Bradford and Middlesbrough, partly because of limited facilities on those grounds and partly because cricket chairman Platt wanted more matches played at Headingley. Despite a vote in committee, factions continued to press the out-grounds' case and one or two refused to let the matter drop, wasting time and energy that might have been put to more profitable use. Long-winded debates covering well-trodden ground can keep committee meetings going on deep into the night, and it is no surprise that able men soon lose interest in the whole boring business. The captains of industry who might contribute importantly to Yorkshire's development expect sensible business practice to be followed, and they are not prepared to become members of a vested-interests talking shop.

In a sense, by helping to reduce the size of the committee I went a long way towards voting myself out of office, but that, I suppose, is democracy, and while my emotional attachment to the county remains, I can honestly say that I have never missed the actual committee involvement. My departure undoubtedly came as a relief to Appleyard and company, but Yorkshire, in their haste to see the back of me, made a rod for their own back. As part of their revision of the club rules, the committee introduced needless restrictions on the election process. Rule 6.4, for instance, states: 'A member who is a registered player or paid official of the club shall not be eligible for election to the committee, nor shall any member of the committee be eligible for registration as a player or to be a paid official of the club.' Reg Kirk, shortly before resigning as general committee chairman in January 1986, neatly summed up what I thought was the shallow thinking and petty-mindedness of those in charge, angrily pointing out: 'The only reason this package of rules is being bludgeoned through is to get rid of a forty-five-year-old cricketer.' Tightening the screw still further, Yorkshire then added: 'In each district there shall not be elected more than one candidate who has been a registered player or paid official of the club.' For more than 120 years Yorkshire prospered without the need for such narrow-minded bureaucracy, and every single scrap of evidence confirms that the rule changes were aimed exclusively at me.

The sorry consequence of this farcical and prejudiced mismanagement is that only three of the twelve district representatives, Bob Platt, Geoff Cope and Phil Sharpe, possess first-hand experience of first-class cricket. Platt is cricket chairman, a somewhat reluctant replacement for Close, and fulfils an active role, but Sharpe is well-known for saying virtually nothing about anything. He sits on the fence so often I am surprised he does not have splinters in his backside. In the circumstances it is probable rather than possible that Yorkshire will one day in the not-too-distant future find themselves running a county cricket club without the help of any ex-cricketers. Little or no interest is being shown in the club by comparatively recent members of the team, and, on balance, the hours of planning and plotting by some former players against my extremely useful dual role have added up to an exercise in self-destruction. Were it not so tragic, it would be laughable.

CHAPTER THREE

# Wakefield and the Academy

S ir Lawrence Byford exerted a major influence over Yorkshire cricket
from the moment he was elected president of the county club in
early 1991. Ironically, the committee declined to renominate the
popular Viscount Mountgarret for the prestigious office in 1990 after he
refused to limit his active involvement and retire into the background.
Sir Leonard Hutton took over, content to act as no more than a
distinguished figurehead, but, sadly, on 6 September that year he died,
aged seventy-three. The committee has not always found it easy to
identify a suitable president and Sir Lawrence, formerly Her Majesty's
Chief Inspector of Constabularies, presented himself as something of an
unknown quantity when he accepted the nomination, although he was
very much a man of the people, having supported Yorkshire as an
ordinary member for many years. He immediately made it clear that,
whatever the committee's intention, he visualised his role as that of a
'hands-on' president tackling a serious financial shortfall.

Not long after his appointment, on 10 July 1991, the general
committee met and voted 16–6 in favour of probably the most
momentous decision ever taken by the club. I had proposed that
'Yorkshire County Cricket Club compete in first-class cricket under the

rules as laid down by the Test and County Cricket Board, namely that the club is allowed to employ, as deemed fit, one overseas player, two Category A players [those seeking to move to another county despite being offered a contract by their current county] within a five-year period and any Category B players [those released and not offered terms by their county].' Tony Vann seconded the motion. Sir Lawrence wrote and thanked me for 'your helpful attitude at yesterday's historic meeting', and then campaigned tirelessly by talking to members at matches to convince them it was indeed time to dispense with tradition. As a result of all our efforts, in 1992 Sachin Tendulkar, the brilliant Indian batsman, became Yorkshire's first overseas player.

In making his mark, Sir Lawrence introduced a practical policy with which I wholeheartedly agreed, as Yorkshire had competed at a crippling disadvantage during a sequence of barren years on the playing front. To my mind, Sir Lawrence has done an excellent job for the club, proving to be a thoroughly decent man in all his dealings. It is not his style to be devious or to do anything behind anybody's back, and his obvious integrity has done much to restore Yorkshire's credibility. All his actions reflect the best of intentions in trying to smooth things over, and it is my experience that he has given everyone a reasonable chance to press his case in committee.

However, his attempts to be honest and straightforward carried him away in his efforts to establish Yorkshire at a new ground of their own near the M1 motorway on a greenfield site outside Wakefield. Albeit with the most honourable of motives, he jumped the gun over increasing difficulties at the county's headquarters at Headingley, plunging Yorkshire into another public dispute they could well have done without. I should here declare my interest: I have no doubt that Yorkshire should own their own ground, no matter where it is situated. I backed the Wakefield venture in principle because putting money into Headingley never has, and never will, bring significant long-term benefits. Yorkshire do not own any part of the complex – 'not a stick, not a brick, not a piece of mortar', as the late secretary Joe Lister used to observe.

No tenant in any walk of life is keen to improve his landlord's property beyond the stage of making himself temporarily comfortable. The average citizen seeks the security of unrestricted property ownership, so I am convinced that Yorkshire missed a wonderful chance to take charge of their own destiny in 1987. At that time, Norman Shuttleworth, then chairman of the Leeds Cricket Football and Athletic Company, the owners of Headingley, persuaded his fellow directors to offer Yorkshire total control of the cricket side of the dual-purpose complex, negotiations being conducted with Viscount Mountgarret, as president, Brian Walsh, as chairman, and treasurer Peter Townend. The figure mentioned for a ninety-nine-year lease was around £250,000 per annum, with an annual adjustment to account for inflation. As the income from ground advertising at the time stood at some £200,000, with every prospect of a steady increase, it is impossible to see how Yorkshire could have lost out, but they rebuffed Leeds on the basis that accepting responsibility for regularly finding that sort of money was too big a gamble. Importantly, the matter was not put to the committee. Although Peter Townend subsequently advanced a range of financial arguments against grasping the nettle, the issue should have been decided by those people elected by the members to run the club – a point I stressed forcefully in committee. As far as I was concerned, the three of them had misused their powers; I did not win any brownie points for telling them so!

By then, of course, it was too late, the status quo surviving until May 1995, when Yorkshire announced their support for a £30 million redevelopment plan for Headingley. Both parties recognised the necessity of repairing the fabric of the ground and, if possible, of removing the old running track which separated the spectators from the playing area, acting as a passageway for a constant flow of human traffic. Finance chairman Keith Moss stressed the importance of retaining Test cricket on the ground by saying: 'We have to act in the face of potential competition for international matches, and what has delighted me has been the close co-operation between Yorkshire and Leeds. It is important that Headingley should not now be developed in a hotch-potch way, as has tended to happen in the past.'

The first phase of the project involved the erection of a permanent two-tier stand on the Bowling Green terraces between the county offices and the ballroom at a cost of £1.8 million, with work scheduled to finish in time for the Test against Australia in July 1997. The actual details of what went wrong are not exactly clear, but Sir Lawrence, stoutly defending Yorkshire's best interests, could not, it seems, reach agreement with Leeds over the sharing of potential profits, and gradually a rift developed between the parties. Yorkshire's reaction was to push the Leeds board to 'name their price' for selling the cricket side outright, a figure of £6 million being put forward for discussion in March 1996. The county dismissed it as too high by far.

What started out as a gentleman's disagreement steadily developed into open warfare as the ownership of Headingley passed into the hands of Paul Caddick, the millionaire head of a construction and development business, in October 1996. In the first instance, Sir Lawrence acted, typically, in good faith, calling an emergency committee meeting on 7 October 1996, at which he said that 'in view of the imminent announcement from Leeds Rugby Club that they are to enter into a new ownership, Yorkshire should make their intentions known so that the new directors will be under no illusion as to the county's intention to move from Headingley to a new greenfield site'. It is clear that Sir Lawrence wanted to put the record straight on the county's behalf, leaving no room for misunderstanding, and at that meeting the committee unanimously agreed to accept the offer Sir Lawrence had secured from Wakefield Council of a site at Durkar, 'at no cost to the club'. A figure of £46 million for the development was accepted as realistic, with the help of funding from the National Lottery, European grants, receipts from land sales and development and 'other related sources, including the Arts Council and Heritage Fund'. Sir Lawrence confirmed that, while National Lottery support projections were somewhat optimistic, the council leader and officials were confident that 'contingency funds would be available to cover any shortfall'.

The minutes for that meeting also contain a sentence which now stands as an unheeded warning: 'The president also touched upon counsel's opinion relating to the county's lease at Headingley.' Yorkshire had signed a ninety-nine-year lease at Headingley in 1982 for use of the cricket facilities, paying a service fee of £25,000 and a peppercorn rent of £500 per annum. On the other side of the coin, they also contracted to promote county and Test cricket on the ground, and this commitment brought a landslide of trouble down on their heads. Fierce disagreements had surfaced periodically over whether the lease represented a good deal for Yorkshire, but the fact that Paul Caddick went to great lengths to keep them at Headingley suggests that Leeds enjoyed the greater benefits, and it hardly helped that Michael Crawford, the Yorkshire chairman when it was agreed, later received a seat on the Leeds board. It was reported that Dennis Greenwood, Norman Shuttleworth's replacement as chairman of the Leeds board, had told Sir Lawrence that if Yorkshire wanted to leave they could do so, but no official record of this verbal 'release' exists and Leeds might well have thought that Yorkshire had nowhere to go anyway.

It might well be more than a little unfortunate that finance chairman Keith Moss was away on holiday, and that David Welch, a former finance chairman, and Peter Quinn, for many years a local government officer, missed that first emergency meeting. They were three men with the knowledge and background to have sounded, perhaps, a sensible note of caution by asking some pertinent questions. Looking at it now, I would have required assurances on two points: the lease and the money. It was absolutely vital for Yorkshire to possess an unequivocal, written release from their undertaking to Leeds before embarking on a highly publicised declaration of intent to move. A verbal agreement is all right in certain circumstances, confirmed, say, at a public meeting with plenty of witnesses, but a passing remark at a private meeting is very different. In the case of Dennis Greenwood, Yorkshire also needed to be sure that he had the full authority of the Leeds board to make such a grandiose gesture. Additionally, with no documentation to support their contention, they could hardly expect Paul Caddick to honour, without compensation, a pledge to which he was not party. To compound their folly, Yorkshire rushed into action before any hard cash appeared on the table. They sustained their enthusiasm on the back of nothing more than an attractive idea.

Certainly Sir Lawrence promoted the county's best interests by taking up the Wakefield option as he wanted to establish Yorkshire at their own headquarters and leave something really worthwhile for coming generations. The annual report for 1996 stated: 'As early as 1902, Lord Hawke, then president of the club, commented that "we would soon need to be looking to purchase our own ground". It has taken over ninety years for positive steps to be taken.' Thus, all the indications were that Yorkshire, with Sir Lawrence at the helm, were embarking on a crusade to fulfil at last a half-forgotten pledge. It is hardly surprising, therefore, that the committee overlooked essential elements in the planning process, and this is where they made their big mistake. Yorkshire CCC and Wakefield Council charged forward without any financial guarantees on paper.

A similar picture had unfolded in the early 1980s when Yorkshire took the decision to establish an indoor cricket school. The Bradford representatives on the committee pushed forward fanciful schemes trying to set up the school at Park Avenue as part of a commercial enterprise including a shopping centre and bowling alley. The plans looked wonderful, but any architect can put an attractive design on the drawing board. The Bradford project turned out to be pie in the sky, and while its supporters were dreaming, Tony Vann, Philip Akroyd and I produced the funding for a centre in Leeds and got it up and running by 1987.

The president's haste also caught the members on the hop. They remained in the dark as Yorkshire negotiated with Wakefield, and, accidentally, Sir Lawrence alienated a lot of people by presenting them with a *fait accompli*. However worthy his motives, he stirred up a hornets' nest of resistance from those who lived in the Leeds area, from those attached to the traditions of Headingley and from men and women who merely wanted their voices to be heard. Without doubt, the committee demonstrated that they had learned nothing from the dark days of 1983 when they rode roughshod over the members and sacked me. Different personnel, same errors.

The administration, I feel, relies too readily on Rule 2: 'The management of the club and of its property, funds and affairs shall be vested in the committee, whose decisions on all matters relating thereto shall be final and binding on every member of the club.' That is fair enough when dealing with everyday matters, but huge decisions with far-reaching consequences are different. Yorkshire could, for example, have gone ahead and signed an overseas player without consulting the members, but Sir Lawrence, in particular, saw the need to carry people along with him and went out of his way to persuade the members that a change in policy had to be made. In the case of the proposed move to Wakefield, he lost his way along the public relations path.

At a full committee meeting on 26 November 1996, Keith Moss queried the position. He referred to the 'verbal agreement to discharge Yorkshire from their obligations', but noted that 'nothing has been discussed with the new owners, Caddick Holdings'. The minutes reveal that 'the president reassured the committee that he did not foresee any problem'. Sir Lawrence's confidence was misplaced. Viscount Mountgarret was among those annoyed at Yorkshire's attitude, claiming they had been 'inept and impulsive' in going ahead without formal consultation with the membership. Striking at the heart of the issue, the former president stressed: 'The committee does not have a mandate to take a unilateral decision affecting the fundamental structure of the club.' With the Headingley is Home action group making waves, Yorkshire had to start selling the idea of moving to Wakefield to get support at the 1997 annual meeting. This came readily enough in the end, but all the embarrassing turmoil could have been avoided. Eventually Yorkshire found it prudent to advise the membership that 'our meetings with Mr Caddick have been interspersed with both verbal and written threats', among the more serious being writs for £17 million in damages in September 1997.

An indication of the confusion which existed can be gained from Tony Vann, a Leeds-based businessman who sought re-election to the committee in 1998 after losing his place as a Central district representative in 1996. During his campaign, Vann, despite keeping very much in touch with events, admitted:

> *I had assumed, wrongly as it turns out, that getting out of the lease would not be too much of a hurdle. When members voted 3–1 in favour of the Wakefield move at the 1997 annual meeting they were putting their trust in the information supplied by the club, but they did not know the other side of the story, and since then the deadlines for applications for lottery funding have come and gone and it has emerged that the lease issue is far from straightforward. I don't know anything about Paul Caddick, but he clearly has a valid case in wanting to protect his interests with eighty-four years of the lease to run, and he holds the aces.*

Realistically, Vann was right, for whatever games of bluff and counter-bluff had taken place, Yorkshire discovered that Caddick had no intention of allowing them to walk away, taking a lucrative source of income with them. He stuck to the point that over the years the Leeds board's investment in facilities at Headingley demanded a reasonable return.

By mid-summer concern grew in Yorkshire's ranks. As Wakefield Council ran into difficulties after the resignation of Councillor Colin Croxall, the driving force on their side, and with no sign of sufficient funding on the horizon, Yorkshire announced on 16 October 1998 that they had reached agreement with Leeds in respect of the redevelopment of Headingley. Explaining this change of heart, Keith Moss said: 'New funding limitations resulting from changed National Lottery policy and planning uncertainties following the calling in by the minister of the

Durkar planning application, as well as changes in the financial prospects of cricket generally, meant it made sense to look again at Headingley.'

The Headingley scheme is in the same melting pot as the Durkar development and might not be brought to fruition if there is not enough financial support. The original target comprised in part £4 million from the Sports Council and £3 million from Leeds City Council, sums that required the provision of facilities for the general public. What these could be is a matter for conjecture, so there are more questions than answers. After all the guessing games, though, the one certainty is that in spite of all the haggling and hostility, Yorkshire are still not set to own anything. In the circumstances I believe Yorkshire ought to be investigating the possibility of part-ownership. If Caddick is not ready to sell them the cricket side outright, he might be open to persuasion to sell them 49 per cent. That would not be ideal, but at least then Yorkshire would have something tangible to pass on, something they have never had before. That, surely, was what the Wakefield venture was all about, and now Yorkshire have fudged the compromise. Caddick is the only winner, having bluffed and bullied the county club into submission. Yorkshire lacked an entrepreneur, a man of bold vision and tenacity to bring plans to completion, such as Paul Sykes, who built the Meadowhall shopping centre at Sheffield.

As Sir Lawrence's spell as president draws to a close – he had to be persuaded to continue into 1999 – he might look back and wish he had the chance to do things differently. It was not wrong to want to give the members a dream of owning their own ground, but the stupidity was allowing them to believe it was a reality before it was an option. Many members feel humiliated that they were brought into this fiasco by the committee. Some feel foolish, others feel they were conned. This two-year farce has cost the club a lot of money and a great deal of credibility.

The Yorkshire committee's decision to set up a cricket academy at Bradford Park Avenue in 1989 was also botched, and reflected political prejudice and parochial thinking. The temptation to say 'I told you so' is great, but I take no satisfaction in being proved right ten years down the line. A decision to switch operations from this season back to the logical venue, Headingley, became inevitable as all the foreseeable difficulties arose.

Basically, I am all in favour of creating a well-funded, carefully structured system for developing emerging talent, but it is not easy to see just where the Yorkshire Academy has succeeded, despite astronomical costs – £436,738 up to the end of 1998. From the start, as a member of the committee, I fought to house the Academy at Headingley, not least because the county had created the best cricket school in the country across the road from Headingley in 1982. Unfortunately, in the face of a clear administrative bias, I lost out.

Bob Appleyard, one of the Bradford representatives on the committee, had taken the initiative on 24 October 1988, pointing out that Yorkshire had never had a groundstaff and that the time had arrived to introduce one to provide an opportunity for regular practice for and coaching of young players. In political terms, however, Appleyard failed to declare an obvious interest: he also served actively on the committee of a pressure group, the Friends of Bradford Park Avenue, formed following the demise of the compact venue at the end of the 1985 season. The Friends made no secret of their desire to revive first-class cricket in Bradford, although, initially at least, they robustly denied that their vigorous backing for the Academy had anything to do with ambition in that direction. It did not escape attention, though, that Yorkshire's cricket chairman at the time, Brian Close, was also the Friends of Bradford Park Avenue president, so two leading decision-makers on the cricket sub-committee hopped about with a foot in each camp. And yet another ex-player on the cricket committee, Bob Platt, had strong links with Park Avenue, tilting the balance further against Headingley. No matter how impartial the other cricket committee members might be, the weight of argument perceptibly leaned one way.

Ignoring the democratic need to balance the pros and cons, the cricket committee, encouraged by a reportedly enthusiastic promise of backing from potential local sponsors, recommended that a groundstaff scheme be started in 1989, based at Park Avenue. The fact that the playing area and surrounds stood derelict and vandalised received no mention, nor did the need for constant security cover. Once the die had been cast, the cloak of secrecy lifted and Close expressed the hope that 'county cricket can be played at Bradford in 1991'. A leaflet appealing for donations echoed this sentiment, and went further by promising sponsors 'preferential treatment (hospitality and advertising) and a prominent position on the Academy's founder members' board when first-class cricket returns to Park Avenue'. No doubts there; no pretence any more about a key issue. I thought it was clearly exposed as a sordid charade.

When I challenged general committee chairman Brian Walsh over the agreement with Bradford, he wrote a long letter, painting what to my view was a misleading picture, part of which read:

> *The cricket sub-committee was given the task of assessing the feasibility of establishing a nursery. That we wanted such a nursery, hopefully employing some ten or more youngsters, was agreed by all, should the necessary funds be available. I believe that the true reason why the cricket sub-committee favoured Park Avenue was because of its availability for use at all times during the season. Headingley would not be so available. Both the Leeds club and Leeds City Council have been aware of the Park Avenue question from an early stage.*

I was not alone in wondering about the accuracy of this statement. Norman Shuttleworth, the chairman of the Leeds Cricket Football and Athletic Company, wrote to Walsh as early as 10 January 1989 to express his concern after 'reading the news which has been recently published about the possible use of Bradford Park Avenue ground'. Clearly, then, the whole business surprised the Leeds club chairman, who politely indicated exactly what was available at Headingley: 'all the equipment necessary to service the ground, much of it purchased with Yorkshire's money'. Shuttleworth continued: 'You pay the service charge of £13,000, plus a mere pittance of £500 in rent, whether you use the ground frequently or infrequently.' In my letter to Walsh dated 28 February, among my concerns I stressed that surely, out of common courtesy, we should have extended the same opportunity to Leeds CF and AC as had been given to Bradford CC. I pointed out that parochial views and vested interests should be submerged; the priority should be deciding which was the better venue for Yorkshire's groundstaff. Getting county cricket to Park Avenue should be a separate issue entirely.

Councillor Bernard Atha, chairman of the Leeds City Council Leisure Services Committee, publicly contradicted Walsh too. In his letter to the chairman, also on 28 February, Councillor Atha, who repeated his comments to the press, stated: 'I am instructed by the Leisure Services Committee to express our surprise and dismay to hear of plans to transfer a groundstaff from Headingley to Bradford. We regretted that we learned of this proposal informally. We were surprised that no approach has been made to the Leisure Services Committee about participation in the Academy, given the very close co-operation and links which exist in connection with the Cricket School.' Recognising my more open-minded position, Councillor Atha contacted me to insist that he had 'received no request for discussions or financial assistance towards the Academy. I find this, in itself, extremely strange. I very much hope that Yorkshire will agree to have proper discussions with the Leeds City Council.' So much for the often repeated assurance that every factor had been taken into consideration by the cricket committee before Bradford got the vote. The evidence from witnesses of unblemished character is clear, and it does Yorkshire no credit.

Brian Walsh rose to prominence in Yorkshire cricket circles by means of some outstanding anti-committee outbursts at the time of the 1984 club crisis over my sacking. His powers of oratory captured the spotlight at some meetings and helped to reinstate me as a player, and he went on to stand successfully for election in Leeds for the new administration which took office in the wake of the 1984 'revolution'. His reputation as a barrister earned him the role of chairman in 1986, by which time his politics had changed and he had distanced himself from me. Although under the old district system he represented Leeds, Walsh threw his weight behind Close and Appleyard, his thinking shaped by a well-developed sense of self-preservation. A number of people on the committee, having watched him in action, no longer had the same trust in him, so he needed powerful allies to retain the chairmanship. Close, Appleyard and Platt were useful because their stature as former players overawed their less self-assured committee colleagues.

By putting himself first, Walsh betrayed the Leeds connection and structured public pronouncements to suit the convenience of a few. Close, Appleyard and Walsh spread the word that Headingley could not provide sufficient nets, yet Alf Davies, chief executive of the Leeds CF and AC, put together a detailed dossier to destroy another bit of propaganda. Davies stated:

> *The number of artificial wickets at Headingley could be increased as required on the Bowling Green area. There is available an area of fifty-five yards of first-class practice wickets. This is comprised of the areas outside the Yorkshire County Cricket Club pavilion and at the Kirkstall Lane End and gives some twenty-five pitches. Additionally Keith Boyce, the groundsman, states that practice pitches can be prepared on virtually any other part of the outfield. There are, towards the end of the square, five pitches of county standard which could be used. Additionally, five further pitches of club standard could be prepared, giving a total of ten pitches in the middle.*

Close, Appleyard and Walsh completely ignored the possibilities in Leeds.

After a winter working abroad, I returned to a general committee meeting in February 1989 to be surprised at just how far plans had advanced. The Bradford committee representation wanted Yorkshire CCC to take complete financial responsibility for any shortfall not met by sponsorship from Bradford City Council and local businessmen. Appleyard gave his personal assurance that he would be responsible for obtaining sponsorship, to which I replied: 'That's all well and good, but what happens if you get knocked down by a bus? Who do you think is going to go out and get sponsorship every year in your absence? You will not get people to keep giving money year after year.' I applauded the good people of Bradford who were prepared to contribute, but I knew that it could not last. Eventually it was agreed there would have to be a ceiling of £15,000 applied to Yorkshire's commitment, otherwise the club was potentially exposed to unlimited expense. As a result, Bradford City Council eventually had to give a grant of £40,000 to pay for new dressing rooms, equipment and machinery, refurbishment and new personnel.

Despite these concessions, in desperation I went to see the president, Viscount Mountgarret, at his home, warning him that Yorkshire cricket was being used to further other causes. I added that in my opinion Leeds had been deliberately snubbed, and I outlined the advantages of Headingley. It did not take a genius to understand them. I do not know of any other county which would deliberately organise a groundstaff away from the centre of its operation. In committee, when I had asked what the Academy instructors would do at Bradford when it rained, one bright spark suggested bussing the boys to Headingley's Indoor School! A tremendous advantage at Headingley was the fact that the Academy boys would be able to join the senior players in the nets to learn valuable lessons. They would be able to watch first-class matches in the company of the coaches to gain further experience, while potential involvement in Test match preparations represented a huge bonus. In comparison, the facilities at Bradford were nil, but the president, while taking on board the points I made, allowed himself to be swayed by the supposed greater experts. All our efforts were in vain. Close, Appleyard and Walsh refused to be deflected and a sufficient number of committee men fell into step. Leeds district representative Tony Vann, saddened by the Bradford bias and weary of being a voice in the wilderness, resigned from the cricket committee in March 1989, explaining: 'It makes no sense to send ten boys to a derelict ground day after day to learn the skills of the game. It will be a soul-destroying experience for them.'

As ever with Yorkshire cricket, no one stood back and thought things through. Predictably, the wheel slowly turned full circle, wasting time and money every inch of the way. When first-class cricket ceased to be played at Park Avenue at the end of the 1996 season, Bradford as an academy venue was doomed. Costs were piling up and Bradford Council and businessmen could see little commercial gain in continued sponsorship. There was no kudos or publicity to be gained from just keeping the Academy afloat. And in May 1998 the county acknowledged that 'following the withdrawal of major sponsorship and with rising expenditure an unacceptable situation has arisen', and 'the Academy could continue at Park Avenue only if the problems of vandalism and funding could be addressed'. It took them ten years too long to reach those conclusions.

As I've said, the concept of an academy was fine, but the running of it left a lot to be desired. Bob Appleyard claimed that creating the Academy would stop other counties poaching Yorkshire's best youngsters. That has hardly been the case, for although the England Under-19 selectors regularly turned to Yorkshire, many boys either moved on or dropped out of the professional game. It is impossible to streamline the production of talent to meet the particular demand on the contracted squad. Sport does not work like that, and the danger always exists that lack of opportunity will persuade promising players to try their luck elsewhere. Very few of Yorkshire's youngsters have gone on to become top-class cricketers, and the most successful ones would probably have made it without the help of the Academy.

In Australia, for example, they do not believe in the four- or five-month grind that characterised the Bradford operation, and I feel that shorter, more intense periods of training would be much more useful. The aim ought to be to keep the coaching fresh and alive by avoiding a boring routine. I would advocate a few days' in-depth instruction on specific techniques before sending the boys away to put into practice the lessons they have learned. One man must, of course, be in charge to maintain continuity, but many great players come to England and quite a few would, I imagine, welcome three or four days' well-paid work with a handful of the county's top prospects. The Academy could build up a priceless video library, a storehouse of knowledge from around the world to present to future generations. Former Test wicketkeeper-batsman Rodney Marsh organises the Australian Academy, getting through all the spade work in their close season. Then the boys get competitive cricket with either a grade or a state team, the theory being that the ability to carry technical adjustments forward into demanding match situations is important. Putting a fault right or trying something new in the nets is one thing, doing the same thing when it really matters is another. Marsh also calls in the very best players to add an edge to the coaching – for example, Greg Chappell for batting and Dennis Lillee for bowling. Players of that calibre have the wherewithal to impress and influence young boys, but Yorkshire prefer to rely entirely on ordinary coaches whose qualifications don't equip them to help the truly gifted junior.

I am sure that it is also wrong for the county to run a team in the Yorkshire League. That was Close's idea, as he feels the club must have control of the youngsters all the time. He went so far as to come out of retirement to captain the side occasionally, but if you collect all the best youngsters together in one club, the standard of the League must suffer. In the old days, by spreading the most promising talent around Yorkshire CCC ensured that the boys they were interested in got the 'star' position in a side. Only two batsmen can go in first for the Academy, but what if there are three or four openers all demanding recognition? The lad batting at six for Yorkshire in the League line-up might be just as good as the one at number three, but he does not get in as often. In sharp contrast, Barnsley ensured my progress by batting me at three all the time. Additionally, youngsters benefit from playing alongside hardened League veterans. The weakness of age-limit cricket right up to international level is that all those taking part are involved because of their date of birth rather than their ability, which is a disadvantage, and the same applies to Yorkshire's League squad. It was far better for me growing up with Billy Sutcliffe and Johnny Lawrence at Leeds in the Yorkshire League. A word or two from them in a match situation was worth more than a week's coaching from someone with a badge and a scrap of generally accepted knowledge.

Yorkshire could save themselves a lot of toil, tears and hard cash by becoming more selective, by picking out the very best young cricketers with quality rather than quantity as the guideline. The Americans have a saying: 'If it ain't broke, don't fix it.' Well, back in the 1950s, when Yorkshire were a great power, boys received invitations to the winter nets, working hard through January, February and March. Many fell by the wayside, but the reward for those who created the right sort of impression came in the shape of time in the senior nets in April, and the chance to bat against Fred Trueman acted as a spur which drove me, for one, on night after night. The impression exists that cricket lacks the appeal and high-profile personalities of soccer, so Yorkshire must put some magic back into their set-up. The new beginning at Headingley should be regarded as a challenge.

# CHAPTER FOUR

# Rebel Cricket

Kerry Packer is arguably the most controversial character to stride across the world of cricket, hated and admired in equal measure, but never ignored. The Australian media tycoon trampled ruthlessly over cherished traditions in 1977 when he challenged the established governing bodies, raised the stature of the leading players and led the way in terms of marketing the game. By creating a 'pirate circus' of world-class performers, Packer swept away a suffocating complacency at the highest level and went a long way towards saving cricket from financial ruin. At the same time, though, he threatened to tear down the whole house of cards.

A burly, aggressive figure with a clear sight of what he wanted, Packer appeared initially as an unlikely saviour, and there were dangers that his medicine would kill rather than cure an ailing patient. His involvement stemmed not from any emotional attachment, rather from his refusal to accept the Australian Cricket Board's rejection of his attempts to buy exclusive rights to television coverage of Test matches for his Channel 9 company. Rumours of a breakaway movement, circulating in April 1977, were confirmed on 9 May with the announcement that thirty-five players, including England's Tony Greig, Alan Knott, John Snow and Derek Underwood, had signed contracts to take part in games organised by Packer. A rather panic-stricken official response took the form of a resolution passed by the International Cricket Council at Lord's on 26

July, which baldly stated: 'No player who, after 1 October 1977, has played or has made himself available to play in a match previously disapproved by the Conference shall be eligible to play in any Test.'

There was support, too, for banning Packer players from county cricket, so the two sides in the developing argument were obviously on a collision course, one which carried them into the High Court in London. There, Mr Justice Slade found against the ICC and the Test and County Cricket Board, ruling that their action amounted to an illegal restraint of trade. I turned down an approach from Packer because his contract represented a 'body and soul' agreement, giving him far too much control over my movements, and the TCCB called me as a witness. By then, with news of my rejection circulating worldwide, I was regarded as public enemy number one by Packer and his main recruiting sergeant, Tony Greig, who sacrificed the England captaincy to underwrite his long-term future. As soon as it became clear I was to give evidence, Greig telephoned me to ask: 'How the hell have you got involved in this?' He then added: 'We'll have to work over the weekend to find some mud to throw at you.' The judge, on being appraised of this approach, decided that Greig's remarks were jocular, satisfying legal dignity with a warning, but that little exchange in the most hallowed halls of justice comprised the first shots in a campaign against me which escalated into all-out war with serious repercussions.

Greig eventually went so far as to suggest that I was afraid of fast bowling, citing as proof my absence from the 1974–75 tour to Australia during which pace bowlers Dennis Lillee and Jeff Thomson destroyed England with their sustained hostility. His preposterous suggestion took no account of the facts. When I made my decision to stay at home hardly anyone had heard of Thomson, who finished with figures of none for 110 against Pakistan in 1972 and missed out on Test cricket until the first Test in Brisbane against England in November 1974, having spent twenty-three months in the doldrums. Lillee had broken down with back trouble in the West Indies, emerging from the last Test in Kingston in February 1973 with none for 132. He, too, ended a twenty-one-month absence at Brisbane, and it was only later, once the tour had got under way and England were collapsing all over the place, that my critics saw an opportunity to fabricate the malicious story that I had made myself unavailable to tour Australia through fear of top-notch fast bowling – a myth that still persists today. Greig also failed to take into consideration the 1977 series in England when, with Thomson in full cry, I managed to average 147 over five innings.

I told the High Court that I thought the ban on Packer players reasonable because they wanted both the penny and the bun. For example, England's Packer players wanted to make themselves unavailable for winter tours, but wanted to be picked to represent their country during home Test series. They expected the security of conventional cricket plus the rich rewards of an unofficial venture which might do untold harm. I told Mr Justice Slade: 'There is nothing wrong with cricketers wanting to earn more money, but they cannot serve two masters. Players who earn big money with Packer's proposed Australian super-Test series during the English winter cannot expect to resume playing Test and county cricket which is dependent on income from recognised Test matches.' That was my firm conviction then, and nothing happened to change it throughout a very emotive time.

Players inevitably took sides, and the High Court judgement did leave a loophole. Mr Justice Slade made it impossible for the authorities to ban the 'rebels' from any form of the professional game, but a good deal of power remained in the hands of the Test selectors and county committees. They could dispense with the services of any individual on the basis of form or team spirit, which is so often a matter of opinion. The Professional Cricketers' Association, formed in 1968, came out strongly against Packer almost immediately, voting that his recruits should be ousted from the championship and showing an impressive solidarity which persuaded me to join their ranks after I had ignored their existence for nine years in the belief that the PCA was little more than a talking shop. In the end, player power probably did more than anything to preserve established cricket, and I have no regrets over the part I played, although my role was not quite so prominent as Greig tried to make out.

Bearing in mind the way the fates have treated me, I should not really have been surprised to find myself finally becoming captain of England at such a critical time. Mike Brearley, the captain of the tour of Pakistan in the winter of 1977–78, broke his arm in a meaningless fixture at Lahore, so I stepped up to deputise in the third Test at Karachi on 18 January. In doing so, I picked up a poisoned chalice. Whatever the High Court's view, all concerned with the England party were under the impression that Packer players would not be selected during our three-match series, although the Pakistan authorities had lifted the ban on their five rebels and invited four of them – Mushtaq Mohammad, Majid Khan, Zaheer Abbas and Imran Khan – to join their squad. Asif Iqbal indicated that he would not be available and dropped out of the picture. Initially, however, it appeared that this represented little more than a gesture as the series clashed with the so-called super-Test fixtures, and it was reported that the five Pakistani stars had turned down an offer of around £270 per Test from their board. Majid spotlighted the dangers of the deteriorating situation when he admitted: 'I am always available for selection unless I am under contract to someone else at the same time.' In other words, he was happy to let Packer dictate his programme, a point Mushtaq underlined when he pressed the Pakistan board to negotiate with the Australian.

Still, a good deal of whispering continued in dark corners, people's suspicions increasing when Mushtaq, Zaheer and Imran flew into Karachi. Their arrival on the scene indicated the distinct probability that Pakistan were going to include them in their final line-up for the third Test. The entire England party was against contact with the Packer men, and the degree of uncertainty in the Pakistan camp prompted Brearley, on his return to England, to voice our opposition:

*When we became aware of rumours concerning the Packer players,*
*the England squad held several meetings and agreed that it would be*
*wrong in principle for them to play against us. The lads are not*

*scared of being beaten, but they are worried about the future and wanted to make it quite clear where they stand. They are unanimously opposed to Packer's players being considered for selection in ICC Tests. This is certain to be the case in forthcoming series against countries like Australia and West Indies.*

To a large extent, Brearley did no more than hint at the depth of feeling and his words emphasised his unease at any talk of a strike, but, putting it bluntly, England were not prepared to take the field against any Packer players and industrial action represented the most effective option.

Meanwhile, a good deal happened behind the scenes. Cricket officials in Pakistan are always wary of their public, who might riot, cause trouble and virtually wreck the ground if their favourite personalities are not picked, and the would-be spectators on this occasion were certainly not interested in the complications of politics. Those running the game in Pakistan are always, in fact, under just as much pressure as the players, so we appreciated that nothing could be taken for granted. We had to plan our strategy in the knowledge that the Pakistan selectors could not afford to be seen to be backing down. It was the old story of two sides being trapped between the proverbial rock and a hard place, and, as expected, a good deal of steam issued from under the collars at Lord's. Doug Insole, chairman of the TCCB, despatched an urgent telegram to the Intercontinental Hotel, which read: 'Messrs Barrington and Boycott, please ring me any time after 0300 your time.' Ken Barrington, of course, was tour manager, but he didn't really know how to cope with such a dramatic turn of events. A fine, determined player and a good man on the cricket side in his managerial role, Ken preferred to distance himself from the turmoil, very worried about the prospect of England refusing to play.

The telegram emphasised the fact that nerves were reaching breaking point at home, and later on a telephone call from Insole interrupted my dinner. He wanted to know why he had not heard from Barrington and added that Freddie Brown, chairman of the ICC, was at Lord's expecting to speak to him. I went to fetch Ken from the dining room and left him to deal with Insole. In view of the confidential nature of the business in hand, I imagined Ken would conduct the conversation from his room and asked the hotel operator to transfer the call to room 705. I went up at once, only to find the door locked and the telephone ringing. I managed to get a maid to open the door, and when I looked inside the room, Barrington was nowhere to be seen.

I spoke again to Insole, who anxiously asked about developments. I told him that nothing had changed and that the players were adamant about not playing. Insole's concern centred on the legal position as he thought Pakistan could sue the TCCB for a substantial sum. He did not want England to become the first country to refuse to play, stressing: 'It would be bad for England and it would be bad for you, as history will record that you were the captain and Barrington the manager. Those are the two names that will be remembered. Surely you don't want that to happen. You are a responsible, mature person and I implore you, as a personal favour, to persuade the players to play.'

I insisted that I did not feel it was up to me to dictate to the rest of the squad, adding that no words of mine would have the desired effect as feelings were running very high. 'They are all aware of the implications, but don't want to turn out against Packer players. When you get reliable, steady people like Bob Taylor, Graham Roope and Brian Rose saying they are not going to play, you can see how strong the feeling is.' The news of the solidarity in the England camp clearly surprised Insole, so I tried hard to make him appreciate the position from our point of view. 'Look at Bob Taylor,' I said. 'If he were being selfish after getting the chance to step into Knott's shoes, he would want to play and keep his nose clean. Then he'd have a good chance of keeping his place next year. I've got most to lose. I have just realised my life's ambition to be captain of England, so it is not in my best interests to rock the boat. At the moment my prospects of taking over from Brearley would be improved if I were to toe the official line, but I don't operate like that. I am trying to do what I honestly believe is best for cricket.'

Insole listened without really hearing what I was saying. He continued to plead the case for appeasement. 'I take your point,' he admitted. 'We are all aware of your sentiments at Lord's, but you need to show some leadership. You can carry the rest of the team with you.' That made me angry, because Insole was implying that to prove my qualities as captain I had to make a resolute England dressing room follow me against their clearly expressed better judgement. To leave no room for any doubt, therefore, I put several players on the telephone to Insole in the course of the ongoing discussions. The resulting exchanges reflected our collective distress at the circumstances in which we were placed, through no fault of our own.

Brian Rose: 'What are the legal implications if we don't play?'

Insole: 'I'd have to take advice.'

Mike Hendrick: 'Packer needs his players to appear in Test cricket so they can be kept in the public eye. If they no longer play Test cricket they will lose their pulling power.'

Insole: 'I agree with you, but there are legal implications.'

Bob Taylor: 'I am a man of principle and I don't want to play against Packer men. It is wrong.'

Ian Botham: 'I agree with everything Bob Taylor says. The TCCB spent £200,000 in court and got nowhere, so here is a chance for us to do something as players.'

Insole: 'I can see all that, but I don't think it is the right way to go about it.'

Chris Old: 'As one who turned down Packer to play for England in Test cricket without his players, I find it hard to go back on that.'

Insole: 'Taking drastic action like not playing will not help. We are thinking of doing something to solve the problem. By not playing you will lose the good will of the public.'

Round and round in circles the conversation went, and I invited all the other players to speak to Insole, but Graham Roope, Phil Edmonds, Geoff Miller, Geoff Cope and Derek Randall declined, all agreeing that there was nothing else to say.

Having reached a stalemate, I advised Insole to send the Pakistan board a telegram to cover the TCCB, which he did. It read: 'The UK Cricket Council warns your board England players adamant will not play Test if additional players from Australia are selected. Team has been instructed to play, but Cricket Council cannot guarantee them complying. If such players selected, consequences at Pakistan board's own risk.' The England squad also received their 'instructions' in the same way: 'Following the phone call with England captain, should players decide against playing the Cricket Council confirms the instructions that the England cricket team should fulfil their obligations to play the final Test match with Pakistan and honour both the board's contractual obligations and also those of the England players to TCCB, despite whatever selections made by the Pakistan board for their side.'

The England party agreed to stand firm, and it is worth noting that we received total support from the Pakistan squad. Obviously some of them were motivated by self-interest, because if three Packer men were recalled at the last minute then three of the original side would have to be dropped, but the captain, Wasim Bari, was in no danger of losing his place. Even so, he put his cards clearly on the table the day before the Karachi Test was due to start:

> *If Imran, Mushtaq or Zaheer is picked for the Test without giving the Pakistan board a written undertaking to be available full time for the next two years, I will resign as captain as soon as the match is over and I will refuse to tour England next summer. I have the backing of my vice-captain Sarfraz Nawaz. Irrespective of the contracts the rebels have with Packer, I believe the board has an obligation to the thirty-eight players who have worked so hard for a month to prove their willingness to rebuild our side.*

During nets at Karachi, I took the opportunity to meet the Pakistan selectors. Gazing around the empty ground, I warned them: 'You see these stands, they will be full tomorrow, but the spectators will not be seeing any cricket if you pick the Packer players. There will be no chance of England turning out.' It was not exactly my intention to threaten the Pakistani officials, but they needed to understand that we were not bluffing. I did not want them to be relying on a late reprieve in the shape of a change of heart on our part. Our minds were made up. The Pakistan officials, therefore, were left in no doubt as to the extent of the potential explosion and destructive fall-out.

Greig dropped a bombshell himself, although by aiming it from Sydney, which was a long way from the scene, he missed the target by a mile. Unable to restrain his frustration at England's unyielding attitude, he claimed: 'The threatened strike is the work of Geoff Boycott and his cronies. I refuse to believe that Mike Brearley had anything to do with it. Boycott put the team up to this. Brearley insisted that I and the other Packer players should turn out for him and has always stood for compromise and no division.' Greig joined Insole in mistakenly assuming I could control the England party and bend them to my will. He was wrong, too, if he imagined that Brearley could guarantee him, or anyone else, a welcome in the dressing room. Being charitable, I suspect the Packer empire, which was not making the expected impact on the field at that time, needed to create a public stir and, as ever, my name seemed most likely to capture the headlines. But Greig's high-profile beating of Packer's drum worked against him. Sussex, having stood by Greig in December by reappointing him captain in defiance of a private agreement between the counties to hold the future of the Packer men in abeyance, suffered acute embarrassment as a result of his behaviour. Lancashire and Nottinghamshire reacted most strongly, seeking to have Sussex expelled from the championship, and, while they probably never expected backing for such an extreme step, they confirmed that Packer had ruffled too many feathers for comfort. For their part, Sussex stripped Greig of the captaincy on 31 January.

Everybody in Pakistan knew the score all right, and the home authorities turned their attentions to the task of keeping the show on the road without losing face. Finally, after an act of brinkmanship without parallel in the history of the game, they narrowly avoided disaster. Pakistan board president Mohammad Hussain announced that Mushtaq, Zaheer and Imran would not play, explaining: 'They were asked to extend an unconditional and unreserved apology to the nation for not making themselves available for the whole series. They were also instructed that they should uphold the authority of the International Cricket Council in future and not accept invitations or sign contracts with any other cricket authority without approval. We regret the players have failed to give this assurance.' Mohammad Hussain insisted that the selectors had not bowed to any pressure from outside. 'We made the decision on the facts. Our young players have done well in the first two drawn Tests and we never wanted the Packer players in our team, but there were so many things to consider. We invited some of our friends to give us their views and that is all that they did,' he said, but I am convinced that had the England players not stuck out their necks so loyally and bravely the rebels would have been welcomed back to the fold.

Another powerful voice, probably the most powerful of all, belonged to General Zia Ul-Haq, Pakistan's chief martial law administrator. He watched play during the first morning and specifically asked me to visit him to give him my views on the Packer circus and outline our version of events in the tense build-up to the Test. I went for tea with the general, along with Wasim Bari, and sought his opinion. He told me he was against the Packer trio being part of the Pakistan team, an opinion which certainly had reached the ears of the selectors, who must have looked to him for guidance, particularly as the fear of civil unrest hung over their deliberations. He added that he had spoken with Mushtaq and Zaheer:

*I reminded them that they had signed a contract with our board before signing for Packer and that they should be available for Pakistan. Mushtaq said that they were in Pakistan and wanted to play, but I pointed out that their presence was possible only because Mr Packer agreed. It is not up to Mr Packer to decide who plays for*

*Pakistan and when. I was very firm with them. I know we live in a materialistic age, but some things are more important than money. If it is only money you want, you are no better than a prostitute. Mr Packer is not promoting cricket, he is prostituting it. You cannot just come to Pakistan for one Test match, take thousands of rupees of my money and then go back to Australia.*

Mushtaq and Zaheer must have departed in some haste after that, and General Zia clearly understood things perfectly. Both Wasim and I took the opportunity to emphasise that we did not want Packer men to be included in the Pakistan squad to tour England in the summer of 1978.

Nor, for that matter, did the rest of the official game, and as England travelled on to New Zealand the players' hard line became cemented into a series of resolutions put forward for consideration by the Cricketers' Association. These confirmed the widespread opposition to the breakaway organisation. Mike Hendrick proposed and Ian Botham seconded that 'Members of the Cricketers' Association will only play Test cricket with or against players not contracted to professional cricket outside the control of the ICC and the TCCB'; Bob Taylor proposed and Mike Gatting seconded that 'Members of the Cricketers' Association will not play first-class cricket against any touring side which includes players contracted to professional cricket outside the control of the ICC and TCCB'; and John Lever proposed and Geoff Miller seconded that 'Members of the Cricketers' Association will not play with or against players contracted to professional cricket outside the control of the ICC and TCCB in first-class cricket, John Player League, Benson and Hedges Cup and Gillette Cup while their contracts preclude their availability for Test matches and their own countries' domestic competitions.' I deliberately did not put my name to any proposal as I did not want World Series Cricket and Greig to have any more ammunition. However, on behalf of the squad I wrote to Doug Insole to confirm our position, which we all felt was justified.

It is interesting to look back and reflect on what might have happened to world cricket had the English players followed the party line and featured in that Karachi Test alongside the Packer trio. Would Test cricket have had to accommodate the circus and its players? Could the English domestic game have survived? I cannot pretend to be ready with all the answers, but I believe that England's stance greatly assisted in containing the Packer empire within acceptable parameters and ensuring the survival intact of the traditional forms of the game, and that the final peace settlement in 1980 owed something to our input. But Packer won. By taking on and beating the establishment over television rights, he proved himself to be a tough and hard customer, a street-wise businessman, but what I admire most about him is the fact that he is very fair and loyal to all his employees. You can always deal with a man like that because you know where you stand with him. There is no back stabbing with Packer. He is up front with everything, and if he doesn't like something he says so very firmly. He possesses values that I respect, including great vision and the courage to pursue apparently impossible dreams. By adopting extreme measures to get what he wanted, Packer made many enemies among those who believed they had an almost divine right to run cricket, and he threatened the existence of the professional game, but, to balance the picture, it should be acknowledged that he managed to take cricket forward.

Emotions ran high at the time, and I understand Greig and his outbursts. He had burned his bridges, so he was fighting for his very existence. He was misinformed, though, about my acting as any sort of ringleader; for once I could parade my innocence for all to see. Greig's gamble in throwing in his lot with Packer brought rich rewards eventually, but his initial worries blinded him to the realities. He did get some things right, although I don't think any altruistic vision inspired him. The South Africans, banned from international cricket because of apartheid, discovered a platform in the shape of Packer's cricket on which to advertise their skills. Additionally, top personalities in Pakistan and West Indies, who felt they were being poorly paid, enjoyed the extra riches, and Packer certainly helped to break the shackles in which cricketers were bound by their masters, but the super-Tests really only improved life for a few and threatened the livelihood of the many by creating two warring factions. Any extension of the Packer enterprise could easily have undermined the established game, particularly at Test level, by stealing its leading players and devaluing the official international programme. As most domestic cricket was, and is still, financed by profits from Test matches, the consequences for rank-and-file professionals could have been extremely serious.

I am, however, glad to say that Tony Greig and I are good friends again these days. It would be unfair to blame Tony for not feeling the same way about English cricket as those of us born and bred in the country. His father was English, but he grew up in South Africa, and I wonder if he would ever have come to England to pursue his career had South Africa not been banned from the international sporting arena. During our spells in commentary boxes around the world, I often teased him with the question: 'Who are you supporting today, Australia, South Africa or England?' Our colleagues invariably chorused: 'Whoever is winning.' His attitude owed something, too, to his desire to move on into the world of business. He never really visualised himself as the long-serving performer on the field, despite lots of ability and a tremendously competitive spirit, so he settled comfortably into a senior position with Packer in Australia.

The English authorities took a small revenge on Greig by denying him honorary life membership of the MCC until 1998. This distinction is granted to all England captains, but Greig had to wait for twenty years. I wrote to tell him: 'Making you wait that long is wrong and unfair. Your record with England will stand any scrutiny from friends or enemies. It is an excellent one – something you can rightly be proud of. I had to wait seven years, but finally it came.' In the end, though, officialdom did not change the course of history. That was something the players did.

Players created cricketing history again in 1982 by going on an unofficial tour to South Africa. When the seven of us – myself, Graham Gooch and John Lever of Essex, John Emburey of Middlesex, Dennis Amiss of

Warwickshire, and Alan Knott and Derek Underwood of Kent, soon to be joined by Peter Willey and Wayne Larkins from Northamptonshire, my Yorkshire colleague Chris Old, Leicestershire's Les Taylor and Derbyshire's Mike Hendrick, who flew out of London shortly after we touched down (later still, Kent's Bob Woolmer, Warwickshire's Geoff Humpage and another Yorkshireman, Arnie Sidebottom, increased our numbers) – stepped from a jumbo jet on to the tarmac at Jan Smuts airport on 28 February 1982, we caused a cloudburst of indignation in many quarters. Without trial, we were found guilty of allegedly defying the politically inspired Gleneagles agreement, a document drawn up by people who did not understand sport or sportsmen. The agreement prohibited sporting contact with South Africa, whose government's determination to maintain a comprehensive colour bar had made the country's white population unacceptable throughout much of the civilised world.

As we stood in the South African sunshine on that fateful February day, all of us were convinced that we were doing no more than pursuing our legitimate business as professional cricketers. We had no hidden agenda, and the motive behind our decision to visit South Africa was purely financial. My own reasoning took into account the fact that cricket was being used as a tool to put apartheid in the spotlight and exert pressure on the South African authorities. This did not seem either fair or reasonable because cricketers were powerless to change the way the country was run. There were many anomalies, too. It was not against English law for companies to trade with South Africa, and many leading South African sportsmen were able to prosper on the international stage, golfer Gary Player being a notable example. In addition, a number of South African cricketers were earning good livings on the county championship circuit, including Allan Lamb at Northamptonshire, and Chris and Robin Smith at Hampshire, while English players regularly wintered in South Africa, supplementing their incomes by taking on coaching engagements. Nothing in the situation made any sense.

In his welcoming speech, Joe Pamensky, the president of the South

African Cricket Union, also underlined another important factor in the equation:

*The SACU, a body which recognises no distinction of race, colour or creed, has made strenuous efforts to enable this country to participate in the international arena. A delegation of the International Cricket Conference visited this country in March 1979 and acknowledged that no further changes were necessary for South Africa to take its place in the international cricket community. The delegation recommended that a team chosen from members of countries of the ICC should tour South Africa. Political pressure became so great, however, that the intention of the administrators could not be carried out. We will continue our efforts to gain admittance to the ICC, but at the same time the SACU has emphasised that there is a demand from players, public and sponsors for an end to our isolation. The English players have risked their future careers and we believe they have taken a stand against the hypocrisy and double standards that have kept South African cricketers from taking their rightful place in the international cricket community.*

Two days later, as the self-appointed guardians of public morality continued to shriek their protests, Pamensky added: 'South Africa has been the scene of numerous fact-finding missions. Without exception these commissions have found South African cricket to have achieved and, in fact, exceeded the requirements for readmission into world cricket.' Looking at things from a sportsman's point of view, it was difficult, if not impossible, to understand the anger our activities aroused.

Peter Cooke, a passionate cricket enthusiast and the manager of a large South African recording company, first raised the possibility of a tour with me in December 1980 while I was on holiday in South Africa preparing for England's trip to the West Indies starting the following month. Peter took time off work to bowl to me in the nets, play golf and tennis and generally help me to gain full fitness. We got on very well and obviously talked a lot about cricket. Cooke revealed a deep and genuine concern about the increasing effects of isolation on South African cricket. He explained:

> *Eddie Barlow, one of our greatest cricketers, is on the point of retiring and his loss will be greatly felt. How long will it be before other outstanding players like Graeme Pollock, Barry Richards and Mike Proctor follow suit? Allan Lamb is making himself available for England, Kepler Wessels has been lost to Australia, and both Robin and Chris Smith have decided to become honorary Englishmen, just for the chance to play Test cricket. I fear that our children will never have the opportunity to watch or play Test cricket in South Africa. Kids in the schools are losing interest in the game and something drastic has to be done if the game is not to die in this country.*

I understood Peter's anxiety and sense of frustration. He was not a revolutionary intent on changing the political climate, merely a man who wanted to revive cricket in his own country.

The details of an unauthorised tour began to take shape in February 1981 when Cooke arrived in Trinidad and caught up with the touring England party. Maintaining secrecy was essential, so we chose a codename – Operation Chess – which covered all the clandestine negotiations, and set up a players' company called Oxychem in London. It sounds now a bit like the plot of a spy novel, but at the time we were all feeling our way carefully in uncharted territory. David Gower and Ian Botham were among the first to sign an individual letter of intent, which read:

> *This letter serves to confirm that I, (player's name), the undersigned, agree in principle to the proposed tour of South Africa as explained by Geoff Boycott – i.e. approximately one month from early to mid-October 1981 to finish in time for England players to return home*

*for a few days before touring India. I understand that I will be*
*required to sign an agreement under English law and the said*
*contract will be binding. Upon signing the agreement I will receive*
*an advance payment to be determined, and that will be paid in*
*whichever way I so wish it to be – as will the rest of the monies due*
*to me. I understand that the knowledge of this tour will be kept*
*confidential and not be made public by me or anyone connected*
*with the proposed tour until one month prior to the commencement*
*of the tour.*

John Emburey, Graham Dilley (Kent) and Gooch also put their signatures on the dotted line.

We wanted to recruit as many current England Test players as possible, but were determined that the tour should not in any way clash with any part of the English season or with any Test matches. Our intention was not to become another pirate organisation like Kerry Packer's, and we definitely did not want to challenge the authority of the TCCB, except where it directly affected our rights as individuals to earn the best possible living from our skills as cricketers.

During our tour of the West Indies the intense nature of the apartheid argument was brought home to us by the refusal of the Guyanese government to allow Robin Jackman into their country. The Surrey seamer found himself banned because he had a South African wife and earned part of his living out there. It appeared for a time that the whole West Indies tour might be cancelled, and as the England squad sat around kicking their heels it became clear that our original plans regarding South Africa would have to be modified. The trouble in Guyana suggested that it would be wise to postpone, temporarily at least, our South African venture to spare the TCCB any possible embarrassment. We reckoned the Indian government might also take exception to the composition of the England party for the full official winter tour coming up in 1981-82 if it included anyone involved in matches in South Africa. In fact, every move we made, unlike the Packer circus, was governed by the need to protect the established game, and we did our best throughout to avoid complications for the various governing bodies.

Those cricketers who expressed interest in the South African project also had to take into consideration a letter sent in August 1981 by the TCCB to every county player which warned that anyone taking part in tours to South Africa 'could thereby make himself ineligible for future selection for England'. The people at Lord's clearly knew that something was going on without being aware of any details. So, quite reasonably, the potential South African tourists wanted some financial guarantees, and a meeting took place in Bob Willis's room at the Express Hotel in Baroda, India, on 21 November 1981. Botham, Dilley, Gower, Gooch, Emburey and myself were present, and by this time Holiday Inns had agreed to sponsor our proposed tour, putting up £500,000 to cover the costs of a party of fourteen, plus Bernard Thomas as physiotherapist-manager. It was generally agreed that we wanted a financial guarantee to fall back on if we were banned from Test cricket, and Gower offered a figure of £150,000 spread over three years as a realistic sum. The Holiday Inns' representative, Stuart Banner, finally put forward £45,000 up front for each player with the option for a second and third year if we were suspended from international cricket.

An agreement had almost been reached when, under a cloud of uncertainty, the whole business collapsed at the end of December. Holiday Inns had stipulated that their backing was dependent upon myself and Botham being in the English party. During the second Test against India at Bangalore, Botham withdrew to protect his income from endorsements and other sources outside the game, and so did our sponsors. This was a crippling blow which put an end to our plans, and it was not easy to take Botham seriously when he later claimed that his change of heart had been brought about by his friendship with West Indian batsman Viv Richards – we all knew that his hand was on his wallet rather than his heart. Gower followed Botham's lead and backed out, using his business interests in the Caribbean as the reason.

Peter Cooke might easily have shrugged his shoulders and walked away from the wreckage at this stage, but he refused to give up hope and continued to search for ways to boost cricket in South Africa. On 22 February 1982 he met Peter Savory, managing director of South African Breweries, in the Long Room at The Wanderers Stadium in Johannesburg. Savory asked how much money would be needed to fulfil Cooke's ambition and was told that the figure was around one million rand. Savory immediately said 'No problem', and followed up with a letter of confirmation the next day. The wheels were in motion once again.

Within forty-eight hours Cooke was on his way to London, where the arrangements were quietly put into place. I played no part in this development as I was at home recovering from a viral infection which had caused my early return from the Indian tour. I felt that nothing worthwhile could be achieved, and was surprised when a newspaper report claimed that I intended to fly to South Africa to organise and play in a 'rebel' tour. Donald Carr, the secretary of the TCCB, telephoned me immediately, but I was able to tell him truthfully that I had no intention of going to South Africa. Unaware of Peter Cooke's activities, I contacted Willis in India to warn him that Carr was making enquiries which might eventually relate to our abandoned venture. Willis knew at that point that a new tour had become a possibility, and Peter filled in more details when he arrived in England. Still far from well and preoccupied with the ongoing dramas at Yorkshire, I remained very much in the background as Peter, showing impressive determination and energy, steadily recruited a useful squad.

England's tourists returned from India on 24 February and Peter Cooke's group was due to fly out on the twenty-eighth, the departure advanced twenty-four hours as TCCB questions became more searching and unnerving. Several players endured agonising hours of soul-searching, and Peter struggled to handle the pressure behind a crumbling wall of secrecy. Willis withdrew fewer than twenty-four hours before the flight was due to take off, feeling that he had a future in English cricket as an administrator, and Northamptonshire opener Geoff Cook also backed out at the last minute. Short of a batsman and close to breaking point, Peter telephoned me to plead: 'I want to get a team out of the country and I need you to be in it.' My mind was in a whirl because on 24 February I had learned that an in-depth inquiry into the state of Yorkshire cricket had recommended that I should be sacked. The reality was that I could be out of a job at the age of forty-one. I also realised that Raman Subba Row, the manager of England's tour party in India, and captain Keith Fletcher were likely to produce unfavourable reports on my contribution to the common cause on the Indian Tour, and the press was doing rather more than just hinting that, despite my best endeavours, I had made my last Test appearance. Although I would much rather have continued to play for England, I realised that too many influential voices were being raised against me, so I decided I could not afford to gamble on what might happen. Peter Cooke had allayed my doubts about the strength of the squad, and I accepted his offer.

Everything became a hectic rush as I packed a couple of cases and scrambled on board the 1.06 p.m. train from Wakefield to London. In my haste I left my suit bag on the train, but by some miracle a taxi driver managed to rush back from the Royal Garden Hotel to King's Cross to find it in time. From the moment our plane took off we realised that we had made ourselves outcasts so far as the TCCB and the ICC were concerned, but we refused to abandon our basic principles. We gradually came to realise that the South African Cricket Union was trying to pass us off as an England team, which was something we could not accept, and at our insistence Peter had to make sure that our title was emphasised as the South African Breweries' England XI on every scoreboard.

Interestingly, Peter Cooke had added West Indian-born batsman Alvin Kallicharran, who was playing in South Africa, to our party. Having lived in England for fourteen years, playing for Warwickshire, he qualified as an English player and was duly issued with his tour kit. However, the South African Cricket Union and the sponsors had a change of heart during a gathering called to discuss playing conditions and other tour arrangements. Joe Pamensky raised the subject of Kallicharran and informed us that the South African Breweries wanted him out. By insisting on this point, Pamensky interfered with our selection policy and, as far as I was concerned, broke an important agreement. Up to that stage it had been intended that I would captain the SAB England XI, but, believing strongly that we had been badly let down, I told Pamensky that I was no longer available to lead the party and left the meeting.

Inevitably, various accounts of this incident have been aired publicly, mostly to my discredit, but the truth is that I did not cause a major row or lose my temper. On the contrary, as Peter, the man in the middle of it all, has consistently confirmed: 'Behind the scenes Geoff was strong and full of sound advice as to what to say and do.' I remember informing the rest of the England squad of my decision and trying to take any heat out of the situation by turning the issue into a joke. 'Imagine me going back to England and being invited to Buckingham Palace,' I said. 'I would be kneeling in front of the Queen and, with her sword on my right shoulder, she would ask: "Are you Geoffrey Boycott from Yorkshire?" I would reply: "Yes, ma'am." Then, with her sword on my left shoulder, she would ask: "Did you play cricket in South Africa with the rebels?" Again, I would reply: "Yes, ma'am." Finally, with a quick swish of the sword, she would cry: "Off with your head then!"'

It is ironic, however, that at a time when I was standing up for Kallicharran I should be accused of supporting apartheid and helping to oppress black cricketers. To emphasise the collective position of the English squad, we issued a statement, which read: 'All players in the South African Breweries' English team wish to make it clear that our purpose in being in South Africa is to play cricket and earn our living. Even though we are guests in South Africa, we would like it to be known that we do not support apartheid.' Unfortunately, menacing phone calls and bomb threats were received on the first day of the opening fixture, a one-day international against South Africa at St George's Park, Port

Elizabeth. These, together with the 'poison pen' approach of the English press, emphasised the political implications of what other people were doing to make capital out of our presence in South Africa.

The TCCB added its weight to the argument within a few days of our arrival, relaying a communication individually to each member of the party through A.R. Thomas, the deputy consul general. It read:

*We must make you aware of the very strong reaction in England and other countries to the proposed participation by you and other English cricketers in international-calibre matches in South Africa. In particular, the India and Pakistan tours to the UK this summer could clearly be in danger if the proposed matches take place, thus seriously affecting county finances and the possible future livelihood of fellow cricketers. If it is practical for you to do so, we urge you to reconsider your position and refrain from playing in any such matches.*

Signed by Carr, as secretary, and George Mann, as chairman, this represented moral blackmail of the worst kind.

On 19 March 1982, the TCCB officially announced that all on the rebel tour would be banned from Test cricket for three years. It was a savage sentence, although the TCCB, ducking and weaving through a fog of possible legal consequences, insisted that the ban was to protect the game rather than to punish us. We investigated the possibility of dragging the whole matter through the courts and took advice from Robert Alexander QC, the barrister who appeared for Packer in his battle with the TCCB. He was sure we would win an action for restraint of trade, but he also recognised that the TCCB, acting as a trades union, would be seen to be protecting the game. In that case the ban would probably not be lifted. We had the SACU firmly on our side throughout, and Pamensky spoke out strongly, saying:

*The penalties imposed on the players are unfair. The players have done no more than exercise their inalienable right to earn a living wherever they choose. The International Cricket Conference adopted a unanimous resolution last year which committed member countries to recognising the right of all countries to pick for Test matches any players they see fit to choose without interference from any other country. By abandoning this principle the TCCB have endorsed the oft-expressed view that the ICC has no teeth. The meek submission of the TCCB to threats is deeply regretted. It confirms the widespread view that cricket administrators throughout the world are hiding behind the politicians instead of committing themselves to the cause of cricket. The SACU stand behind the principle that all cricketers – and especially those who hail from England – have the free right to choose where they play. Some sixty cricket professionals from England have chosen to play and coach in South Africa this very season. In principle there can be no difference between individuals visiting South Africa and playing cricket and a group of individuals playing in a team.*

It might be argued that Pamensky's was a vested-interest stance, but his words were echoed by another observer, Tommie Campbell, chairman of the International Steering Committee of Freedom in Sport. Campbell, watching the second and third days of the match against South Africa at Newlands as a guest of the Western Province Cricket Union, commented: 'By imposing a ban from Test cricket on players currently touring South Africa with the SAB England XI, the TCCB have committed a complete turnabout of policy. They are condoning the basic felony which was committed by South Africa at the time of the D'Oliveira affair.' This was a reference to South Africa's refusal to accept Cape-coloured all-rounder Basil D'Oliveira, then with Worcestershire, as a member of the England touring party in 1968, a decision which rightly resulted in the tour being cancelled. Campbell continued: 'The TCCB decision means that for the first time in history an England side will not be selected on merit. The TCCB will be imposing a makeshift Test team on the British public. No one has the right to tell an individual, law-abiding citizen where he may play his games, earn his living or enjoy his leisure.'

Those were fine sentiments, but the TCCB continued to make expediency their guiding principle. As late as 1 August 1986 they were issuing directives to all county players warning them against accepting coaching or playing contracts in South Africa after 1987 – even as individuals – if they wanted to preserve their prospects of Test selection. Overall, it was a rotten business, the more so as when I went to South Africa in 1964 under Donald Carr as manager, England played without a murmur of protest in front of crowds segregated on the basis of race and colour by high-wire fences! How times had changed. As players in 1982, we were left to take our medicine and get on with completing the tour, which we did with our heads held high, our spirits constantly raised by the messages of good will and support which flooded in from South Africa and every other corner of the cricketing world.

The stupidity of it all was brought home to us during the 1982 English season. As we served the first year of our ban from Test cricket, Allan Lamb, born and bred in Cape Province, South Africa, featured in six matches for England against India and Pakistan. Although India had raised petty objections about Geoff Cook and myself touring with England the previous winter because we had played privately in South Africa, neither of the touring parties made any reference to Lamb. All along the line, cricket was hamstrung by double standards which, sadly, still exist today, and which might seriously affect South Africa again.

The dramatic and welcome political changes brought about by the election of Nelson Mandela as president created favourable circumstances for the readmission of South Africa to the world of international sport. They had ceased to be a member of the ICC on leaving the British Commonwealth in 1961 and were elected as full members in 1991, a four-match series against India in 1992–93 marking the country's resumption of Test cricket. Rapidly, their well-organised and skilful team established itself as a formidable force, challenging Australia for the title of world champions.

Much to the annoyance of some politicians, however, South Africa's senior squad remains largely white, and positive steps are being taken to introduce apartheid in reverse. Those in charge should remember why the South African Cricket Board was renamed the United Cricket Board. The decision was made so that cricket in South Africa would be truly united, with all races together, black, coloured and white. The ANC talked abouit equality and of creating a united South Africa, so their concern should be with all the people.

The Minister of Sport, Steve Tshwete, revealed on 3 January 1999 that he could not support the South African team playing the West Indies in the fourth Test at Newlands, Cape Town, 'because the selectors have failed to give opportunities to more black players, despite clinching the five-match series'. Tshwete, who has publicly disagreed with United Cricket Board managing director Ali Bacher over 'lily-white' team selection, continued: 'I am worried we will be sending white teams to the rugby and cricket world cups.' Tshwete's theory clearly was that as South Africa, already with a 3–0 series lead when they reached Cape Town, could not lose they should have taken the opportunity to blood a number of black players not good enough to be chosen in a competitive situation. His thinking marked him out as someone with none of the feelings of a professional sportsman.

In response, Bacher rightly pointed out that 'the board has enormous respect for Steve Tshwete, who played a crucial role in the unification of cricket, but we disagree on this issue. If we had picked a below-strength side for the Newlands Test, it would have been demeaning to the West Indies and unfair to the commercial stakeholders in the game. It would also have devalued the honour of representing South Africa in a Test match.' Bacher was unquestionably right. Three days later, the UCB set an immediate and minimum target of twenty-two black players to play representative cricket in next summer's domestic schedule. Explaining official thinking, Bacher said:

*We, as a board, feel we would like to have at least twenty-two*
*coloured players as regular choices at first-class level next season. We*
*will then be looking at a figure like thirty-three the following season*

*and will have long-term targets for the next three seasons. There are two key issues. One is to maintain the high standard of South Africa's domestic competitions, and the other is to give more opportunities at first-class level to more players of colour. This latter point is absolutely imperative.*

Without doubt, therefore, the intention of the United Cricket Board – and, I imagine, other sporting codes – is to concentrate on getting black players on the field at every level of competition, even if this means selection on the basis of race rather than ability. To this end, a Transformation Charter for South African Cricket has been produced with ten main objectives covering all aspects of the game which must be achieved within the next three years. As part of this grand design, a four-man monitoring committee has been set up to oversee selection. This means that the selectors operate while constantly looking over their shoulders, despite all their experience and knowledge. The chairman, Peter Pollock, and Mike Proctor played Test cricket, and Clive Rice would certainly have done so but for South Africa's years in the wilderness. This trio is joined by Rushtie Diemajiet, representing the black sections of the game, and Maurice Garda from the Indian (Gauteng) Board. To most people these selectors, in consultation with coach Bob Woolmer, who sits on meetings without having a vote, would be capable enough of picking a satisfactory Test team, but their efforts are scrutinised by four 'monitors': UCB president Ray White, vice-president Percy Sonn, board member Gerald Majoli, and Bacher. The inference is clear: if the 'monitors' want to make changes, they can overrule the selectors.

Ray White is on record as stating: 'Our historic and moral duty is to ensure that South African cricket grows and flourishes among the truly disadvantaged of our society while recognising that the majority of the disadvantaged people come from our black African communities. This involves a commitment to promote and develop cricket among black African people at all levels.' These are fine words with which the great majority of observers agree, but by introducing positive discrimination with minimum quotas of black cricketers in all teams, South Africa are reviving apartheid in another guise. They are promoting the very system they fought against with understandable fervour. It was unjust then, and it is unjust now.

Another example of cricket being influenced by politics was provided by the Gauteng Cricket Board, who decided not to renew the contract of white coaching manager Ray Jennings when it expired at the end of March this year. Barry Skjoldhammer, the chairman of the Gauteng Board, said: 'Ray's uncompromising approach in facing difficulties has not always endeared him to people universally and may, in some cases, have been interpreted by some as inflexibility, especially in some of the more sensitive issues faced by cricket and, indeed, all sports administrators in South Africa today.' Gauteng enjoyed a successful season under Jennings, who pointed the way towards the truth by claiming: 'South African cricket has this cancer of hidden agendas at the moment.' My guess is that Gauteng will appoint a black person to replace Jennings once the fuss has died down.

The problem for South Africa is that logically they cannot advance the cause of black cricket quickly enough to satisfy the politicians, as was demonstrated in January 1999. Western Province opening batsman Herschelle Gibbs, Free State fast bowler Victor Mpitsang and Boland seamer Henry Williams, all good black cricketers, featured in the seventeen-strong squad for the one-day series against the West Indies. This trio was joined by Western Province batsman Ashwell Prince, Boland fast bowler Roger Telemachus and Border paceman Makhaya Ntini in South Africa's provisional World Cup squad. In this way, the cricket selectors showed their good intent, but even then Mluleki George, the National Sports Council president, complained that the parties were still 'far from the ideal of racially representative national sports teams'. George also stressed: 'There is still more to be done because we maintain that the national teams should reflect the demographics of the country.' Taking George's opinion as a guideline, South Africa's teams will shortly include ten players on merit plus one token black representative, followed by a nine to two ratio, and then eight to three, and so on. I wonder sometimes if the day will come when some organisation or another pushes for at least one woman to be chosen in national teams to ensure an element of sexual equality.

In the meantime I fear that the South African government will not be satisfied until the various national teams are made up of whites and blacks in ratios that relate exactly to the breakdown of the population. It is, of course, all utter nonsense. There is no virtue or benefit in legislating against the white youngsters who are trying to build careers in cricket in South Africa. If someone who is demonstrably less talented is promoted above them they are likely to be devastated and confused. The quota system works against them, but they have nowhere to go and no one to turn to. The probability is that some promising sportsmen will have their lives ruined by ill-conceived policies, as their chances of playing cricket outside South Africa without a proven track record are virtually nil. As I see it, those now in power in South Africa are allowing themselves to slip into the very standards they once so viciously attacked. The emerging generation of white South African cricketers is not responsible for the faults of their parents and grandparents, and they deserve to be considered on merit in the same way as black Africans.

Former West Indian batsman Conrad Hunte spent seven years in South Africa working on a development programme before returning recently to Barbados. His background and working experience equip him to make an objective assessment of black potential, and he says: 'The UCB faced two tensions, the first being the high expectations of the population, who want more black players in the national team. The other problem is that although the development programme has been going for fifteen years, it takes at least three generations to produce superstars. We have to have black players at the top level, but they have to be qualified to be there.' This is a view shared by most people in South Africa, but all South Africans should listen to Hunte. Black cricketers need encouragement, but it will not help their development if they are exposed to pressures they cannot handle. South African cricket will go backwards instead of forwards if a national team containing players who are obviously not good enough is consistently beaten in Test matches.

Soccer is increasingly a major attraction out there, drawing big attendances at matches and huge television audiences. SABC television conducted a poll during a top game as to whether national teams should be selected entirely on merit. The studio calculated that 90 per cent of their viewers responded to produce a 97 per cent yes vote. The majority of those seriously taking part in sport as either professionals or amateurs appreciate that the crucial element is maintaining the highest possible standards; anything else is a waste of time. Patience is an elusive virtue, but unless the South African government takes the necessary time to nurture talent among the black members of their society, cricket will not prosper. Any success achieved by the national team now, whatever the colour, will do far more to encourage an enthusiasm for cricket than any legislation. Black African and coloured African youngsters must learn to walk before they can run.

# CHAPTER FIVE

# The Men in White Coats

From the earliest days of organised cricket, the umpire's job has been reasonably straightforward, and when I began my first-class career back in 1962 their decisions were largely unchallenged. Certainly the general public accepted their collective judgement without comment, even when television offered a closer black-and-white view of play.

The advances in technology, however, have put modern umpires under tremendous pressure, particularly in Test matches and one-day internationals, where the more contentious rulings on lbw and catches by the wicketkeeper are analysed in minute detail. Incidents in important domestic competitions also come under close scrutiny, and the game is screened all over the world on a regular basis, exposed to an audience which is not necessarily aware of the difficulties facing the officials out in the middle. Inevitably, mistakes are spotlighted, and with television companies paying huge sums for the privilege of covering cricket, there is little or no chance of either the cameras or the commentators being restricted in their approach. Understandably, the television companies want to show cricket as it is, warts and all, for incidents are the lifeblood of their industry. Therefore, the responsibility for creating the best possible image lies with the leading authorities within the game, and one of their major tasks is to raise the stature and profile of umpires.

The lead must come from the International Cricket Council, a body which has hitherto been both too weak and too political, lacking the will and the strength of character to push through essential reform. The various cricket-playing countries nominate people for places on ICC committees, and many of them, seeking to advance their own prospects, are interested mainly in not upsetting anyone. For this reason, I would like to see the formation of a loosely knit, interchangeable sub-committee of former Test cricketers from different countries, men who could look at situations objectively because they would not be seeking permanent jobs within the organisation. I cannot, for example, see any reason why the chairman of the ICC could not be given the power to contact, when necessary, a broad spread of experienced ex-Test cricketers able to give impartial advice. Sunil Gavaskar, Imran Khan, Richard Hadlee and Clive Rice are the sort of strong characters who possess knowledge the game cannot afford to neglect, and, although they are not available on a regular day-in-day-out basis, they would, I am sure, be prepared to contribute part-time.

Undoubtedly, the current administration is a long way short of being satisfactory, never mind perfect. Evidence of muddled thinking abounds, not least with the policy of appointing match referees for international occasions. Basically, it is little more than a public relations exercise, a matter of being seen to do something about the control of matches and behaviour on the field. A lot of expense is involved, and being a referee is a nice job, with a select few doing little more than watching the game; for 99 per cent of the time, the referee's role requires only the filling in of forms and reports. Having spent time travelling around the cricket-playing world for television, I suspect that some of them feel they have to justify their existence every now and then by imposing a fine, making a statement or enforcing a suspension. Too often the action of the referee eventually becomes a bigger issue in the news than the actual incident. The ICC guidelines limit what the referee can say publicly, so the press are left to speculate endlessly on something that otherwise might well have been forgotten in a matter of minutes. As a consequence, the whole business can drag on for several days.

Perhaps the most famous incident of all was the 'dirt in the pocket' drama at Lord's in July 1994, when England captain Mike Atherton was spotted in close-up on television apparently rubbing some substance onto the ball in the course of England's humiliating 356-run defeat at the hands of South Africa. Umpires Steve Randell, from Australia, and Dickie Bird did not take any action as the condition of the ball remained unchanged and the South Africans registered no complaint, but the referee, Australian Peter Burge, opened up a real can of worms by deciding to conduct an investigation during which Atherton, when interviewed, was economical with the truth in his insistence that he had had nothing in his pocket. In the face of further television evidence, the England captain then admitted that he had picked up a handful of soil to absorb the sweat on his hands. Chairman of selectors Ray Illingworth fined Atherton £2,000, but otherwise supported the captain by ignoring calls for his sacking, and the media storm raged for several days.

When the dust literally settled, the case for getting rid of referees and giving greater power to the umpires had been well and truly made. The ICC originally brought in match referees to help umpires, but the weakness of the system is that in doing so they actually undermined them, leaving them without a deterrent of their own. What can an umpire do if a player uses bad language? Realistically, not a lot, other than threaten to report the offender in the same way generations of harassed mothers have warned naughty children: 'Just wait until your father comes home!' That hardly deals with the immediate problem. An umpire could, I suppose, give him out to a frivolous appeal when given the chance, but that would be ludicrous, and no self-respecting official would base decisions on anything other than the evidence. The truth is that another tier of authority has been introduced, making life harder all round.

The umpires have one obvious advantage over the referee: they are nearer to the action, dealing closely with the players, and are in a position to react instantly. But there are no well-defined rules to empower them to stamp out, for instance, gamesmanship or 'sledging'. Instead, they are obliged to wait for an interval or the close of play before calling in the referee, who then has to investigate the matter by interviewing the player or players concerned and their captain. Justice delayed is justice betrayed, and on-the-spot punishment invariably stops things getting out of hand. Other sports, including rugby league and ice hockey, have shown the way by using the sin-bin and putting offenders out of the game for a spell, while soccer prefers the 'totting up' principle via the use of yellow cards for relatively minor fouls with penalty points adding up to an automatic suspension when a sufficient number are accumulated.

This is one idea worth looking at for cricket, because a tough, easily understood disciplinary procedure in soccer has promoted skill and enhanced the sport's entertainment value. Importantly, the impetus in soccer has come from the top, with FIFA instructing referees to clamp down on those who try to operate outside the laws. A cricketer persistently stepping out of line could be prevented from bowling for a specific period, or a fielder could be 'sent off' to cool down. A batsman showing serious dissent could be forced to miss his team's next innings. The point is that the umpire is best placed to know exactly what is going on. It is not possible to be sure from the boundary edge what a fielder at short leg is saying. It might be possible on television to see his lips moving, but only the umpire can know whether he is being polite or abusive. Alternatively, the umpire could hand out penalty points for misconduct, and here, too, the possibility of eventually being banned ought to concentrate the minds of those who are too often ready to ignore the spirit of the game.

It would be much more convenient for the umpire to be in total control, letting everybody know where they stand and leaving far less scope for ill feeling. Take, for instance, ball tampering. The Pakistanis were vilified for weeks when they toured England in 1996, but, while arguments raged in the newspapers, those in charge kept their heads down and in the end nothing really happened. Surely experienced umpires, with the full backing of the ICC, could have sorted matters out in a few minutes by explaining that they wanted to look at the ball at the end of every over and by warning that any illegal interference with its condition would result in the bowler or bowlers being banished from the attack. I am aware that a raft of legislation exists within the laws of cricket, which state that 'captains are responsible at all times for ensuring that play is conducted within the spirit of the game as well as within the laws', that 'the umpires are the sole judges of fair and unfair play', and that 'umpires shall intervene without appeal by calling and signalling "dead ball" in the case of unfair play'. It is, however, all so vague. There is no 'bite' in this legislation, which effectively leaves the umpires out on a limb.

No one event on the field of play highlighted the problem more clearly than the dismissal of Sri Lanka's brilliant batsman Aravinda de Silva in the third Test against India in Bombay in 1997. Sri Lanka were chasing a remote victory target of 327 in ninety overs on a pitch offering some turn, and the Indians clearly regarded de Silva as a key figure in the contest, so much so that they resorted to a piece of trickery which amounted to sharp practice. As seamer Javagal Srinath advanced along his lengthy run-up to the stumps, Rajesh Chauhan sprinted from orthodox square leg to deep mid-wicket as part of a prearranged plan. De Silva pulled an inviting short delivery from Srinath into what had been a vacant area when he settled into his stance, only to see the catch comfortably held. The Indians insisted that their success rewarded 'good anticipation' by Chauhan, but most impartial observers regarded their actions as cheating. Although de Silva, rightly, blamed his partner, Roshan Mahanama, for not stepping in with a timely warning, umpires Steve Bucknor and A.V. Jayaprakash were even more guilty of neglecting their duties as Chauhan's deception constituted unfair play. Stretching the possibilities to the extreme, cricket could degenerate into farce, with fielders scampering about all over the place during the bowler's run-up.

I was disappointed to note that match referee Bobby Simpson, the former Australian Test skipper, shrugged away the whole unsavoury business, saying: 'It was within the laws of the game and players must do what their consciences dictate.' Ignoring the spirit of the game in so cavalier a fashion hardly sent out the right sort of message. Armed with increased confidence based on much greater authority, umpires would be able to prevent players taking such liberties – in this case, they could have given de Silva not out, citing the fielding side's unsportsmanlike conduct, an on-the-field verdict I, for one, would have liked to see. There is, simply, a lot more chance of umpires commanding respect if the players know that they possess complete authority.

The benefits that would flow from upgrading the status of umpires throughout the first-class game are, I think, undeniable, but conformity is essential. There is no point in handing officials in one country power denied those in another – that would lead to confusion in Test cricket – so the initiative ought to come from the ICC as the world's governing body.

On the other side of the coin, the standard of umpiring would need to be raised considerably on a worldwide basis to meet the requirements. I have always felt that the highly developed professional game in England ensures that we have the best umpires for two reasons: in the first place they are in action throughout the full five-month season; secondly, the majority are ex-cricketers, familiar with all the tricks of the trade. By keeping an ear tuned to the grapevine on the circuit, umpires learn about the batsman who walks when getting a fine edge with a substantial score at his back, but stands his ground in single figures. Word goes round about any player who has a short fuse, or a bowler who tends to overstep when striving for extra pace. For their part, players achieve a working relationship with umpires, appreciating that they have been around for a long time and responding gratefully to the odd friendly warning. A good umpire is never looking to no-ball a bowler, so he is prepared to have a quiet word when a bowler is getting close to overstepping. In return, a sensible player takes care not to upset him, hoping along the way perhaps just to edge the odd fifty-fifty decision his way, so the wheels tend to turn fairly smoothly. There is also the opportunity for the long-serving members of a county staff to mix socially with umpires, with whom they might once have played, either as colleagues or opponents, and a healthy exchange of information is beneficial to both parties.

It is not quite so simple on the international circuit, though. Umpires fly into a country for a couple of Tests and then go on their way again, so there is no opportunity for the same rapport to build up. One way to help overseas umpires would be to introduce a few at a time to the English scene. An experiment along these lines was conducted several years ago and it seemed to work well enough, with our own umpires standing alongside the visitors, who gained both experience and confidence. In overseas countries there is also a shortage of former players on the list of umpires. India's Srinivas Venkataraghavan, once a leading offspinner, is well established as an excellent official, but he stands as the exception which proves an unfortunate rule. Other umpires from around the world find themselves at a disadvantage, lacking the stature and instinctive understanding a distinguished playing record would provide.

There is also a danger that some umpires, anxious to make a name for themselves, will seek opportunities to snatch their 'fifteen minutes of fame'. Some have pushed themselves into the spotlight, and I cannot approve of the behaviour in this respect of Australian Darrell Hair. He called Sri Lankan offspinner Muttiah Muralitharan for throwing in the second Test against Australia at Melbourne in December 1995, and a short account of the events is instructive. Hair no-balled Muralitharan seven times in three overs while standing at the bowler's end – his actions causing some confusion among those in the ground, who thought the umpire was calling front-foot infringements – so the spinner switched to New Zealander Steve Dunne's end, getting through to the tea interval without further mishap. At that point, Hair made it clear that he was ready to call Muralitharan from square leg, a decision which brought matters to a head. Muralitharan did not play in the third Test and doubts about the legitimacy of his action continued.

Apart from raising an eyebrow at the fact that Dunne did not seem to share Hair's concern at Melbourne, I have no argument with what took place up to that point. Subsequently, however, the ICC fully investigated Muralitharan and ruled that because he has a slightly deformed arm his action, although it appeared unorthodox, was acceptable. This should have been the final word, but Hair went on to insist in a book that he would call the spinner again if he umpired him. By writing that, Hair went way beyond his authority, causing a tidal wave of complications on the international scene. An ICC decision should be binding on players and umpires alike, but in this instance, while Hair achieved a degree of notoriety, cricket suffered. (England manager David Lloyd, voicing his own suspicions at the Oval in August 1998, and again in January 1999 during the three-nation one-day series with Sri Lanka and Australia, should also have abided by that ruling.) Hair was eventually charged on four counts by the ICC and found guilty of bringing the game into disrepute, but he escaped punishment when the ICC discovered they had no code for penalising an umpire!

Practical knowledge gained on the field of play is priceless and cannot be acquired through any teaching methods. Thus, the man who has been a first-class cricketer will instinctively get more decisions right when called upon to adjudicate on, for example, claims for a leg-side catch by the wicketkeeper – and make no mistake, there has to be an element of guesswork in a lot of decisions. Although he stood long before my time, I imagine the legendary Alex Skelding must have regularly got it right. He did not, I am told, exactly look the part in his long white coat and thick, bottle-bottom glasses, which indicated that keen eyesight was not his strong suit, but Trevor Bailey, one of the top post-war performers as an all-rounder with Essex and England, told me: 'It didn't seem to matter what Alex saw, he had a nose for cricket and smelled out what had happened.'

In significant contrast, there has long been a cloud over umpires in New Zealand, even before my first visit in 1966. Their own players felt that they lacked confidence in applying the laws and consequently gave too few batsmen out leg before. Bruce Edgar, who made thirty-nine Test appearances for the Kiwis, suggested at one stage that a negative philosophy had developed, with New Zealand umpires preferring to rule 'not out' as the easier option. An air of uncertainty like this may have sparked a couple of flashpoints during the 1979–80 West Indies tour. In the first Test at Dunedin Michael Holding, having had an appeal for a catch at the wicket turned down, kicked the stumps out of the ground. In the second Test at Christchurch, Colin Croft was called for overstepping and reacted by flicking off a bail as he walked back to his mark and barging umpire Fred Goodall during his delivery stride. Both players were guilty of appalling behaviour, but I am convinced that stronger umpires with wider powers would have prevented tempers coming to a boil.

Since December 1993, each country nominates as a matter of routine two names for the panel of international umpires, the exception being England, who are allotted four places because of the full-time county schedule. The thinking behind the formula is understandable because that way no country feels slighted. I can accept that policy to an extent, national pride being increasingly important, but world cricket actually needs the best umpires, regardless of nationality. The logical answer, therefore, is to let countries put forward their leading officials for consideration but to leave final selection to a small multi-racial group of former players and umpires who would be in the best position to assess candidates and select the most accomplished for the highest honours. To take things a step further, I believe that neutral officials should be allocated for each series. The appointment of one home umpire and one neutral represents an uneasy compromise, paying lip-service to the desire for impartiality. It is basic human nature for visiting teams to question debatable decisions by 'home' umpires which go against them, so some officials, subconsciously perhaps, are guilty of overcompensating to avoid accusations along those lines; some England players, certainly, down the years have felt that umpires have gone too far in that direction. Of course, costs will increase as a result of such a policy, but savings on the charges incurred by match referees should provide adequate compensation.

A proper financial structure should be created, too, to end the huge disparity between payments. It is acknowledged that English umpires can be paid up to six times more than an Indian or Pakistani standing in the same match. Indeed, financial considerations have long been a source of irritation to umpires from the poorer countries, but it is not easy to equate rewards when dealing with umpires from different economic climates. As Australian Dave Richards, chief executive of the ICC, has said: 'I don't think it is our job to standardise payments for umpires because standards of living and the value of currencies differ widely in each Test country.' However, it would surely be fair to pay a match official who can make or break a Test series on a scale equivalent to a player of the same nationality, with substantial extra bonuses for long service. For example, most Indian Test players earn more than £100,000 per year, while their umpires receive very little, a disparity which creates resentment. To get the best umpires cricket must pay the best salaries.

Vitally, if umpires are to exercise increased authority, they cannot be subjected to reports from captains. Instead, I would advocate the control methods employed by the National Football League in America. After every match in the NFL a group of experts analyses the decisions taken by the umpires and then holds a discussion with them. Essentially, they guarantee complete confidentiality and the umpires are able to explain their actions. There is an exchange of views and information, and in each instance it is possible to produce a comprehensive and meaningful report on the umpire's performance. All cricket Tests today are televised and viewed throughout the world, making it possible to have readily to hand highlights of every day's play. The ICC could easily involve senior independent umpires and players in the same way, not merely as a punishment squad – although an umpire making a string of bad errors

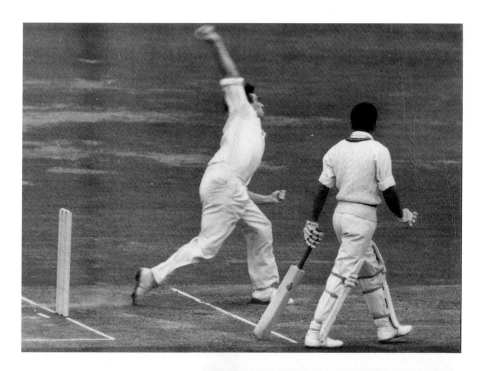

Mr F.S. Trueman in action against the West Indies during the second Test at Lord's in June 1963. Trueman finished with match figures of 11 for 152. (Topham)

Henry Blofeld on duty at Old Trafford during the 1997 Ashes series. (Allsport)

Yorkshire's Richard Hutton, with whom I never managed even an uneasy truce. (Allsport)

Allan Lamb and Ian Botham in July 1996, taking a break from their High Court action against Imran Khan for his *India Today* article, which they claimed had labelled them racist and uneducated. I was called reluctantly to the witness stand. (Topham)

Brian Close, in many ways the ideal Yorkshire cricketer, in mid-shot for England against the West Indies at Trent Bridge in June 1976. (Patrick Eagar)

A more recent shot of Close, from August 1994 when the South Africans were visiting Headingley. (Allsport)

Headingley, a great Test and county cricket ground, in all its finery. (Patrick Eagar)

Back in the nets at Headingley in April 1982 as Yorkshire practise for the new season, under the watchful eyes of coach Doug Padgett (left) and manager Ray Illingworth. (Topham)

Kerry Packer and Tony Greig leaving the High Court in London on the first day of their action against the ICC and the TCCB for restraint of trade. The court ruled in their favour. (Patrick Eagar)

Kerry Packer playing in a journalists' match at Harrogate during the 1977 Australia tour, soon after announcing the birth of World Series Cricket. (Patrick Eagar)

Practising hard in the nets in January 1978 during the 'poisoned chalice' Karachi Test, watched, from left to right, by Paul Downton, Phil Edmonds, Ken Barrington and Geoff Miller. (Patrick Eagar)

ABOVE From left to right, Phil Edmonds, Bob Willis, Mike Gatting, Brian Rose (obscured), Ian Botham, Mike Hendrick, Paul Downton and me – a resolute England party defying the Packer circus. (Patrick Eagar)

BELOW Talking with General Zia, with whom I discussed the situation regarding the Packer players. (Patrick Eagar)

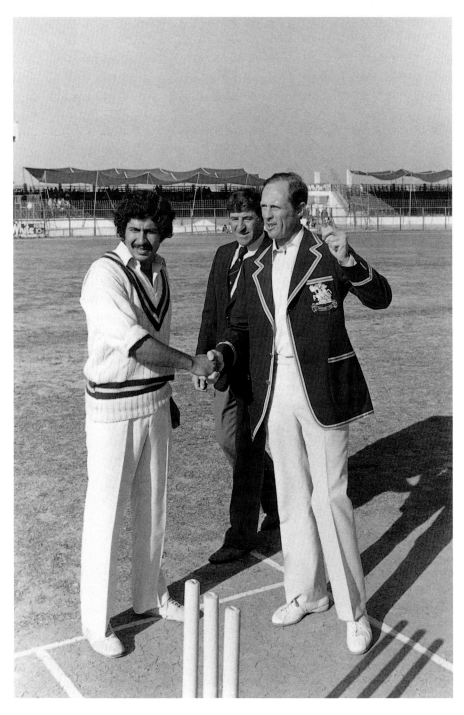

The Pakistani authorities relent and the third Test goes ahead. I am shaking Wasim Bari's hand during the toss, with Ken Barrington looking on. (Patrick Eagar)

ABOVE  In full flow during that third Test at Karachi. (Patrick Eagar)

BELOW  Sachin Tendulkar meets Nelson Mandela in Johannesburg in November 1992 during an historic first visit by India to the new South Africa. (Allsport)

The Sri Lankan spinner Muttiah Muralitharan, whose unusual action was called by umpire Darrell Hair in Melbourne in 1995. David Lloyd has more than raised his eyebrows at it too. (Allsport)

The best-known example of the perils of short-pitched fast bowling: the reckless bravery of Brian Close, pummelled by Michael Holding at Old Trafford, July 1976. (Allsport)

Pictured in 1971 during another battle with the West Indies and Essex fast bowler Keith Boyce. In the early 1970s, I scored double centuries in successive seasons against Essex. (Patrick Eagar)

Educating the cricket-watching public is part and parcel of increasing the sport's audience appeal. Here I am doing a pitch report during the Lord's Test against the West Indies in 1995. (Patrick Eagar)

Analysing the surface on offer for the first Test in Jamaica in 1990 with Michael Holding, a pitch that became infamous eight years later when the opening Test match of England's tour had to be abandoned. (Allsport)

ABOVE Australia was the first country to pioneer floodlit cricket. Sydney at sunset during a World Series match in 1983. (Patrick Eagar)

BELOW Another stunning shot of night cricket at the SCG, taken during England's 1994–95 tour. (Patrick Eagar)

ABOVE  A floodlit Newlands in Cape Town for a one-day international with England in January 1996. (Allsport)

BELOW  A friendly Battle of the Roses under floodlights at Old Trafford in July 1997. (Popperfoto)

would be dropped, at least temporarily – but also as a forum to help improve overall standards.

Equally, there is an indisputable case for making greater use of the television replay. In the days when Alex Skelding established his impressive record, his decisions were not put under the microscope of advanced technology. Today, not only is television looking over every shoulder, but replays can be slowed down and the supposed contact area enlarged to the point where the spectator in his armchair in Manchester has a better view of the crux of an incident at the Oval than the umpire on duty. It does not help anyone if a bad call is highlighted repeatedly, but there is no way of stopping the advance of television. The solution is to turn the situation to cricket's advantage. Already we have a third umpire, who sits in front of a screen and, when called upon, relies on slow-motion television evidence to settle doubts about run-outs. The camera also helps to clear up confusion about dubious catches in the outfield, and passes judgement on the legality of diving stops on the boundary edge, yet, strangely, the official in the middle is left to his own devices when wrestling with appeals for leg-side and bat–pad catches amid a flurry of arms, clothing and equipment.

The ball can be travelling at ninety miles per hour and the umpire has, in most cases, about a third of a second to make up his mind, so guarantees of infallibility are out of the question. South Africa's Jacques Kallis and Jonty Rhodes were adjudged caught behind in the Trent Bridge Test against England in 1998, although replays indicated that on each occasion the ball had brushed the body. Kallis looked distinctly unhappy, while Rhodes, one of the nicest men in cricket, revealed a magnificent sporting attitude and never complained. All the same, as a batsman slightly below the highest class, he must have been very disappointed to lose an innings in such a way. Then Michael Atherton received the benefit of no apparent doubt at Nottingham when caught behind off the glove off the bowling of Allan Donald, who, lacking the self-control of Rhodes, subsequently became involved in some heated exchanges.

The England opener reflected contemporary thinking when he later defended his own part in the proceedings: 'In modern Test cricket batsmen don't walk. They wait for the umpire's decision.' This means that the poor old chap in the white coat can expect no help from the players, even though they claim endlessly that they want fairness and consistency; more use of TV cameras is the only help the umpires can expect. It is easy to label Atherton unsporting, but his approach is a response to the fact that appeals by the fielding side can be part of a campaign to unsettle both a batsman and an umpire. In the circumstances, perfection is even more of an impossible dream, although Ken Suttle, who played in 612 matches for Sussex between 1949 and 1971, recalled only two wrong decisions against him in more than 1,000 innings. He must have been either very lucky or extremely generous in his own assessments; most cricketers accept that luck runs about fifty-fifty throughout a career.

From an official point of view, the aim must be to strive for the best possible results; accepting that lbw will always be a matter of opinion, television could help in almost every other case. Replays would undoubtedly have altered the course of the 1998 England–South Africa series, saving the umpires a lot of embarrassment, and it is a nonsense to have the technology on hand without using it. The less criticism there is of umpires from television commentators, newspapers and the public, the better it is for cricket, but until an acceptable degree of accuracy is achieved media representatives will continue to do their job. To those who resist the introduction of technical aids on the grounds that they would interrupt the flow of the contest, I would say that the nature of cricket is stop–start anyway. Each delivery is an entity in itself following a break, albeit brief, in the proceedings, and adding an extra ten minutes or so to the average day is a small price to pay.

To balance the picture, there are limits, and I do not think that the type of magic eye they employ at the Wimbledon tennis championships would help umpires to apply the no-ball regulation, because there is too much traffic around the crease. I am also very much against the public replaying of incidents requiring an umpiring decision, even though I think the big screens at Test matches add to the enjoyment of everyone. I feel this can definitely hold an umpire up to ridicule, especially from the noisier and more unruly spectators in the ground. It is one thing for a viewer to see a mistake in his own home, and another entirely for it to be brought to the attention of the paying customer at the ground where the game has to continue. After giving his verdict, an umpire is bound to look up at the big screen, seeking confirmation of his judgement, and if he has got it wrong and he hears catcalling from the crowd his confidence is certain to be affected. On a number of grounds throughout the world the spectators believe they have a right to be a part of the action, and any doubts about the dismissal of a local hero are likely to spark a volatile reaction. That is exactly what happened at Melbourne during the 1997–98 series between Australia and South Africa, when Australian umpire Steve Randell, having turned down two lbw appeals by Glenn McGrath against Adam Bacher, became the target of persistent jeering from the crowd.

There is one other important area in which the third umpire could profitably be handed a bigger role: control of the pitch. Currently, a groundsman hands over the pitch to the match officials on the first morning of a Test, and some can be overprotective. I covered the 1997 Test between Pakistan and South Africa at Sheikhapura, near Lahore, where the groundsman became so obsessed with one or two damp patches on the pitch that he delayed the start by refusing to hand it over. On a bright sunny day this caused untold frustration among the players and spectators, who could see for themselves that every other part of the ground was perfectly playable. Eventually, the match referee took it upon himself to get play under way by instructing the captains to toss up. All it needed in the first place was for the decision to be put in more official hands, especially as the groundsman had only one thing on his mind: the state of his precious twenty-two-yard strip. And anyone who doubts the importance of the pitch should try potting snooker balls on a table that is either not level or has very worn patches.

The third umpire is ideally placed to be put in charge of the pitch three days before any Test so that he can shoulder some of the groundsman's burden and help to ensure that the basic requirements for an even contest between bat and ball are provided. I do not advocate the third umpire taking over the groundsman's job, but there have been areas of concern. The Australians lodged a formal complaint before the start of the Headingley Test in 1997 because the pitch had been switched. While their concerns turned out to be unfounded, the presence during the final preparation of an impartial observer in the shape of the third umpire would have eliminated doubts. Much more seriously, the first Test between the West Indies and England in January 1998 had to be abandoned after half an hour or so because the Sabina Park pitch in Jamaica was too dangerous, the ball flying around unpredictably. It turned Test cricket into a farce more readily associated with the humblest village club making the best of a local farmer's field – a case of too much diplomacy and too little common sense.

Employing the third umpire in the role of match manager would also ensure against the chaos which reigned during the India–Pakistan Test at Karachi in 1997 when it was discovered that there were no used balls on the ground, only new ones. It is a matter of routine that a number of balls with recorded use are on hand for all first-class games in case the match ball needs replacing, yet this important point was overlooked at Karachi. On another occasion, Wasim Akram and Mushtaq Ahmed bowled on the Test pitch the day before a match against South Africa to test it out, exploiting a loophole in the regulations. There is nothing in the laws to stop them from doing such a thing, but they breached the spirit of the game. If one side does it, then the other team should be given the same facility; testing the pitch for pace, bounce and spin can give players important knowledge regarding team selection. South Africa forwarded a written complaint to the ICC and did not receive a suitable response. Had the third umpire been in charge, he could either have stopped Wasim and Mushtaq or imposed penalty points for a serious breach of etiquette.

Whichever way you look at international cricket, it makes most sense to simplify the control of the game by giving it to a team of three neutral umpires with the muscle to act decisively on the spot. Similarly, the two umpires operating in domestic cricket should have total authority.

# CHAPTER SIX

# Light, Over Rates, Action

Nothing annoys the cricket-watching public more than needless long delays or an early finish to the day's play caused by bad light, so a lot of damage is done to the game's image because the guidelines on this contentious subject are not being applied properly. Simply, play is supposed to continue whatever the quality of the light, unless there is a danger of physical injury to the batsmen.

That seems sensible enough, yet confusion and inconsistency abound, as was demonstrated in the Bombay Test between India and Sri Lanka in December 1997. With twelve overs remaining and India pressing for the three tail-end wickets they needed to complete a hard-earned victory, steady rain forced the players to the pavilion. Thirteen minutes later the rain stopped, only for umpires Steve Bucknor, from the West Indies, and A.V. Jayaprakash to decide that the light was not good enough to permit a resumption. Spinners Anil Kumble and Rajesh Chauhan were bowling when play was interrupted and it was obvious they would continue, given the chance, because Indian captain Sachin Tendulkar understood that it was too dark for his seamers. As far as I could see, there was no threat of even minor injury against such gentle pace, especially since both Sri Lankan batsmen were protected by the usual paraphernalia – various items of padding and the obligatory helmets. I believe, therefore, that on this occasion India were unfairly denied an excellent chance of success; equally importantly, the spectators were short-changed. Nor does that stand out as an isolated incident, for similar scenes unfold on many an English ground during the domestic season.

Having to bat in difficult conditions often reflects the luck of the draw; it's analogous to losing the toss or getting most of the strike against the opposition's best bowler. Certainly players want to bat at the most favourable time, in the morning when they are fresh for instance, but sometimes an innings starts with about half an hour left, when a side has laboured through a tiring day in the field. Opening batsmen instinctively keep an anxious eye on the clock throughout the final session of a long day, keeping their fingers crossed that they will be spared the nerve-racking task of negotiating a tricky thirty-minute spell before stumps. Sportsmen, however, must take the rough with the smooth, and too much time is spent worrying about the light.

It is surprising how often play is possible, even in the gathering gloom. The most famous example of a team literally making light of an apparently impossible situation is the Gillette Cup semi-final of 1971 at Old Trafford. Lancashire fell steadily behind the required rate in their pursuit of Gloucestershire's sixty-over score of 229 for 6. As they struggled along, it got very dark by normal standards in cricket and an appeal against the light was made. The late Arthur Jepson, a typically dour Nottinghamshire seamer before he became an umpire, pointed to the sky and enquired of all and sundry: 'What is that up there?' The Lancashire captain Jack Bond, batting at the time, replied: 'It's the moon, of course.' Triumphantly, Jepson drove home his point: 'If you can see that thousands of bloody miles away, you must be able to see the ball from twenty-two yards.' Bond nodded his agreement, shrugged his shoulders and applied himself with the determination of the true professional. With the gates firmly locked shut on a capacity crowd of 23,520 and hundreds spilling on to the boundary edge, Jepson and Dickie Bird dared not carry over the contest to a second day. Although the balance of opinion on the packed terraces was in sympathy with Lancashire in the grim conditions, every spectator wanted to witness the final act. The tense drama united players, umpires and fans, and David Hughes conjured up a fitting climax by hammering twenty-four runs off the fifty-sixth over, sent down by offspinner John Mortimer – two sixes, two fours and two twos – to snatch a sensational victory.

The result underlined the glorious uncertainty of cricket and made nonsense of the widely accepted theories on light. That cup-tie stands out more than twenty-five years later as a brilliant public relations exercise, for all those packed into that full house were eager to go back to Old Trafford for more of the same thing, and those running first-class cricket have to pay increased attention to the needs of the spectators. Umpires must not be too generous to the players; they have to get on with things whenever humanly possible. It is important to remember that cricket, in return for getting massive sums from television, has to guarantee a reasonable product. Television is not some remote all-seeing eye, it is a collection of millions of viewers all of whom contribute in various ways to its financial well-being. On that basis, the absence of cricket from the publicised schedule because of poor light is bad business, while a spectator at any ground who has paid for his seat is going to find something else to do with his time and money if he has to wait about for the clouds to lift. People accept that it is not possible to play cricket in rain, but they are unhappy about overcautious assessments of the light.

In a rapidly changing world, it is interesting to speculate about the possible effects of floodlighting, which is being installed at various venues. Lights are not likely to become widely available in this country, but where they are on hand they should be used to keep the game going when the natural light deteriorates. I appreciate that the situation would not be ideal with a red ball against a background of white clothing and screens, but this, too, is a matter of random chance and it cannot be stressed too strongly that in cricket the conditions are rarely, if ever, the same for both sides.

Throughout my twenty-five-year career – 1,014 first-class innings – I seldom batted in what I regarded as dangerous light, although there is no doubt that my generation coped with pitches and light that would be considered unacceptable today, and we did not wear helmets. There were problems against the really quick bowlers, and it could be nasty when you were late picking up the length and line with the aid of primitive sightscreens, but I was over the age of thirty-eight when I first wore a helmet, in the 1979 World Cup final against the West Indies. Since then batsmen have acquired copious layers of sophisticated protection and are far less vulnerable.

Probably because circumstances sharpened my instincts for self-preservation, I was hit only once – at the Scarborough Festival when I completely lost sight of a delivery from Somerset seamer Fred Rumsey which struck me on the shoulder. I was lucky it did not catch me on the head, and I stormed up to the Scarborough office to make very clear my thoughts on the sightscreens at North Marine Road. On balance, however, I believe that players have to make concessions to the paying customer and react to the fact that money through the turnstiles helps to underpin their financial security.

Rumsey's delivery in itself was not especially short or hostile, but short-pitched fast bowling is now an established, indeed essential element in cricket, and although it may come as a surprise to many people, I believe that the limit of two shoulder-height deliveries per over is misguided. Arguments about bouncers crop up regularly, the flames usually fuelled when one side in a Test series is significantly better equipped in the fast-bowling department than the other. The weaker team in terms of pace bowling gets battered and bruised physically, loses the match and complains about intimidation. History indicates that with few exceptions – Jim Laker and Tony Lock in 1956, for England against Australia, and Sonny Ramadhin and Alf Valentine for the West Indies in England in 1950 – Test series are won by the country with the better quick bowlers, and players on the receiving end haven't liked it. Even the

Australians, who pride themselves on being a tough, robust race ready to tackle the world on any terms, squealed long and loud throughout the 1932–33 Ashes battle as Douglas Jardine pounded their defences with the hostile pace of Harold Larwood and Bill Voce.

England won what was immortalised as the Bodyline series 4–1 against a background of diplomatic manoeuvring which contained threats from Australia that sporting relationships would be severed. Jardine firmly denied that he invented leg-theory, asserting in 1933 that it was then more than twenty-five years old. In his book *In Quest of the Ashes*, Jardine wrote: 'I am sorry to disappoint anyone who has imagined that the leg-theory was evolved with the help of midnight oil and iced towels, simply and solely for the purpose of combating Bradman's effectiveness as a scoring machine.' Seeking to justify his ruthless exploitation of a clear advantage in the testing Australian climate, he added:

> *I have a strong suspicion that it is easier for the batsman to decide what ball is just outside the off stump and consequently need not be played, than for him to make up his mind about the course of a ball which pitches the same distance outside the leg stump. Bradman has paid tribute to the amazing accuracy of Larwood and Voce. No doubt he realised the immense saving in stamina which accrued to two such bowlers, who could, when bowling leg-theory, force the batsman to play every ball they bowled.*

This indicates that there was a lot more to Jardine's thinking than meets the eye, and if I could choose anyone to have luncheon with, it would be the great autocrat, because I would love to ask him just how he fitted the tactic into the pattern of his campaign. For all his disdain of the popular theories, it would be fascinating to discuss not only the way he used his outstanding fast bowlers, but also how he handled the Australian reaction, because it appears he was vilified wherever he went. When he walked into the dining room for evening dinner he was subjected to hostile and abusive comments. He was the hate figure of the age. I would love to ask him how he found the strength to be so unfailingly polite in the face of such invective, and how he would have dealt with our aggressive tabloid press today.

Jardine's legacy is you do not change your tactics when you are winning. Bradman, despite averaging 56.5 for the series, did not forget that hard lesson and took his revenge immediately after the war when he turned Ray Lindwall and Keith Miller loose on England, who had nothing with which to fight back. The Australians concentrated their efforts on England's outstanding batsman, Len Hutton, and he went on to repay them in the same coin with Frank Tyson.

It has been an ongoing story, and no captain is going to use a spinner when he has a paceman on hand. Raw speed is a decisive weapon. The Australians were not too concerned with the niceties when Dennis Lillee and Jeff Thomson were wreaking havoc among all-comers throughout the 1970s and into the 1980s. During that period, Australia crushed the West Indies 5–1 in one Test series, but it was not long before Clive Lloyd found himself in a position to terrorise the rest of the world. Lloyd could be counted among the luckiest captains of all time, because he had such a formidable galaxy of talent at his disposal that he could play four pacemen in every game with, for much of the time, bowlers of the calibre of Wayne Daniel and Sylvester Clarke, who would have walked into any other line-up, waiting in the wings. West Indies' incredible strength in depth is confirmed by the fact that Daniel gained a mere ten caps and Clarke eleven. Criticism of short-pitched fast bowling, as I've said, invariably comes from countries without adequate resources of their own. Judgement on the issue is coloured by comparative strengths and weaknesses; no one hears the successful sides backing the campaign for restrictions.

Batsmen, of course, have little say in the matter, forced by circumstances to do the best they can, and their only positive response is to make runs. When they take a painful blow from the bowler, they cannot walk down the pitch and take a swing at him with the bat. They have to grin and bear it, but the good ones learn to cope and at Test level batting is as much about courage as technique. The great Yorkshire left-hander Maurice Leyland, always a wonderful fighter in a tight corner, used to say: 'Nobody likes fast bowling, but some of us don't show it.' That is exactly the right philosophy, because any intelligent fast bowler will exploit even the hint of a weakness.

All the controversy about the so-called bouncer has encouraged the myth that there has always been an abundance of high-class pacemen in the game. This is simply not true. Short-pitched bowling became an issue and helmets appeared on the scene in the late 1970s because there were more fast bowlers in world cricket than at any other time. The result of this increase in the number of pacemen plying their trade was a series of silly suggestions on how to curb their hostility. Probably the silliest of them proposed drawing a line midway down the pitch with penalties against deliveries landing short of it, although the idea was originally put forward by Jardine's vice-captain, Bob Wyatt, at the inquest which followed the Bodyline tour. I respect Wyatt's standing as a former Warwickshire batsman and captain, but he was on a very sticky wicket.

The trouble with drawing a line across the pitch is that when a fast bowler bends his back and lets fly neither he nor anyone else can predict the bounce. So much depends on the type of pitch, on the hardness of the ball, on the rhythm of the bowler, on whether the ball has landed on the seam, and even on the time of day. There are too many variables, not the least of which is the height of the batsman, for a line suitable for a six-footer is hardly going to assist a smaller man. Sometimes the ball will hit a grassy tuft and sometimes a tiny hollow. It all makes a big difference. At up to ninety miles per hour, the best bowlers maintain an impressive accuracy, but they cannot regulate things down to a matter of an inch or two, so contact with the ground is not under complete control. Many times I have known that a particular bowler was trying to get the ball up into my ribs only to see it bounce much higher, flying over my head. On other occasions, a delivery has kept lower than expected for no apparent reason. Variable bounce resulted in Australia's

Terry Jenner being hit on the head by John Snow in Sydney during the 1970–71 Ashes series. He ducked into the ball rather than under it, but it was not particularly short and would only just have cleared the stumps – no blame attached to Snow, who was just as much a victim of the pitch as Jenner. The history of the game is littered with similar incidents. I recall being the non-striker at Trent Bridge in 1980, with Graham Gooch facing the West Indies on a juicy pitch. Michael Holding, from the Pavilion End, produced one which went high over Gooch's head, climbed way beyond the wicketkeeper's reach and crashed second bounce into the sightscreen. Holding's wide-eyed expression revealed that he shared our amazement.

Jim Swanton, retired *Daily Telegraph* correspondent and a senior figure among cricket writers, stresses that the two-bouncers-an-over law covers a third of all balls bowled, but if the current crop of 'fast' bowlers dropped short twice every over batsmen would be queuing up to collect their share of easy runs. Once the shine has gone and the ball becomes a little bit softer, the bouncer represents a gift unless the bowler is really fast and accurate. For the first half of my career I hooked and pulled selectively after negotiating the new-ball phase and I enjoyed some spectacular success, notably against West Indian Keith Boyce in championship engagements with Essex at Colchester. I made 260 not out in 1970 and 233 the following season, and initially in the fixture planning Yorkshire were due to play there again in 1972. Determined to put an end to this sequence, Essex captain Brian Taylor, a character with strong opinions and an infectious enthusiasm, insisted on the match being switched to Chelmsford. When the big day arrived, I was returning to the Yorkshire side after being out with a damaged finger. We won the toss and batted. In the Essex dressing room, Taylor delivered a stirring lecture to his troops and exhorted Boyce to put everything into his opening burst. He called for a battery of bouncers to unsettle me and make sure I didn't get another double century, so the Essex lads were fired up when they took the field. Boyce played his part to the full, beating me for pace to brush the glove as I hooked. The ball flew through to Taylor, who was also the Essex wicketkeeper, only to bounce out of his hands and fall to the floor. As I went on to score 121, I reckon I was lucky to win another round against the bouncer.

But Boyce had the last word, eventually forcing me to remove the stroke from my repertoire in 1973. England endured utter humiliation against the West Indies at Lord's that year, going down by an innings and 226 runs, and I do not reflect on the game with any satisfaction. Vanburn Holder captured my wicket in the first innings with a short ball outside the off stump which I deflected to Rohan Kanhai at slip as I hooked, my dismissal signalling a miserable collapse. By the time Saturday evening arrived England's plight was desperate, our ambition stretching no further than survival overnight in the hope that the weather might throw us a lifeline. To my ongoing regret, however, I tumbled headlong into a trap in the final over, hooking a Boyce bouncer into the hands of Alvin Kallicharran, stationed behind square leg on the boundary precisely for that shot. That represented more than a passing moment of mental agony, it marked a watershed in my career. I reasoned that in my early thirties, with reflexes and eyesight deteriorating slightly, a more subdued approach might pay greater dividends.

The batsman who hooks successfully, however, is able to challenge short-pitched bowling, and it is a case of establishing the right balance. It is a difficult shot to play, requiring guts as well as ability, but there is nothing finer than seeing the bouncer despatched perfectly at the expense of a threatening quick bowler, and plundering a few boundaries is the best way of forcing any bowler to pitch further up. On the 1974 visit to the West Indies, England decided to try to bounce out Lawrence Rowe in Bridgetown, Barbados. We knew he was prepared to hook and felt that he might mistime the stroke in the early stages of an innings. Mike Denness, as captain, stationed me down at deep fine leg as a better catcher than Derek Underwood or John Jameson, with the more specialist fielders nearer the bat. Bob Willis raced in and banged in what he might well have regarded as the right ball for the situation. Unfortunately, Rowe struck it so hard that it was still climbing when it passed over my head on its way out of the ground. That settled the argument. Rowe went on to score 302 and we dared not give him another bouncer.

By being aggressive Rowe had gained the initiative, and Viv Richards had a similar attitude. Hooking was very much a macho thing with Viv, so he represented another potential victim, at least before getting into his stride. We actually outwitted him in a one-day international in 1980 at Berbice, Guyana, where he holed out to Graham Stevenson, mistiming a delivery from Graham Dilley. A repeat in the Test in Antigua, though, badly misfired for England, Viv depositing Dilley into the adjoining graveyard to put an end to that ploy.

Avoiding the short ball is all right so far as it goes, and I never felt in any danger when ducking and weaving, but simply getting out of the line of fire can make scoring difficult. The bowlers are persuaded to keep trying their luck, sorely testing the batsman's patience. On the other hand, when a batsman does connect properly the bowlers, facing criticism from their team-mates, find it convenient to keep a fuller length. I would advise any young batsman, therefore, to prepare himself by practising the hook in the nets. It will certainly advance his career more than hours spent driving a succession of half-volleys, as any batsman who is careful with the hook can dictate to the bowler instead of vice versa. It is also true that the easiest ball to deal with is the one that passes high over the batsman's head without requiring any response; the bowler has wasted a lot of energy and achieved nothing. But the one with which he threatens the rib-cage, which does not draw the same noisy reaction from the spectators, is much more menacing. This is where variable bounce can be really dangerous. The batsman has about one third of a second to decide whether to play backwards or forwards and to gauge the line. An error can mean the end of his innings or a nasty blow, yet this testing length seldom attracts comment.

Most of the comment and proposed reform is, in fact, ill informed, and there is, anyway, legislation in place. Law 42 (8) states that 'The bowling of fast short-pitched balls is unfair if, in the opinion of the umpire at the bowler's end, it constitutes an attempt to intimidate the striker.' That is perfectly clear, and Dickie Bird demonstrated during the Centenary Test at Lord's in 1980 that, properly applied, it is adequate. All summer England had taken a battering from the West Indies quartet of Michael Holding, Joel Garner, Andy Roberts and Colin Croft, who went round the wicket and gave me five bouncers an over at Headingley. (I didn't complain, but in conversation later with Ken Palmer, one of the umpires, while having a drink, I enquired as casually as possible: 'What's going on with all this short stuff? Letting five an over go is a bit much.' 'Well,' he laughingly replied, 'you've a very good technique and I just enjoyed watching you use it.') In that Centenary Test Australia's lively Len Pascoe also went round the wicket and gave me a real working over before I noticed from my end Dickie exchange words with him. The gist of the conversation was as follows:

Dickie: 'That's enough of the short stuff.'

Pascoe: 'How do you mean?'

Dickie: 'You've had a good go at him for several overs and tested him out. Let's just settle back a bit. You can drop a short one in now and then.'

Pascoe: 'I don't think I've overdone it.'

At this stage, the Australian captain, Greg Chappell, decided to chip in with his contribution, and I remember clearly seeing him hurry past me to confront Dickie, who was standing at the Pavilion End.

'I don't think he's bowled enough short stuff,' Chappell argued.

'Well I do,' insisted Dickie. 'That's all there is to it. I am not having any more. In fact, I'll give you a warning.'

And with that he shot across to square leg to put his position on record with colleague David Constant.

Immediately, the Australians cooled down, and I would say that Dickie handled things brilliantly. I was not intimidated and coped with Pascoe, but Dickie's judgement on what was good for the game proved spot on. Pascoe had been given full reign to test me out and that was what he was entitled to, but he couldn't be allowed to carry on all day.

By instructing the umpires to apply firmly the legislation as it stands, the authorities could comfortably cover a wide range of cases. The spirit as well as the letter of the law is important, and two short-pitched balls per over represent a bigger problem for a late-order batsman than a specialist, although if a tail-ender survives for an annoying period by getting cheerfully onto the front foot and blocking, the fielding side is entitled to a bit of leeway. A moderate or emerging county batsman deserves greater protection than an established Test player, so each circumstance must be judged on its own merits. The heart of the matter is that there should be room for manoeuvre without turning cricket into a namby-pamby game by pandering to the faint-hearted.

Having the courage to face hostile deliveries is one thing, increasing the over rate so that there are more of them in a day's play another. Hardly a Test goes by without one side or the other being fined for falling below a modest requirement of fifteen overs per hour. Fines were introduced some time ago with the idea of speeding up the game, but it has not provoked a satisfactory response. The West Indies, concentrating on pace, are among the worst offenders, and we had the ludicrous situation when they were over here in 1995 of their sponsors, the hotel group Sandals, contracting to pay all their fines if they avoided defeat in the series, which produced a 2–2 draw. With such a useful insurance policy to fall back on, Richie Richardson and his team could afford to regard the over rate with a degree of indifference. Indeed, top players are earning so much money from fees, bonuses, sponsorship and outside sources that they don't really care tuppence for the fines when they do have to pay them.

What hope there is of boosting Test cricket lies in speeding things up, and one sensible move would be to reduce the span of a Test match to four days while maintaining the same number of overs. No doubt my critics will raise their eyebrows and make sarcastic comments about my scoring rate as England's opening batsman, but references to the past will not do anything to solve the current problems. It would be perfectly possible to start earlier and finish later by introducing sessions of two and a half hours' duration instead of just two; after all, players already manage to complete sessions of up to three and a half hours in many one-day games, and they cannot complain about a moderate extension such as this if it gives them an extra day off. In addition, the currently accepted over rate of fifteen an hour is simply not good enough. A minimum of seventeen should be within the capabilities of any decent team.

The outcome of all the dilly-dallying we see today is boring periods of inactivity for the paying customer and television viewer. When a spectator attends a Test match, he may have to take a day off work. He would, therefore, be prepared to arrive for a ten o'clock start, because for him the whole experience adds up to a big occasion. Thousands of cricket followers can only manage to attend one day of a Test match in their area, so they want to see as much play as possible, but the ICC doesn't seem to have grasped this most basic of realities. There would be 476 overs available in a Test played over four seven-hour days, while at present a five-day Test with a six-hour day and fifteen overs per hour yields only 450. It is the number of balls bowled which dictates how many runs are scored and wickets taken, so time is not the relevant factor. These days groundsmen prepare better pitches which allow for a more balanced contest between bat and ball, and most Tests these days don't require a fifth day to reach a climax anyway, so what I am proposing is hardly revolutionary. My worry is that the ICC is a toothless body which rarely seizes the initiative. Soccer's governing body, FIFA, has taken imaginative steps to improve its game – stamping out tackling from behind, enforcing the back-pass rule – and is constantly studying the game, trying to ensure that they give the supporters a product which truly satisfies them. They have moved with the times without causing any major upheavals. Sadly, I fear the ICC too readily passes the buck to the home countries, which gets cricket nowhere.

In bringing about such essential improvements, though, the authorities must recognise that bowlers are not entirely to blame for the current air of lethargy about the game. During the Test between the West

Indies and South Africa in Cape Town in January 1999, Otis Gibson was called upon to go out and bat for the last over of the day. The departing West Indian batsman had got up the steps and into the pavilion long before Gibson appeared, and he then proceeded to crawl out to the middle like a man struggling through deep mud. In my opinion he should have been given out for his slouching; the legislation relating to the timing of a batsman's progress to the wicket is not applied properly by umpires. Law 31 states: 'An incoming batsman shall be out if he wilfully takes more than two minutes to come in – the two minutes being timed from the moment a wicket falls until the new batsman steps on to the field of play.' The ICC should undoubtedly take the lead in ensuring that this rule is applied strictly to the letter, the umpires making it abundantly clear that they are timing each changeover. This might also revive the tradition of batsmen actually crossing on the outfield.

And fielders don't get away scot-free either. The arrival at the crease of a new batsman rarely sparks activity among the fielding side until the newcomer has taken his guard; then and only then does the captain start to fiddle with adjustments to the field. There is no sense of urgency, no readiness for play, and there is no more irritating sight than that of a new batsman being forced to stand patiently, bat raised, tweaking his chest pad and adjusting his helmet while the opposition ponderously goes through its motions. Developing as a cricketer under Brian Close for Yorkshire in the 1960s was an object lesson for me in the art not only of advancing the contest, but of unsettling your opponents. When we got rid of a batsman we did not mess about hugging each other, we focused our attention on the pavilion, anxious to get an early glimpse of his replacement. Once the player was identified, and as he was on his way out to the middle, the collective planning got under way. 'He likes to play square of the wicket,' Ray Illingworth or Doug Padgett would say. 'Right,' Close would reply, 'we'll have two gullys and bring point squarer. We'll give him three round the bat, too.' While taking his guard, the batsman became aware that we were already crowding in on him and waiting, straining at the leash to get at him. Without recourse to 'sledging', we often hurried opponents into an error by not allowing them time to take stock. Cricketers ambling about with no apparent sense of purpose are denying themselves opportunity as well as doing their profession a disservice.

The ICC and the England and Wales Cricket Board should accept that fines for slow play do not work. The answer is to impose penalties that influence the outcome of a match. A minimum target figure should be set for each session, with ten extras added to the total of the batting side for each over not completed by the interval. Clearly, due allowance would have to be made for delays outside the control of the fielding side, but the mathematics could be ironed out, probably by the third umpire. He could balance the equation and put the information on the scoreboard to keep players and spectators informed. Those extras would quickly mount up and, with no team wanting to risk losing by handing runs on a plate to the opposition, I am certain that punishment in this way would speed up the action.

Nor is there any reason why individual penalty points should not be awarded too, increasing the incentive for players to eliminate laxness on the field of play. Regulations along those lines, for instance, would have prevented the West Indies pursuing a cynical go-slow policy to scramble a draw in Port of Spain in 1990. England required 151 in their second innings to go 2–0 up in the series. With a full day at their disposal they appeared well set, but rain and an injury to skipper Graham Gooch, who broke a bone in his left hand, checked their progress. The target remained within range at seventy-eight from thirty overs, but, with the light fading, the West Indies delivered only seventeen of them in two hours, loitering with obvious intent and waiting for night to fall, which it did, with England on 129 for 6. Desmond Haynes led the West Indies that day and, although he is a good friend of mine, I accused him of gamesmanship.

When John Arlott, the most revered of commentators, said, 'Cricket mirrors the age we live in,' he was absolutely right. The pace of life is much greater than it was when cricket grounds were packed with enthusiasts quite willing to sit back and relax, yet it is a matter of record that over rates have declined to a disgraceful level comparatively recently. Throughout the 1970–71 Ashes triumph in Australia, England, despite relying heavily on John Snow, Bob Willis, Ken Shuttleworth and Peter Lever, averaged better than seventeen overs per hour. All four worked up a hostile pace and Lever, especially, relied on a very long run, but as a team we never dawdled. Of course, we always had a slow-bowling option, and the necessity of achieving increased over rates would assist in bringing about a minor revival among the spinners at the expense of the medium pacers. This could only be a good thing. Spinners add variety, and cricket needs to readopt them and several other measures to end the monotony of so much pedestrian play.

# CHAPTER SEVEN

# A Nettle
# to Grasp

O urs is a rapidly changing age and I can visualise a time in the not
so distant future when one-day cricket will be accepted as the
international measure of cricketing ability, with Test matches, if they are
staged at all, virtually disregarded. This might seem a little fanciful
following the entertaining Ashes series 'down under' during the winter
of 1998–99, but those who look closely enough can see a definite trend
towards brasher, brighter competition with thrills, spills and all the fun
of the fair. The purists invariably throw up their hands in horror at the
very thought, but, like it or not, the world is moving into the twenty-
first century and the traditional form of cricket is inextricably linked
with the nineteenth and twentieth.

It does not seem to have dawned on the ICC, but attendances at
cricket grounds – at Test matches particularly – are in decline. There is
still good, if occasionally patchy, support in England, but interest
continues to dwindle away in other parts of the world. The 1998–99
visit of the West Indies to South Africa contained all the ingredients of
a great occasion, an historic first visit of a black team following the
breakdown of apartheid. With the exception of the Sunday of the
Johannesburg Test, however, you could virtually count the spectators.

Worrying signs also surfaced at the end of November 1998 in Perth, as England took the field for another enthusiastically promoted Ashes battle. A game without spectators is dead. Marketing men rely on television, advertising and sponsorship to collect essential revenue, but it is a mistake to focus exclusively on those sources of income in the long term. That is easy money. My view is that for every two people lost to the game in the natural course of life, only one person is coming in, with the result that even in India, that most fanatic of Test-playing nations, crowds are well down. Where a Test at Calcutta always drew a capacity audience of 100,000, the authorities there currently expect no more than 50,000 or 60,000, and in Pakistan the picture is gloomier still, except for the one-day internationals.

It is time to start capturing the imagination of children, and I do not think that enough is being done for them. Grounds are virtually empty on the fifth day of any Test, so why not arrange to have parties from schools admitted free? It would cost nothing, and if a small percentage of those children were to grow up to enjoy cricket the financial returns would be more than useful. Prices are also too high in England, making it difficult if not impossible for families to attend Test matches as a unit, so on every day juniors should pay only a token admission charge.

Bigger stadiums with more spectators represent my ideal future for cricket, but to translate that dream into reality it is essential to lay the foundations today. There are so many avenues to be explored, such as blacking out live coverage within fifty miles of any ground from which international cricket is being televised in an attempt to get people out of their armchairs and on to the terraces. I am staggered, too, that no experiments have been conducted in Australia, South Africa, India and Pakistan, with Tests starting at 3.00 p.m. and continuing until 9.30 p.m. These are warm countries with floodlights at the major centres, and the opportunity exists to adapt cricket to fit in with the busy lives of the general public. The cricketing powers-that-be should on no account be asking people to fit their lives around traditional schedules. The social climate that drew people to cricket no longer exists, so the game has to be prepared to improvise. We do not have the best weather in England, but in the height of summer there is nothing to prevent a Test match starting at 1.30 p.m. with an 8.30 p.m. close, enabling spectators to go to work, finish early and see at least the final session.

At least part of the problem, though, is getting through to the people whose interest in cricket is not all that great, and this is where television does have a part to play. The ICC ought to be taking greater advantage of what is a superb advertising medium. Regrettably, they do not seem to recognise the possibilities. At least part of the job of the television commentator is to educate the casual watcher, the man or woman who snatches a few minutes in front of the screen to see what all the fuss is about. The pre-play pitch report, in the institution of which I played a role, has grown into an important and popular feature. Without wanting to boast, I think it is significant to pick up on a little story from India, where, according to the newspapers, many young boys began to imitate my Yorkshire accent. One group received six of the best with the cane from their headmaster for persistently parroting their version of my commentaries on Star TV. I was flattered, but the point is that all these youngsters and, apparently, their parents are taking an interest in cricket because their enthusiasm has been fired by television.

Using the pitch report properly, I was able to pass on valuable information about the state of the twenty-two-yard strip which affected team selection, tactics and the course of the game, but gradually the ICC began to impose petty restrictions. They ruled that we could not bounce a ball on the pitch, which was ludicrous. What difference does two or three bounces make to the pitch prior to play when during the day the surface will be on the receiving end of five hundred or more heavier impacts? Dave Richards, chief executive of the ICC, mentioned that several committee members felt that certain aspects of the pitch report, including the bouncing of the ball, unfairly gave an advantage to one side. How could that be? We staged the pitch report after the toss and after the successful captain had made his decision to bat or field. By pushing a key into the surface of the playing area and bouncing a ball, we were able to create a marvellous visual effect without in any way damaging the pitch. To a tiny degree the ICC surrendered an inch or two of ground by giving us permission to use a key in the batting crease. This reflected administrative ignorance, for anyone with real knowledge of cricket understands that, while the groundsman prepares the standard twenty-two yards, he usually rolls only twenty, leaving a protective grass covering on the ends, where the batsmen stand and the bowlers land. So often the make-up of the batting crease bears little resemblance to the pitch.

If cricket is to prosper in the new millennium it has to adapt to the demands of modern living. Spectators will not magically beat a path to Headingley, the SCG, Eden Gardens, Centurion Park or anywhere else. Cricket has to market a package that will excite the person in the street and persuade him or her to give the game a chance. This is no time for half measures. The legislators must be bold and imaginative if they are to attract more spectators to Test match cricket. It would be folly to rely only on television money. In most countries Test match cricket is quite literally fighting for its existence.

The one man who is doing something positive is Jagmohan Dalmiya, the Indian president of the ICC, who is regarded in some quarters as a devious wheeler-dealer and in others as a bright, far-sighted businessman. He is the subject of controversy, no doubt, because he gets things done, and his brainchild, the ICC tournament, generates millions of dollars for the developing countries. Dalmiya's bold scheme brought into being the Asian championship, which is modelled on the English county championship points system. India, Pakistan and Sri Lanka meet each other twice over a month with the top two in the round robin going forward to the final. There are twelve points for a win plus a maximum of four batting and bowling points, awarded for scoring 350 or more or for taking nine or ten wickets in the first innings. Dalmiya's ambition is to use the success of this pilot venture as the inspiration for a world championship comprising the nine Test-playing nations. Former Indian opener Sunil Gavaskar and ex-Pakistani star Majid Khan are on an advisory panel investigating the practicalities of organising an international mini series, one of the difficulties being that the English season is out of step with the rest of the cricket-playing world. In addition, any world championship would have to be completed over a two-year period to ensure reasonable fairness by avoiding too great a turnover of personnel, and this necessarily demanding timescale is being taken into account.

I was among the leading ex-players invited to join Dalmiya's think tank, but the pressures of prior commitments prevented me from taking part. Even so, I am pleased to offer my support whenever possible in the search for a blueprint which would add another dimension to Test cricket. A world championship would give England the variety of up to three opponents each summer, and I am convinced that Dalmiya possesses the drive and imagination to turn his dream into a reality. I hope also that as he goes about his crusading he can breathe life into the ailing body of the International Cricket Council.

It is a good sign that the authorities are already talking about arranging the World Cup in its existing format on a three-year cycle, and even if they hold back temporarily in that direction, it is certain that a 'mini' tournament will be organised to raise funds for developing countries, to be staged every two years. Events in Bangladesh in 1998, when an international competition drew tremendous crowds, illustrated the potential. I did not get to the opening game as I was in Pakistan for the Australian series, but I was told the ground was three-quarters full on that first occasion and packed thereafter. Sponsors queue up in India to throw money at limited-overs cricket and there is a clamour to see the games in Pakistan; put simply, the public prefers the limited-overs version of the game.

This is true so far as those actually turning up at the various grounds are concerned, and those who sit at home and rely on television to keep in touch. Television, of course, is very important, the more so as coverage is increasingly in the hands of commercial companies, whose policies are dictated by logic rather than emotion. The BBC, as a public service vehicle, could sit back and not worry too much about viewing figures, but in the hands of media men whose existence depends on attracting substantial audiences, television is certain to become more demanding. Matches will have to be played over a specified duration and at times which suit the subscribers; it is worth noting how much in recent years British soccer has found it necessary to arrange and rearrange fixtures to accommodate television's programming schedules. The pace of life has got faster in the past twenty years and people don't want to wait for anything. Cricket watchers are not interested in viewing highlights a day or two old, they want instant, up-to-date action at the touch of a button, and the dramatic advances in technology are making just about anything possible. In England, we once had to make do with highlights from Australia flown in by aeroplane and screened twenty-four hours late. What was regarded as an exciting development then is old hat now. Today, with satellites, live action is always on the menu and nothing else is acceptable, yet it is as recently as 1990 that the series between West Indies and England became the first from overseas actually to be screened as it happened.

Personally, I have come to terms with the limited-overs game and can accept it, although it is by no means the only thing for me, and initially I effectively ignored the significance of this form of cricket, which came into being as my own career began to prosper. Matches completed in one day, with each side restricted to a specific number of overs, although not popular among the players generally and much frowned upon in Yorkshire, were introduced to attract the paying customers. Originally, the idea of boosting flagging county finances grew out of a series of games involving the Rothmans Cavaliers, with sides containing star names and a handful of famous retired players still nimble enough and sufficiently fleet of foot to do themselves justice. The Gillette Cup arrived in 1963, followed by the Sunday League in 1969, cricket as a result steadily reaching a new audience. Importantly, of course, by playing cricket on Sundays the counties for the first time went a long way towards squeezing themselves into the traditional social pattern. It was a day on which the general public were free to enjoy themselves.

People who regarded championship cricket as boring were entertained by the more adventurous approach brought about by the need to maintain healthy run rates.

With our minds focused firmly by habit on the championship, however, we in Yorkshire paid little regard to these limited-overs competitions. To us the championship was all that mattered, as by winning it a team proved beyond argument its all-round ability and mastery of the subtle skills. Success in the Gillette Cup or Sunday League depended more on an element of chance, we argued, but the committee did not share our opinions, and one of the reasons given for Brian Close's sacking as captain of Yorkshire in 1970 was his contempt for what he called 'pantomime cricket'. It took us a long time to adjust to the conflicting requirements, for when opposing batsmen slogged across the line we collectively shrugged and thought they were in trouble. That was exactly what any decent bowler wanted in the championship, but slowly it occurred to us that we could not afford to pay too high a price for wickets. Similarly, our batsmen continued to play as we had been taught during hundreds of hours in the nets under the watchful eye of 'Ticker' Mitchell, the head coach. Mitchell never tolerated anyone who did not play straight and keep the leading elbow high. His acid tongue instilled the accepted techniques into scores of young hopefuls, and his drill-sergeant approach made it difficult for us to switch to slogging, even when hitting out wildly represented the only hope of victory. Our ingrained approach created problems, and we struggled to get our minds around the rudiments of the one-day competitions. In short, Yorkshire relied too heavily on technical skills, and setting defensive fields and bowling negatively was foreign to our nature. True, we won the Gillette Cup in 1965, following Sussex's triumphs in the first two years, but matches stretched across sixty-five overs offered better scope for 'proper cricket', which never figured as part of the forty-over Sunday pattern.

I feel it is fair to say, too, that I adapted fairly well in the end, for I scored steadily enough, trying to minimise the risks and remain reasonably orthodox by pushing the ball into the gaps for ones and twos whenever possible. Accumulating quietly to keep the scoreboard moving is a virtue in any form of cricket. In common with so many professionals, therefore, I treated one-day cricket with considerable suspicion, but I never allowed myself to be blinded to the potential of its appeal, and it is clear that its overall success around the world owes much to the exertions of Kerry Packer.

As I described earlier in this book, I fought hard against World Series Cricket and, as England captain, stood up to be counted in defence of the officially recognised game, but I never underestimated the burly Australian, who masterminded the only serious rebellion within the first-class framework. Some brilliant innovations helped the Packer organisation to breathe life into international limited-overs cricket, which was introduced really by chance at Melbourne on 5 January 1970. Not surprisingly, I went into that first one-day international in a carefree mood. In the circumstances, it hardly seemed to matter what happened. The third Test of that England tour under the captaincy of Ray Illingworth, due to start on New Year's Eve, was washed out by three days of continuous rain which prevented a single ball being bowled. The outfield turned into one huge quagmire, and to while away the time we spent hanging about, I went with Colin Cowdrey to learn the rudiments of royal tennis, his lessons breaking up the grim routine of indoor nets and the odd mile or two of road running. Much to the annoyance of the English camp, the respective authorities agreed to a seventh Test – the initial schedule included six – and to further compensate both the Australian board, who lost out heavily at one of their major money-spinning centres, and the citizens of Melbourne over the holiday period, England and Australia staged a contest with forty eight-ball overs a side on what would have been the last day of the Test.

It was little more than an exhibition game, with all the players tip-toeing carefully over the sodden turf. England batted first, and I faced the first ball from Graham McKenzie, blissfully unaware that it was the start of something very big indeed. We reached 190 all out from 39.4 overs, my contribution totalling eight runs. John Edrich, with 82, earned the distinction of becoming the first player to complete an international limited-overs half-century, but Australia won easily by five wickets. For the record, the teams on that famous occasion were: Boycott, John Edrich, Keith Fletcher, Basil D'Oliveira, John Hampshire, Colin Cowdrey, Ray Illingworth (captain), Alan Knott, John Snow, Ken Shuttleworth and John Lever for England; Bill Lawry (captain), Keith Stackpole, Ian Chappell, Doug Walters, Ian Redpath, Greg Chappell, Rodney Marsh, Ashley Mallett, Graham McKenzie, Alan Connolly and Alan Thomson for Australia. To me it was just another day at the office, and a fairly ordinary day, too, but unquestionably the most notable feature was an attendance of 46,000.

The huge gate receipts opened the eyes of the administrators to the possibilities of the shortened version, and when Australia toured England in 1972 three one-day Prudential Cup ties were organised at the end of the five-Test series. I still treated them with disdain as the games did not fit into my plans. They were bun-fights which had nothing to do with my ambitions as a cricketer, and at that stage I refused to recognise one-day cricket as a challenge because it was too artificial, a pale imitation of the real thing. Like the Sunday League and Gillette Cup, one-day internationals made money, but the standards fell way below those in the first-class arena, and all my thinking related to three-day county cricket and five-day Tests.

I opted out of international cricket between 1974 and 1977, so I missed all the fuss when England hosted the first World Cup in 1975. It passed me by, only two matches sticking in my memory. The first was the low-scoring semi-final at Headingley, where the ball swung prodigiously and Gary Gilmour finished with the remarkable figures of 12–6–14–6 as Australia dismissed England for 93 and scrambled home by four wickets. I also recall the final in which the West Indies defeated Australia by seventeen runs in a magnificent contest which finished just before a quarter to nine at night. Australia suffered five run-outs and the whole event gave cricket wonderful publicity via the television coverage.

Despite the doubts, the importance of one-day internationals grew,

Packer helping to encourage its development, jazzing up cricket to give it a vibrant, colourful image. He saw that a market existed for cricket in the warm evenings in Australia when men had finished work and families were looking for things to do together. More than twenty years later England is beginning to catch up by installing lights at major venues. Traditionalists might not have been able to come to terms with day–night matches, floodlights, black sightscreens, white balls and coloured uniforms, but the package appealed to a wide range of spectators and its novelty value is currently giving counties a boost over here, despite problems with the weather. Derogatory labels such as 'pyjama cricket' or, as Alec Bedser called it, 'Mickey Mouse cricket' did not deter a new type of supporter. Anyone who studies the accounts of county clubs can see that gate receipts are declining, and the truth is that the generations who loved, understood and supported the time-honoured game are disappearing. They are not being replaced because those youngsters who like cricket are drawn by the glamour and excitement of the limited-overs competitions. Boys will not sit through a full day of championship cricket which has no end result and, with a four-day span, is scarred by tedious passages of apparent inactivity, so when today's children grow up they will have no affinity with what some of us would call the finer points.

It is not a question of whether I or anybody else likes it, the situation is there for all to see. I do television commentary all over the world and in every country with the exception of England the administrators say that one-day internationals sell out while Tests draw only small crowds. The writing is clearly on the wall in large letters, for in the year 2000 we are going to follow the pattern of Australia with ten one-day internationals in a triangular tournament which could easily overshadow the Test series, particularly if the West Indies, the principal Test match visitors that year, continue to struggle.

Australia, partly at least as a result of Packer's input, invented most of the new rules which crept in to maintain the excitement. The regulations requiring four men in the thirty-yard fielding circle at all times while allowing only two outside the ring for the first fifteen overs are aimed at producing boundaries. Spectators are not enthralled by seeing an accurate maiden over, they want fours and sixes and plenty of runs, and spread throughout an innings, too, rather than arriving like an avalanche in the hectic closing stages. For that reason, the possibility of different fielding restrictions in mid-innings is being considered. A lot of games are becoming very repetitive between the sixteenth and fortieth over. Nor is this the end by any means. There will be more innovations to add to the spectacle, and I believe that before too long each fifty-over innings will be split in two, with the side batting first having to suspend its effort after twenty-five. Such a system would reduce the value of the toss and give the two teams a more equal chance. It is widely agreed that winning the toss can be decisive in what is now the NatWest Trophy because with a 10.30 start in September bowlers get a lot of assistance in the early stages. Similarly, batting first in daylight is preferable to chasing runs under floodlights when games are prolonged into the night. Dividing each innings into two halves would go some way towards evening things up, at least by giving a team which has struggled on a juicy pitch in the opening session the chance to make up some ground. A change in this direction would also allow spectators prevented by other commitments from arriving at the start to see both sides bat.

There are other possibilities, too. Bowlers have been put under a lot of pressure in one-day fixtures by the strict interpretation of the law relating to wides. A delivery above shoulder height is 'called' as a no-ball, but I am sure that eventually seamers will be permitted to give a batsman one bouncer an over. This is another case of balancing the equation, for bowlers have been turned into cannon fodder with all the advantages handed to the batsmen. A lot of bowlers complain that batsmen who cannot handle the short stuff receive too much protection, and they have a point. Further down the line, it might well be that all the players with the exception of the wicketkeeper will be required to bowl five overs each. That would give the selectors food for thought, with the emphasis having to be put very much on the all-rounders.

Already the benefits of having a top-class bowler are debatable. He is rationed to only ten overs and is prevented from aiming much outside either off or leg stump, and from dropping one or two short. Thus the batsman knows where the ball is going to pitch and can get on the front foot with every confidence. He can almost set himself like a hitter at baseball, and the pace of the ball adds power to a stroke. The possibilities are virtually endless, and it is common sense to realise that the one-day game offers the means by which cricket can be both underpinned financially and developed in various countries. The bigger the World Cup becomes, the more it will capture the imagination.

But those in charge need to display some caution. There is nothing to be gained from expeditions to Japan or China. Sri Lanka and Zimbabwe have achieved impressive progress, but they would still be grateful for injections of cash, while New Zealand, who first competed against England in 1927, are handicapped by a shortage of companies with sufficient commercial muscle to provide adequate backing. West Indies scaled the heights in the 1970s and 1980s without shaking off their impoverished image, and Holland, Kenya, Bangladesh and Denmark are among other countries working hard to advance along the road to full International Cricket Council status. The essential thing for those in authority is to doggedly pursue measures to stabilise the situation, and to remember that whatever action is taken, one-day cricket is now the key to the future.

# CHAPTER EIGHT

# The State of Play in England

E nglish cricket is in a mess, and the most worrying aspect of our ongoing national decline is the fact that no one with the power to change things is ready to acknowledge this basic fact. Many ex-players, men with outstanding careers behind them who are motivated entirely by a deep affection for the game, are expressing concern at the poor standards in our domestic competitions because they know that we will never be a major force at Test level until we create the circumstances which foster the development of exceptional talent. The reality is that there are no top-quality players coming through the system, and things are not likely to improve until the authorities face up to the situation. As with an alcoholic, nothing can be done to achieve a cure until the 'patient' admits that the problem exists. Unfortunately, the people in charge are burying their heads in the sand. 'This is just a cycle we are going through,' they claim, but it seems to me that England have been going through this particular cycle for a long time now.

It would not be fair to say that nothing has been done, because a number of committees and commissions have investigated the state of the game, but none has actually produced anything worthwhile. There was the Altham committee back in the 1950s, when cricket was doing comparatively well on the field, the Clark committee in 1966, the Palmer committee in 1986, the Murray committee in 1992, the Acfield report more recently still, and finally the proposals put forward in 1997 by Lord MacLaurin, the English Cricket Board chairman. No doubt all those involved did their best to improve things, but largely it has been a question of tinkering with the various competitions, a matter of tentatively shuffling the same deck of cards in the vain hope of finding a winning hand. This is not exactly a surprise, because I honestly feel that all these committees lacked the sort of expertise that could have been offered by distinguished former cricketers.

I know Ian MacLaurin well and like and admire him. He is obviously a brilliant businessman, but his knowledge of cricket in the broadest sense is limited. On New Year's Eve 1996 in Zimbabwe, circumstances accidentally brought myself, Lord MacLaurin and his wife together for dinner. While the conversation was on a more social level, we touched on a couple of things and I invited him to come and have a proper cricket discussion with me any time he liked. He did not take up this offer, and I was disappointed that he did not think it helpful to come and talk over anything with me before publishing his report, *Raising the Standard*, although he did telephone me on the morning of its general release. I enquired as to how many ex-England players had been interviewed; the answer was twenty-six, although I am not sure who they were or just how much notice was taken of their opinions. In the same way, David Acfield, although an experienced county cricketer, never operated at international level.

It really is pathetic when you think about it, because I cannot imagine for one moment that Lord MacLaurin's great commercial outlet, Tesco, would let me run their business on the strength of my success as a batsman. Nor, I am sure, would a leading commercial enterprise launch any sort of campaign without the benefit of extensive market research, yet most of the proposals in *Raising the Standard* puzzled and upset a lot of cricket supporters. I suspect that Lord MacLaurin was misled by an 'inner circle' of influence anxious to be seen to say the right thing. Strong support for the document appeared in the serious newspapers. Christopher Martin-Jenkins in the *Daily Telegraph* opined, 'There is every reason for [the proposals'] endorsement,' while Alan Lee in the *Times* referred to MacLaurin's ideas as 'attractive and ingenious'. All well and good they may have been, but all the members of the public to whom I spoke thought the recommendations were so complicated they couldn't work them out. Inevitably, the counties turned their back on the blueprint, too.

So why should it be thought so readily that someone with a high profile in the business world possesses the knowledge to put cricket back on the right path? Indeed, it is perfectly easy to demonstrate that many mistakes have been made. The decision to cover pitches provides one excellent example. Before 1979, on uncovered pitches, we had a lot of very good players and we won plenty of Tests as well as losing a few. Then the move began to make county cricket more like Test cricket. Pitches were covered, but the game did not improve, it deteriorated, making life easier for batsmen. I loved it, and even at the age of thirty-eight and well past my prime I managed to average over a hundred per innings for the season. The next step brought the introduction of four-day cricket in 1991, initially on a limited, experimental basis. The reason put forward by Ossie Wheatley, as chairman of the then Test and County Cricket Board, was that the players wanted and needed more time off to rest and practise. So there were more free days, but what happens, in my experience, is that players go home and rest and play a bit of golf. I don't see all that much evidence of players making sensible use of the scope for more practice.

Another widely publicised theory suggested that four-day cricket would be better for spinners, but again the opposite turned out to be the case. Slow bowlers are now regarded largely as cannon fodder, operating on flat pitches. On uncovered pitches you had the 'stick and carrot' situation which maintained a proper balance. Spinners were able to exploit rain-affected strips and the good ones took full advantage to pick up their five- and six-wicket hauls, while on other occasions, when conditions favoured the batsmen, a slow bowler might well have to work very hard to finish with 2 for 60 or so. Importantly, though, the good days gave the slow bowlers the confidence to cope with difficult situations and encouraged positive thinking. Overall, slow bowlers were able to confirm their place in the scheme of things as part of a recognised pattern: two quicker bowlers, one all-rounder and two spinners.

Equally, batsmen learned to cope with changing circumstances. There were the days when they knew they had to 'fill their boots' on a good strip and others when, with the ball turning sharply or seaming or swinging, it took a lot of technique and character to make thirty or forty runs. A good batsman had to be able to wait against the swing bowlers and play the ball late. He also needed 'soft hands' to survive against the spinners; few players today are adequately equipped in that direction. With conditions changing regularly, sometimes every day because different grounds also had different characteristics, all players had to think about exactly what they were doing. The dull routine of much modern cricket simply did not exist. Probably the most important thing that Brian Close, as captain of Yorkshire, taught me was that a thinking cricketer is a better cricketer. It is all about being positive, knowing your own strengths and weaknesses and being able to assess accurately the opposition. Because today's players have a fourth day, there is a tendency to let games drift along instead of making things happen. At times it is almost as if they are going through the motions. In three-day cricket time was an important factor and it gave everyone a sense of urgency.

The argument that county cricketers are required to play too often is also nonsense. Yorkshire got through an average of 114 days each season at the start of the 1960s, while most other counties were not far behind. The schedule at the moment includes sixty-eight days of championship cricket, plus seventeen matches in the one-day league. Add a few days for the NatWest Trophy and other competitions like the Super Cup, and you arrive at a total of about ninety days. Admittedly, the knockout competitions increase the physical demands on players, particularly those turning out for the successful teams, but they hardly add up to the difference, and back in the 1960s travel up and down the country meant long hours on the roads and late-night arrivals as well. The older players simply regarded the inconvenience and discomfort as part of life's rich pattern. By modern standards we were on a treadmill, only we did not recognise the fact and got on with the game.

My concern today is that the obsession with preparing players for relatively few important engagements is counter-productive. In the middle of the 1998 season, for example, Michael Atherton, as England's leading batsman, was in wonderful form when he was advised to take a rest from Lancashire, which he did. That amazed me, because when runs were flowing for me I could not spend enough time out in the middle. I wanted to make up for all the times when I got out cheaply. There are spells when every good batsman feels that he cannot get out. As they say, the ball does look like a football and you feel that it is almost impossible to fail. Yes, you know that you might be dismissed, but you sense that it is pretty unlikely. I cannot imagine for one moment that Denis Compton ever considered taking a break in 1947, when he scored 3,816 runs and averaged 90.85. The great Middlesex and England batsman played fifty innings against the background of a notoriously busy social life without feeling the slightest degree of weariness. Fred Titmus, the distinguished England offspinner and a colleague of Compton's at Middlesex, recounts many stories which underline the great man's zest for life and relaxed relationship with sport. Titmus insists that it was not unusual for Denis to arrive in the dressing room at the last minute, just in time to change, borrow a bat and rush out to play another dazzling innings.

I regret not playing alongside another great character from that rich post-war era, Surrey and England seamer Alec Bedser. He represented my ideal as a professional because all he wanted to do was bowl – bowl in matches and then practise bowling in the nets. All I wanted to do was bat, and I feel we were very much on the same wavelength. Alec had a very hard introduction to county cricket. When he joined the staff at the Oval he found himself busy from morning until night. He was required to bowl to the senior players in the nets in the morning before taking part in the junior nets in the afternoon. Finally, before going home to bed, he bowled in the nets in the evening to the members who turned up to pay for practice time. In the final analysis, of course, that demanding routine stood him in very good stead, building up his body strength to the point where he could keep going virtually all day. No one ever heard Alec ask for a rest. When his captain wanted him to bowl, he bowled, and, as a matter of record, Alec completed 1,220 overs at a decent enough pace in that 1947 season, taking 130 wickets at 24.42 – an impressive total without being exceptional for the period. For a comparison in terms of overs bowled per English season (first-class and one-day) between Bedser's era, Trueman's era and today, look at the following tables.

|  | **Bedser** |  |  | **Trueman** |  |
|---|---|---|---|---|---|
| 1947 | 1,220.4 |  | 1960 | 1,068.4 |  |
| 1948 | 1,139 |  | 1961 | 1,180.1 |  |
| 1949 | 1,005.2 |  | 1962 | 1,141.5 |  |
| Total | 3,365 |  |  | 3,390.4 |  |
| Av. per season | 1,121 |  |  | 1,130 |  |

|  | **Cork*** | **Fraser** | **Gough** | **Mullally** |
|---|---|---|---|---|
| 1996 | 761 | 775.4 | 825.5 | 753.5 |
| 1997 | 732 | 751.5 | 511.3 | 488.1 |
| 1998 | 705.2 | 634.3 | 504.5 | 655.5 |
| Total | 2,198.2 | 2,162 | 1,842.1 | 1,897.5 |
| Av. per season | 732 | 720 | 614 | 632 |

*Dominic Cork's figures relate to the 1995, 1996 and 1998 seasons respectively as he was injured for much of the 1997 season, playing in just ten matches and bowling only 160.2 overs.

Today, players are very good at training in the sense of enhancing agility and speed over the ground, so there is no doubt that the standard of fielding has improved tremendously, but the standard of batting and bowling has gone down. There are numerous examples of good cricketers in the 1950s and 1960s who played hardly any Test cricket yet were better players than anyone in the current England squad. People such as Don Kenyon, who scored thousands of runs as an opener for Worcestershire but could not force his way past Len Hutton and Cyril Washbrook. Don Shepherd maintained a very high standard year in year out as an offspinner for Glamorgan, taking 2,218 wickets at 21.32, yet he did not manage a single cap. Les Jackson and Cliff Gladwin formed a much-feared fast-bowling partnership for Derbyshire, but they also spent most of their professional lives in the background. Although I am well aware of the dangers of constantly claiming 'things were better in my day', it is nonetheless pertinent that cricket remains one of the few sports in which modern technology has made little impact, and comparisons are still legitimate. I remain convinced that anyone who looks objectively at the situation will agree that the level of skill in English cricket stands at an all-time low. Thus we have to face the most important question: How can we hope to create a strong, successful national team from such relatively shoddy material?

It is, of course, impossible under current circumstances. County cricket, in the shape of the championship, is the only breeding ground for emerging talent. It provides the opportunity for young cricketers to extend the range and depth of their ability, and, incidentally, it is also the medium through which general interest in the game can be encouraged. Thus, it is absolutely vital that the English Cricket Board realises what is happening. There is an acute shortage of star quality, the factor which above any other attracts the public through the turnstiles. Currently there is very little to capture the imagination – just a group of genuine, enthusiastic, ordinary lads who love to play cricket. Effectively we are devoid of spinners, seamers are thin on the ground, and far too much batting is workmanlike.

For once, the England selectors were safe from criticism when they named the party for the 1998–99 Ashes tour to Australia; they were hard-pressed to find sixteen decent names for the trip. We possess a hard core of thirteen or fourteen who represent the best available, and anyone who follows the game would pick them automatically. Only two players omitted from the original squad could really argue that they had been unlucky: Middlesex left-arm spinner Phil Tufnell and, maybe, Somerset seamer Andy Caddick – although there was some debate concerning the relative merits of Graeme Hick and John Crawley that hardly amounted to an issue of great importance. More to the point, the selectors could not even find a third opening batsman or a high-calibre alternative to Tufnell. With the greatest of respect, I hardly think the Australians spent many sleepless nights worrying about Robert Croft or Peter Such. The cupboard is as near bare as makes no difference.

It is, therefore, quite clear that we do not have in England a sufficient number of quality players to sustain eighteen first-class counties. The minimum requirement is for around 300, which, even then, allows for fewer than twenty per county, the majority of whom ought to be good enough to engage in meaningful competition. The undisputed evidence that we can raise nothing like the necessary numbers casts a long shadow over English cricket's future. It is vital to have a keen competitive edge to force players to fulfil their potential and to provide a worthwhile spectacle for the paying customers. If the legislators could put the county game on a healthier footing, it would stretch the up-and-coming youngsters and better prepare them for the greater demands of international cricket. A relaxed, easy-going championship in which most sides have little left to play for come July makes it possible for anyone with reasonable ability to drift along doing enough to justify his existence, sometimes encouraging false hopes.

Nothing illustrates the pitfalls better than the career of Graeme Hick, who scored heavily after joining Worcestershire in 1984. As he qualified for England, the Rhodesian-born batsman earned the highest praise from the most discerning of cricket commentators, even being compared to the legendary Don Bradman in such a respected newspaper as *The Times*. Embarrassingly, a number of counties proved too ready to spread the field once he established himself, offering a succession of easy singles to get him away from the strike. This approach gave Hick and his admirers a misplaced sense of security, for immediately he stepped up a level to experience the unrelenting hostility of the West Indies' pace attack on his Test debut in 1991, he failed to make the expected impact. As a consequence, Hick has never really established himself in the England side, despite his demonstrable class. Certainly in the 1950s and 1960s he would have faced a more searching examination of his technique long before he entered the international arena.

In one sense, therefore, I was lucky to begin my career in the 1960s. There were plenty of excellent bowlers around who caused me many, many problems, and they forced me to become a better batsman. I learned more from occasional confrontations with Worcestershire's Jack Flavell and Len Coldwell and Derbyshire's Cliff Gladwin and Les Jackson than I did accumulating steadily at the expense of ordinary pacemen, and to face Kent's Derek Underwood was to become embroiled in a master-class. You waited a long time for a bad ball, and 'Deadly' bemoaned the concession of a single to the extent that any fielder who let him down finished up on the receiving end of an angry glare. On a rain-affected strip each delivery fitted into the fabric of a desperate fight for survival and provided the most complete test of a batsman's technique. I did not exactly look forward to the 'pleasure' of their company, but the challenge of testing my skills against the Stathams and Loaders brought out the best in me. I was stretched to the limit because they were able to make batting difficult. It put you on your mettle – there was no comfort zone. You either got out or forced yourself to become a better, more rounded batsman.

An international sportsman has to face up to the best the opposition has to offer and prove to himself and the rest of the world that he has what it takes. Modern English cricketers are denied those opportunities in domestic cricket and, to make matters worse, the marketing men at

Lord's are steadily promoting the idea that international cricket is the only thing that matters. They point out, reasonably enough from a financial point of view, that all the counties exist largely on the back of the profits made from the international programme, with its high-profile sponsorship, extensive television income and substantial gate receipts, and they appear to believe that it doesn't really matter if county cricket drifts into mediocrity. I honestly don't think some administrators would be bothered if no one came to watch county cricket and games were played like practice matches simply to get the best players ready for Test cricket. Some are even happy to see the county championship relegated to the status of 'feeder' cricket, as a means to an end.

It is on this basis that the leading England performers are being offered contracts by the ECB, who will subsequently control their availability for county cricket. This means that the top players are likely to appear on the domestic scene very briefly, probably in the early weeks of the season as they seek match fitness, and occasionally in the later stages of the campaign if, for example, someone is recovering from injury or has lost form and needs match practice. Superficially it looks like a workmanlike arrangement, for the bonus the county clubs can expect is something approaching double the money from central funds, and financial security is an attractive proposition, particularly when attendances and membership figures are moderate to say the least. Additionally, in return for exercising control over the best cricketers, as is the case, for instance, in South Africa and Australia, the ECB feel they can guarantee healthy profits by increasing the number of Tests and one-day internationals from the year 2000.

But it is not as simple as that. In England we have a professional domestic game which none of the other countries has on anything like the same scale. In Australia and South Africa players receive a match fee for appearing in the Sheffield Shield and Currie Cup and then go back to other full-time jobs, while the English counties operate a contract system which has become more expensive in relation to gate receipts. A decision has to be made as to whether the authorities want a professional game to continue in England. If they do, fine; ways and means must be found to help the counties stand more firmly on their own feet. Certainly, those supporting a significant shift in the scheme of things should understand that without a proper championship they will be unable to put a respectable England team on to the field. Whatever the marketing people might claim, county and Test cricket go hand in hand and their long-term futures are inextricably linked.

In essence, the administrators, as they address this problem, ought to ask themselves, in the first place, whether first-class cricket can continue to sustain eighteen counties. Personally, I suggest the number should be reduced to ten. Obviously, cricket would surrender a permanent presence in some areas, with a subsequent loss of membership, but the plus side of the equation is that a smaller championship must improve the level of competition, making it tougher by cutting out the weakest links in the chain. I suspect that there would be outrage at such a move because of all the history and tradition associated with many of the county clubs. In any case, as the counties hold the balance of power at the ECB, there is no chance of a sufficient number voting themselves out of existence – turkeys don't vote for Christmas. It will not happen. If every county knows that however poor the standard of cricket and however mediocre the playing staff a large cheque will arrive each year from the English Cricket Board, larger than the year before, then there is bound to be complacency. They want their cake and they want to eat it, too.

The reality, then, is that consideration must be given to an alternative way of dealing with the fact that too little talent is spread over too wide an area. If the ECB is going to demand first call on the services of the leading players, it follows, inevitably, that standards in the domestic game must fall even further, with dreadful consequences. It is a vicious circle. To my mind, therefore, the one obvious solution is to attract more overseas players on to the circuit, just as soccer has done in the Premier League. Counties would have to select the imports very carefully as these days Test cricket is staged throughout the year and there is no universal close season to accommodate English requirements. The world's top talent would not necessarily be available for long-term engagements, but there are a lot of players who would welcome the chance to play in England for part, if not the whole, of a season. I know, for example, that Sachin Tendulkar retains a great fondness for Yorkshire after becoming their first overseas player in 1992 and, despite his crowded schedule, might well be persuaded to play a few games at some stage. As the best batsman in the world, the gifted Indian stylist would do wonders both for the standard of cricket and for attendance figures. Overall, Yorkshire did themselves a big favour when they broke with tradition and stiffened their ranks with a series of imports. Recently Darren Lehmann made a magnificent contribution to their cause as he advertised his claims for consideration by the Australian selectors, and once he had earned recognition they recruited Greg Blewett, another quality operator on the fringes of Test cricket.

The advantages of introducing such players are twofold: they force English cricketers to raise their own game and they are also on hand to offer help and advice. Bearing that in mind, it is interesting to note that Shane Warne, the world's outstanding legspinner, more than once expressed a keen interest in playing some county cricket, and I recall him saying: 'From what I have seen when touring England there is plenty of talent about, so I'd like to see if I could kick-start some of the under-achievers.' Injury, unfortunately, forced a change of mind, but it is significant that an Australian on tour can spot a weakness in our game to which the huge staff at Lord's are apparently blind. Players of the calibre of Warne, Lehmann and Blewett are certainly good enough to serve England's purpose, and if a county were to sign three overseas stars of similar standing they could then weed out the weakest of their home-grown players, who are merely time-serving on contracts while holding back the game's progress. Unquestionably there would be opposition from the Cricketers' Association, for their job is to protect the interests of all the players, good, bad and indifferent. Soccer has already crossed that bridge, weathering protests from Gordon Taylor, the secretary of the Professional Footballers' Association.

While I can empathise with the 'drawbridge mentality', my concern is with the top of the pyramid. Quality beats quantity every time. Even so, I am aware that I am swimming against the tide in this instance, for there has been sturdy and vociferous support for the campaign to remove all overseas players on the basis that they deny scope to the youth of England. It appeared likely at one point that the counties would go so far as to enforce a ban, but protectionism would solve nothing. To take another example from soccer, Italy and Germany sustain their league systems with the aid of international personalities from all over the world, yet their own national squads have won the World Cup in recent years. The ready recourse to importation can hardly be said to have stunted the growth of their players. The English Premier League has also gained strength from the influx of foreign recruits. Soccer is buoyant, exciting and attractive because standards are high. Our own football players have to stretch themselves to the limit if they want to survive and stay at the top. Is it unreasonable to suggest that the same could apply to cricket?

Nor can I sympathise with the fears which exist about the development of a transfer system in cricket. On the contrary, I believe it would be a good thing; certainly, any restriction on a cricketer moving from one county to another must be unlawful, always providing that contractual obligations are observed. It is ridiculous for the ECB to support the listing of players in restricted categories by any county wishing to retain an individual against his wishes, and sooner rather than later the whole business will be challenged in the courts. Surely, then, it would be wise to make a virtue out of necessity, to move with the times and allow players to switch allegiance at the end of their contracts. The new multi-million-pound television deal put a lot of extra money into cricket and counties should be willing and able to use their share to attract and suitably reward the best batsmen and bowlers.

A lively transfer market would also put cricket more often into the newspaper headlines alongside soccer, with speculation as well as news. This might upset the traditionalists, but it might also attract a new generation of spectators. The general public is interested in financial figures and cricket has lost out to soccer in this direction. Huge transfer fees and rumours that top stars are earning £30,000 or £40,000 a week capture the imagination; rightly or wrongly, the vast sums involved give the players in question a stature which is denied even the outstanding cricketers, who are far less well paid. Rich rewards fuel great expectations, too, so there is pressure on the high earners to maintain impressive levels of performance. So we come back to competition, and the fact that cricketers on contracts, operating in undemanding circumstances, enjoy too wide a comfort zone.

I played a handful of games for Yorkshire in 1962 before really getting into the team the following summer. I did not get picked for the early matches, but when the chance came I knew I had to be very much on my mettle. Like all uncapped players, I received only match fees, supplemented by win bonuses as and when they came along. There was nothing for losing or drawing. From 1964, after I was awarded my Yorkshire cap, only about 40 per cent of my income was guaranteed as salary and the rest depended on my being selected. That gave me a big incentive to do well by contributing to team success. Brian Close, as captain, often sat reading the racing paper while the rest of us knocked up before a game, with one or two perhaps wondering if they were going to be in the side. Before the start, Close would ask: 'Anyone not fit?' He rarely got a reply. If anyone had a bit of a niggle he kept very quiet about it, because if you did not play you did not get paid, and the harsh facts of economic life acted as the best painkiller in the business. Yorkshire did operate a modest sickness scheme, but it did not match the money you received for playing and winning. There were, too, members of the second team pushing hard for senior recognition, so no one wanted to take the risk of dropping out and possibly not regaining his place.

The rewarding of performance is, incidentally, another aspect of cricket worthy of investigation. A strong case can be made out for offering far less in terms of basic salary with generous win bonuses. Winning is what it is all about. There is little enough merit in finishing second in a two-horse race. Looking back again to the 1960s, Yorkshire's players had to maintain a consistent level of form and it was no good a batsman hoping to secure his future by prospering on the better pitches in August because the committee decided on 31 July whether to retain your services for another season. It was a case of getting in and playing well throughout with little room for manoeuvre and certainly none for complacency.

No matter how well-motivated or determined the individual, however, he can really improve only in the correct environment, and the organisation of county cricket today is a shambles. The Sunday League is well beyond its sell-by date. The administrators are selling the game and the cricket-watching public short by continuing to insist on forty-over matches on Sunday. They short-sightedly don't want to change from an easy money-making format. Sunday is the best day to encourage families, so it is far better to give them the opportunity of a full day's entertainment in the hope that they will get the taste for watching proper cricket. But for two years before the Sunday League started in 1969 there were some counties who played three-day county cricket starting on a Saturday, and they attracted very good attendances. It is time for the counties to start looking at the long-term future of cricket. They should scrap this 'Mickey Mouse' type of cricket which lacks variety and any great skill. The desperate gamble to revive its fortunes by festooning the players in garish clothing failed miserably and, as a minor side-issue, I would suggest that much more subdued uniforms be introduced at all levels. Display county colours by all means, but have predominantly cream shirts, as at Wimbledon, and, if necessary, names on shirts, but give the matter proper thought. Do it tastefully, with more attractive uniforms to boost leisure shirt sales as a bonus.

I also have serious doubts about the stampede towards the use of floodlights. Day–night cricket is well and good if the weather is suitable, as it is in Australia, South Africa and on the Asian subcontinent, where they can almost guarantee warm evenings. In England, over three floodlit games you are likely to get on average one lovely, sunny day and warm evening; one with mixed conditions – a little light rain with some sunshine; and one complete wash-out. No one, therefore, should be misled into thinking that day–night cricket will on its own bring thousands of spectators back to grounds on a regular basis.

It is much more important to tackle the confusion which surrounds the fixture programme. All the evidence confirms that the public does not know on what days matches are going to start and finish. Championship fixtures begin on a variety of days, and many last only three or even two days, so at times there is little for county members and casual spectators to watch on a Saturday, when the majority have time on their hands. Even when the action stretches into a Saturday the competitive element has often disappeared, the result already a foregone conclusion. What was the AXA Life Sunday League might more accurately have been called the Any Day You Like League, because games were not necessarily played on Sundays. Matches were switched to midweek at the whim of the counties, and the new two-division National League is equally confusing, with fixtures scheduled all over the place.

To me it makes most sense to begin championship matches on a Friday, ensuring that Saturday and Sunday play contains a lot of significant action. I am perfectly happy to go along with two divisions and I am convinced that the first-class season should run from the first Friday in May – there is no sense in staging first-class cricket in April, when it is too cold for players and spectators alike – to the end of August, with the top two counties in Division Two promoted in place of the bottom two sides in Division One. There would then be room in September for play-offs, particularly for the third-placed county in Division Two, which could be awarded home advantage against the seventh-ranked county in Division One for a place in the top section. I would in addition stage a mid-week fifty-over league for all eighteen counties on Wednesdays, again with play-offs for the top four in September. There are the necessary elements in such a scheme to attract the paying customer.

The English Cricket Board, in addition to establishing a firmly fixed start day for all county games, should take the necessary steps to ensure that groundsmen prepare interesting pitches which last for four days. So-called 'result' pitches do nothing to help players or attract spectators. Ideally, a championship match starting on a Friday should run comfortably into the Monday, and still be competitive. The authorities should also realise that cricket is not like soccer. Football clubs can easily rearrange fixtures because they are able to use floodlights in the evenings for games, which only last ninety minutes. A supporter wanting to watch a cricket match has to devote his whole day to the exercise, so he requires greater notice in terms of dates. The simple, straightforward solution is to get back to weekend cricket so that spectators can plan ahead with as good a guarantee as possible of seeing two full days of proper stuff involving exciting and committed domestic and overseas professionals.

So there are things that can be done to improve professional cricket in a reasonably short space of time. Putting things right at the top is a priority, but the ECB have to look much further ahead as well. They have a responsibility to the game which stretches beyond our lifetime and far, far into the future. They successfully lobbied Chris Smith, the Secretary of State for Culture, Media and Sport, to get cricket taken off television's protected list, thus creating a massive increase in income through the sale of rights to the highest bidders – Channel 4 and Sky. They deserve credit for that, but, building on that breakthrough, they should turn their attentions to the Minister for Education, seeking government help to improve cricket at grass-roots level. We have to face up to the fact that over the past twenty years or so fewer and fewer children have played cricket. Once upon a time, all over England, boys were batting and bowling in the street, with a dustbin or chalk marks on a wall for the wicket and, if they could find nowhere else, cobblestones for a pitch. Parks, recreation grounds and even rough strips of grass were permanently trampled by young feet throughout the summer months. Some great batsmen sharpened their reflexes using rubber balls which bounced and flew at unpredictable angles off uneven surfaces. Nowadays you'd be lucky to see an impromptu game of cricket anywhere. Those who take an early interest do not seem to follow it through, so the authorities need to persuade more boys – and girls – to take up the game.

In the first place, the task is to convince the government that summer sports – cricket, tennis and athletics – are getting a raw deal. To do so, it is necessary to persuade the government to make radical changes to the school curriculum. At the moment, for instance, children find themselves swotting in April and May and then taking examinations in June, thus missing out on the nice weather. How much better to have the same examinations in March, with preparations taking place in January and February, when outdoor activity is almost non-existent. An academically relaxed summer term could do much to improve the health of the nation in general, and schools would also be able to stage competitive matches on Saturdays, as used to happen years ago. I have spent a good deal of time in South Africa where they put a high value on sporting excellence, and schools there play matches on Wednesday afternoons and on Saturdays – rugby as well as cricket – and it has not taken them long following the end of apartheid to get back among the world leaders in sport. The evidence is there for all to see. We must get back to competitive sport for all children. Competition is the lifeblood of sport, and life is a competition. Learning how to win and how to smile in defeat builds character. Too many people have the view that you shouldn't encourage winners because it demoralises the losers. What a load of tripe!

I also noticed that the average school day in South Africa runs from eight a.m. to five p.m., and that is a timescale we could look to adopt on a nationwide basis. It would be possible to have normal lessons until, say, two p.m., having had a short break for lunch, before devoting the afternoons to sport, which might reasonably be treated as seriously as every other subject as a whole range of careers in sport are now available. The ECB has a good case ready and waiting to be put to the government. Nothing is healthier than sport, and boys and girls taking part on a regular basis would be fitter and stronger than those glued to the television or computer screen. It's time, too, that someone pointed out that school holidays are too long anyway. Seven weeks is ridiculous when working parents receive only three or four weeks a year, and most mothers I know complain that their children are left with nothing much to do. How much better to have them in school with a timetable that is both educational and enjoyable. A real mix of academic studies and physical exercise to reflect the world in which we live today could work wonders.

The demand for organised coaching is there – not just for cricket, but for tennis and athletics too – and if it means paying teachers more, then so be it. It is money well spent. The priority should be to teach people how to teach sport, because coaching is definitely not straightforward. The key to success is making each session enjoyable. I was very lucky to have Johnny Lawrence looking after me as a youngster because he never made life too difficult. He introduced things gradually, taking great care not to overawe me and making sure that I did not become confused. Batting is a complicated art, so you do not attempt to master it all at once, and I am sure that Johnny Lawrence's influence enabled me to derive great enjoyment and satisfaction from practice even to the end of my career.

At a higher level on the education ladder, something has also to be done to compensate for the loss to cricket of the university players. Not so long ago six or seven emerged every season from Oxford or Cambridge, but now the teams they put out are too weak to do more than go through the motions. It is a question of adapting to make the best out of current circumstances, and it is no use meekly saying, 'That is too big a change.' Look how sport has changed in the past fifty years and ask yourself: Could the people watching and playing sport in 1949 have imagined all these various developments, even in their wildest dreams? I don't think so. The danger is that no one will grasp the nettle and stick out their necks. People become too attached to what they are familiar with, so any deviation from the normal pattern frightens them.

That, presumably, is why my offer to coach in Jersey was turned down in 1997. Around that time I noticed an advertisement on behalf of the ECB development department seeking a development officer on the island. As a part-time post it offered only £8,500, but the money was irrelevant. I like Jersey, where I have coached in the past, where I am well known and where I have many friends. I submitted an application because I imagined that we could arrive at some sort of compromise arrangement outside the recognised scope of the operation. Naively, I thought that my high profile and first-class record would compensate for the fact that I did not live on the island. I indicated my readiness to be available on a regular basis and argued that I would be an attraction for the youngsters the department was trying to reach. Not so, according to the rejection letter. 'The post requires an ongoing weekly commitment of twenty to twenty-five hours throughout a three-year period,' Terry Bates, the development manager, told me. No discussion, no attempt on their part to meet me even part of the way. They stuck to their set criteria and ignored everything else.

That experience literally sums up the situation. Cricket has to be bold and imaginative. It must use whatever tools come to hand in order to preserve its intrinsic values and advance into the new millennium at the same time. Unless there is a massive collective change of heart at Lord's and throughout the counties, the future remains bleak.

# CHAPTER NINE

# The Wider Picture

Cricket holds an endless fascination for me which defies all the changes in format and fashion introduced over the years in the search for a more modern image. The legislators are constantly striving to attract a new audience, which is understandable in these days of high-pressure marketing, but the simple, uncomplicated battle of wits between bowler and batsman is enough to stir my senses and emotions. I count myself so very fortunate because every morning of my working life I have looked forward to immersing myself in this wonderful sport. There was nothing else I wanted to do, and I have never lost my appetite for the game. Invariably the joy and thrill of competing lifted my spirits, even during spells of disillusionment and near despair when runs proved elusive or I found myself in conflict with the Yorkshire committee. I also endured the frustration of missing out on the England captaincy, of being able to pick my own side and put my theories to the ultimate test at the highest level; four matches deputising for Mike Brearley provided no more than a glimpse for me of my promised land. Throughout my disappointments, though, I never lost a genuine, deep-seated love of cricket. Even now, thirteen years on from my retirement, I miss playing to such an extent that I can honestly say I would exchange the rest of my life for five more years of playing for Yorkshire and England at the height of my form. Given the power to turn back the clock for such a comparatively short period, I would die a happy, if relatively still young, man.

Nothing in my experience can compare to the sense of achievement which stems from success at cricket, and, having played with and against the best and put together a record of which I am intensely proud, I can say only that retirement represented the first step on a long, downhill march. Commentating, however, does offer a small degree of compensation. It is not the same thing at all, but my work with radio, television and newspapers keeps me in close touch with Test and county cricket, and for that I am grateful. Although watching from the sidelines does not set the adrenalin surging through my veins, I enjoy the media involvement in general and commentating on television in particular. It is in this area that I feel I can continue to serve the best interests of cricket by informing and educating the public so that they, too, can appreciate the finer points.

My interest in television began while I was still playing, stimulated by occasional invitations from the BBC to offer my thoughts on the day's play. These arose when injury kept me out of the England side, or when Yorkshire's failure in a knockout competition left me available for the later rounds. These opportunities encouraged the thought that I might be good enough to earn a regular place on the commentary team at some later stage, so I took great care to study the techniques of well-practised performers like Jim Laker and Richie Benaud as I operated alongside them. They were both extremely helpful in teaching me the tricks of the trade, but the best advice came from Richie, who said: 'Always try to add something to the picture.' Initially, I feared that my blunt Yorkshire accent might well count against me at the BBC, whose traditions put heavy emphasis on well-modulated public school accents. Things, of course, have changed at Broadcasting House, as they have everywhere, but even today some critics point out that I do not arrange my words in a grammatically correct manner. They are right, of course, but I think it is more important to concentrate on being informative and entertaining.

For whatever reason, after my playing career finished it proved difficult to catch the eye of those in charge at the BBC. They relied on a tried and tested team, and one or two letters and telephone calls to Keith McKenzie, the executive producer of cricket, ran into a polite stonewall. Keith always replied that he would keep me in mind for any opening that might materialise, yet nothing happened. Then, by pure chance, I noticed that Sky were setting up their new satellite channel to cover West Indies v. England in 1990. David Hill, the head of Sky at that time and now a major figure at the American television and video company Fox, responded more enthusiastically to an approach, recommending me to Trans World International, the production company that was putting together its own commentary team. Bill Sinrich, the top man at TWI then and now, subsequently gave me the chance to break into broadcasting on a more permanent basis.

It was all very new to both them and me as we were breaking new ground by providing live coverage of an overseas series. Formerly enthusiasts at home had been restricted, at best, to a few edited highlights, often screened a considerable time after play had finished. No style had been established for ball-by-ball coverage from abroad, so Sky allowed us to set our own, with Tony Greig acting as the front man. His long association with the Packer circus and Channel 9 in Australia proved invaluable, and we gelled very well, mixing some relaxed humour into our commentaries. Greig pushed and probed during our discussions, bringing out the best in me as we delved into the techniques of both batsmen and bowlers, something which had not really been done much before.

Another innovation concerned the use of the telestrator, the facility for turning the television screen into a drawing board to explain a particular point. Over the years I developed an interest in American football without knowing too much about the finer points of the game's rules, and I paid close attention to one of the commentators, John Madden, who used the telestrator to great effect during his explanations of various aspects of the play. As an ex-professional with Hall of Fame status and a former coach of the Oakland Raiders, Madden knew everything about the sport's tactics, and he taught me a lot about American football. It occurred to me that I could use the same facility for cricket, and I brought what became the famous white pencil into action more and more. I regarded it as a marvellous tool, particularly for illustrating thoughts on field placings.

As we established our own way of commentating, those of us with TWI received wonderful support from Bill Sinrich, who was a great boss to work for – hard and demanding, but scrupulously fair. That is exactly what I have tried to be as a commentator, and I never let personalities cloud my judgement. It does not make the slightest difference to me whether a player under discussion is a friend of mine or someone who does not get on with me. My responsibility is linked to performance on the field and nothing else, and I care too much about my reputation for honesty to let bitterness or anger influence my views. The *Concise Oxford Dictionary* describes 'comment' as an 'explanatory note or remark; criticism of events', and it is necessary for the commentator to explain, criticise or praise instantly. A handful of journalists attached to evening papers are required to meet deadlines, too, although their schedules are less demanding than ours, but the majority of the press enjoys the luxury of being able to sit back and compile a relatively carefully studied report. Reporters working for Sunday newspapers have literally days at their disposal, but the television commentator must deal with situations as they arise and respond immediately.

It is fair, therefore, to argue that in order to respond instantly in a fair and honest way to whatever is happening out in the middle, commentators need the greater depth of knowledge about the game. They must also be very quick thinking. The viewer, of course, can see events unfold, so it is impossible to waffle without being made to look foolish. The whole business of commentating has advanced tremendously from the early days of radio when the man at the microphone could, within reason, say whatever he liked and the listener had no choice but to take him at face value. The radio commentator existed simply to describe the run of play and his opinions were rarely required. His counterpart on television, on the other hand, fills a much more demanding role because the viewer needs something that enhances the visual images. That is why in television we operate in pairs, with the lead man setting the scene and adding an extra layer of description, while his colleague concentrates on the techniques and tactics. In these circumstances, I believe it is my job to be frank and say what I think, no matter how unpalatable my comments may be. I see no purpose in being nice and friendly to all concerned, although I accept that I regularly find myself as a result in a minefield of controversy.

Some viewers, for example, seem to feel that I should support England's cause at all times, and they become upset when I suggest that an England batsman or bowler should be doing something differently. Equally, there are those who accuse me of being disloyal when I put forward an idea on, for instance, how the opposition bowlers might attack a particular England batsman. I don't understand these attitudes. Commentators must be neutral when they are on air. Certainly I always want England to win, but that heartfelt desire is part of my private life, something that must be shut out when I pick up the microphone. As a professional broadcaster, it is up to me to give an expert impartial opinion. After all, television coverage is not confined to the home country. It is now beamed all over the world; my comments are heard by supporters of both sides in every Test and viewers on each side of the fence are entitled to an unbiased appraisal. Some commentators do take the easy option of sticking to the obvious as it guarantees them a quiet life, and it does indeed take much more courage to stick out your neck by stating what you think should be happening or why things are going wrong for one side, but those are my principles.

The most difficult trick is to predict the course of play accurately, to foresee an incident before it actually happens. In that sense commentating is a bit like captaincy, and to do it well you need both experience and the right instincts. You either possess these qualities or you don't. The good commentator also has to walk what is a thin line between saying too little and being patronising. Basically there are two types of people watching cricket. On the one hand there are those who have played, perhaps to a good league standard, or watched a lot and thereby gained a sound knowledge of the game. They notice subtle aspects of the exchanges themselves, but there are others who quite like cricket but who are puzzled by so much of the game's ritual. It is therefore all too easy to annoy a large section of the audience by satisfying the needs of what is probably a minority, but everybody has to learn sometimes and television is the most effective means of bringing a greater understanding of cricket to the public. From the outside, the game might look boring. It is certainly often accused of being so. If the commentator does not explain what's going on sufficiently well, that particular myth can only grow. I passionately want to fuel the interest of the less knowledgeable and get them to share the love I have for cricket.

By doing things largely my own way, I have to accept that I cannot please everyone, and I do receive more than my fair share of brickbats, but fortunately these are outweighed by a healthy number of compliments. One of the main complaints is that I go out of my way to be controversial, while some of my supporters claim that I give voice to opinions that are widely held but rarely publicised by those anxious not to rock the boat. I cannot agree with either suggestion. My natural manner is to be frank and forthright, so I always try to tell the story as I see it without fear or favour. My personal guidelines are that what I say must be fair and I am never afraid to repeat my opinions in front of the individual concerned. I never broadcast a single word that I do not believe is the truth. Whether I am correct is a question of judgement, but my honesty is a matter of record, and I refuse to hide behind a mass of prevarication.

No one can be right all the time, and, in company with the rest of mankind's teeming millions, I do make mistakes under pressure. People have every right to disagree with me, but you cannot be a good commentator without ideas of your own, or if you always err on the side of caution. My main aim is to grab the viewer's attention by stimulating intelligent discussion; while I never try to hurt or damage anyone in the process, I firmly believe that players have to accept that they live in the spotlight. Exposure to criticism as well as praise is part of their job and I have been in the same position often enough during my own career to know how they feel. Once you enter the public arena, however, you have to develop a thick skin to survive. Criticism hurts, and it usually hurts all the more when it is justified, but life goes on and anyone who struggles to come to terms with the hard facts of reality should avoid watching television and reading the newspaper.

No cricketer alive today has been the subject of more intense media speculation and attention than me, and still today a few reporters bring up my past to underline any point they might be making about me in the present. Somehow the number of batsmen I am supposed to have run out, my alleged slow scoring or my absence from the England scene for three years are made relevant to a more immediate issue. Opinions formed long ago remain firmly cemented in the minds of those who go out of their way to knock me, yet they have nothing whatsoever to do with my activities as a television commentator. Whatever I did or did not do as a batsman for Yorkshire and England is important only in relation to discussions about me as a cricketer, yet half-remembered and often imagined incidents from my playing days continue to spill over into the modern era.

Patrick Collins, of the *Mail on Sunday*, is one columnist who regularly goes out of his way to snipe at me, so I understand better than any of today's players that it is very hard to live in the goldfish bowl of public and media attention. The off-the-cuff nature of my work on radio and television makes it impossible for me to select the right words carefully; given more time, I might soften some of the impressions I give, but any offence caused is accidental. Collins, though, can spend up to six days sharpening his knife as he attempts to carve up my reputation. I believe the offence he causes is the result of careful consideration, and I regard him as a paid assassin, hired to stab in the back personalities in the limelight. Significantly, journalists with no experience on the field queue up to attack ex-players, probably feeling that we are intruders into their private domain, but they lack any sensible arguments to put forward and instead search for other weapons to use against us. I can accept to a degree their argument that it is not necessary to have played the game to write about county and Test cricket, but surely they ought to admit that as a distinguished batsman at the highest level I am bound to approach things from a different, if not necessarily better, perspective. Sadly, they refuse to bow to logic and try to deny me the basic right they take for granted themselves. It is acceptable in their eyes for them to rubbish the England team, but they rush to the barricades when I do the same, using me as the subject of their columns.

A case in point relates to an interview I did with Sue Barker on *Grandstand* on Saturday, 14 June 1997 during which I made a passing reference to Dominic Cork, describing him as a show pony, a term which in cricket at least is hardly regarded as being particularly unpleasant. I acknowledged his talent, but weighed that against his attitude problem. My remarks reflected a carefully considered opinion rather than a throw-away line, for the previous winter he had missed the Zimbabwe leg of the England tour having been given time off to sort out his fitness and personal life. Then, after letting down the management by failing to turn up for two fitness assessments before the departure for New Zealand, he had struggled to find any sort of worthwhile form when he finally joined the squad. David Graveney, the chairman of selectors, had openly expressed concern at Cork's situation, and I had spoken to him as well, and three other senior players, to ensure that I had all the facts in my possession. Sue Barker asked a question and I gave an honest answer, which spawned an outburst of indignation and a host of lurid headlines.

Peter Johnson led the way in the *Daily Mail* the following Monday, pouring fuel on the fire with a double-page spread highlighted by a banner which revealed: BOYCOTT PUTS IN THE BOVVER BOOT. Johnson wrote:

*Considering that Cork has recently suffered the breakdown of his marriage, the sudden collapse of his England career and is now facing critical surgery, it might have been kinder not to usher him towards the operating theatre with the accusation that he was a prima donna. This, remember, is the same Boycott who, at the time he was the world's best opening batsman, literally took his bat home and went into a prolonged sulk because Mike Denness was given the England captaincy ahead of him.*

Incredibly, in the wake of references to my being 'the biggest batting bore of the post-war era', Johnson confirmed the very points I had made, saying: 'Cork was a mixed-up and petulant character all through the New Zealand tour. He bowled without fire and apparent hope. He behaved on and off the field with the listlessness of a man who would much rather have been somewhere else. Some of us said so and wondered how much of the trouble stemmed from a private life in turmoil. Boycott made no such allowances.' Johnson found it necessary, once again, to dust down all the old canards about my batting to insist that I had no right to point out Cork's limitations, even though he agreed with what I said. He concluded his article with the question: 'Should people who live in glasshouses throw stones?' It added up to a piece of arrant nonsense. Even if every single derogatory word written about me as a player or captain had been justified, I was still entitled to express an opinion on *Grandstand* in 1997, as I am at this moment.

It was noticeable, too, that Johnson remained discreetly silent on 10 September later that year when England omitted Cork from the Test and one-day squads for the winter tour of the West Indies and the limited-overs party which went to Sharjah. The all-rounder did not even make the A team squad, and Graveney was quoted in the same *Daily Mail* newspaper as saying: 'He is simply not the same bowler he was three years ago. All the feedback I have had from his last tour is that he has problems being involved in a team situation. We still feel he can be an asset to England and we want to spend some time this winter helping him over his technical and temperamental problems.' The chairman of selectors touched on two key issues, Cork's difficulties with team situations and his temperamental problems, putting the official seal of approval on my *Grandstand* comments. Graveney also mentioned that Cork had been very upset by the whole incident, but he could not deny the truth of the matter. Inevitably I met up with Johnson that summer and asked him if he had seen the *Grandstand* programme in question. He admitted that he hadn't, claiming that he had been instructed to make me the target of an outburst of moral indignation. Journalists like Johnson are not all that well equipped to act as guardians of the public interest.

The farce dragged on and on, for on 16 and 17 April 1998 the same Peter Johnson published in the *Daily Mail* two interviews with Cork, who ranted on about wanting to stage a television debate with me. Claiming that I was conducting a vendetta against him, he accused me of seeking revenge on behalf of Australian batsman Dean Jones, who left Derbyshire in 1997 in angry circumstances: 'I find it very significant that Dean Jones and Geoff Boycott are good friends. First Deano walks out of the club criticising senior players, then Boycott makes his attack – there has to be a connection somewhere.' It was all a figment of his vivid imagination. I respect Dean Jones as a batsman and get on with him well enough as a person, but we are not at all close and I had not spoken to him once during his stay with Derbyshire. Among all the rubbish about a few uncomplimentary words from me ruining his Test career, however, Cork contrived to hang himself with a rope of his own making. Talking to Johnson about that tour of New Zealand in 1997, he said: 'Sometimes I went to Athers and the management and admitted that I was not as focused as I should be and that things were not right. At one stage I told the captain I was sorry for not being as respectful as I should be, but the problem was not him. At times we did not get on as we should have. I came home to hear stories that I was the bad boy of the tour.' To me that summed it all up. Cork wanted to blame anyone but himself.

Cassius Clay surrounded himself with arrogance and showmanship

My life in cricket as a pundit and commentator suits me down to the ground. Pictured during the first Test at Kingston, Jamaica, in 1994. (Patrick Eagar)

Behind the microphone in the West Indies, 1990. (Patrick Eagar)

Inspecting the wicket for BBC television. (Patrick Eagar)

Ray Illingworth gets a grilling from me at Old Trafford during the May 1996 Texaco Trophy match against India. (Allsport)

ABOVE  Helping Graham Gooch with his preparations in New Zealand on the 1991–92 tour. (Allsport)

BELOW  Micky Stewart adds his thoughts to the proceedings. (Allsport)

ABOVE Discussing tactics with Micky Stewart during the 1992 World Cup. (Allsport)

BELOW Coaching aspiring youngsters at Lord's in 1993, for the *MCC Masterclass* book and video. (Patrick Eagar)

Keith Fletcher, rashly appointed to the England job in the autumn of 1992, in the nets in Madras on the disastrous 1992–93 tour of India. (Patrick Eagar)

When Ray Illingworth was appointed chairman of selectors in the spring of 1994, Fletcher's days were numbered. Fred Titmus mulls over England's prospects in the 1994 Lord's Test against South Africa with them. (Patrick Eagar)

The uneasy relationship between Mike Atherton and Ray Illingworth on display before the second Test at Melbourne at the end of 1994. (Patrick Eagar)

David Lloyd directs operations during the sixth Test against the West Indies at St John's, Antigua, in 1998. (Patrick Eagar)

The sublime Sachin Tendulkar during the MCC v. Rest of the World match at Lord's, 1998.
(Patrick Eagar)

Warwickshire's Brian Lara at Edgbaston in 1994 in front of the scoreboard showing his record-breaking 501 not out. (Patrick Eagar)

Tendulkar, the dignified captain, lifts a Man of the Match trophy after the first Test against Australia in Madras, March 1998. (Allsport)

Lara, the troubled captain, leads his team out for a one-day international against England in Trinidad, April 1998. (Allsport)

# Just some of the stars who could shine in the 1999 World Cup

ABOVE England's Graeme Hick and RIGHT Darren Gough (Allsport)

ABOVE Australia's Shane Warne and ABOVE RIGHT Michael Bevan (Allsport)

ABOVE South Africa's Jonty Rhodes and
RIGHT Jacques Kallis (Allsport)

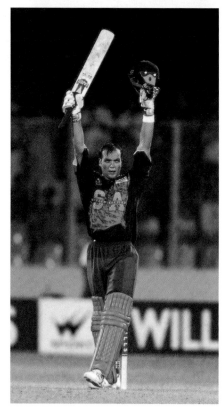

ABOVE Pakistan's Saqlain Mushtaq and
RIGHT Shahid Afridi (Allsport)

BELOW Sri Lanka's Sanath Jayasuriya and
RIGHT Muttiah Muralitharan (Allsport)

BELOW India's Saurav Ganguly and
RIGHT Javagal Srinath (Allsport)

ABOVE West Indies' Shivnarine Chanderpaul (Allsport)

New Zealand's Stephen Fleming
(Allsport)

Zimbabwe's Heath Streak (Allsport)

Hansie Cronje lifts the Wills International Cup in Dhaka, Bangladesh, October 1998. I think he'll be doing the same with the World Cup come Sunday, 20 June. (Allsport)

during his reign as the best boxer in the world, but he consistently delivered the goods. Prince Naseem, from Sheffield, is an up-to-the-minute version of Clay and also gets away with his antics, so long as he is winning. The end product of Cork's endeavours hardly matches up to his inflated ideas of his place in the scheme of things, and in many ways he is still growing up. For the record, to date he has scored 634 runs in twenty-seven Tests at an average of 17.61 with two half-centuries and a top score of 59. His ninety-eight wickets have cost him 31.81 runs each, and 7 for 43 stands as his top return in a list of five hauls of five wickets or more.

In the *Daily Express* on 18 June 1997, Jim Lawton asked the question: 'Was Boycott not one of cricket's great prima donnas?' He came to the conclusion that I might well have been, but drew attention to important differences between Cork and myself:

> *Personal problems never intruded into his professional sense of what needed to be done. He never mistook a promising spring for a summer of achievement. What Boycott has railed against in the desperate years of English cricket failure has been the shortfall in genuine graft and the hasty willingness to make overnight stars. Boycott placed the talented Cork firmly in this category; he has said that what the Derbyshire player did at Lord's the summer before last, when his hat-trick sent excitement pulsing into every corner of the English game, was merely a down payment on glory, that what has followed has been a squandering of the credit.*

Among Cork's grievances, Lawton also listed the failure of the English Cricket Board to come to his defence, conveniently ignoring the fact that he had no defence. Really, I am saddened by Cork's apparent inability to make the most of his talents, and I take no pleasure from his failures. I wish he had squared his shoulders, taken my criticism on the chin and gone out to prove me wrong, but he didn't, preferring to grumble to the press.

These days newspapers have traded the old-fashioned virtues of balanced reporting for a more gung-ho approach. They react to results rather than performances, so that victory for any of our national teams justifies ridiculous extremes of praise, while defeat provokes howls of hysterical outrage and sparks calls for heads to roll. Realistically, each reaction is as silly as the other. In the long run the means are more important than the end product. Success for England in a Test series does not alter the fact that there are problems, and every professional team should be constantly seeking improvement. *Wisden*, the most authoritative publication on cricket, ranks England at number seven in the world, ahead only of Zimbabwe and New Zealand, and while it may be true that statistics do not tell the full story, they do not lie either. The *Wisden* formula may not be perfect, but it is a worthwhile guide to our current standing. It is, therefore, impossible to pretend from the commentary box that England are one of the world's top sides, although I would stress that whenever possible we do try to find something encouraging to say.

As part of the defence mechanism which protects the dressing room, the England players and those closely involved with them claim to avoid listening to the television commentaries. The official line is that they object to hearing ex-players comparing them unfavourably to previous generations, yet they are always well aware of what has been said. Certain individuals are likely to be distant or cool at the ground whenever they have been the object of criticism, but our responsibility is to the general public, not to them. The players' attitude indicates that either they are not telling the truth and do listen to the commentary, or their wives, girlfriends or families pass on our comments. If the latter is the case then trouble usually follows, because hearing things second-hand invariably gives a distorted picture of what was said. In any case, if they do not set any great store by our opinions they should not be affected by them. If they are confident about the way they are playing they should be able to ignore the press.

A significant exchange in this respect took place between Cork and myself at Port Elizabeth during the England tour of 1995–96. I was working for BBC radio and South African radio, and Cork tackled me one day without being too unpleasant. 'I hear that you have been having a go at us,' he said, adding, 'You should be supporting us and encouraging us.' I pointed out that England already had a coach, a manager and a captain to provide the necessary psychological support and encouragement, and that the players could also rely on each other for a bit of mutual backslapping. I insisted, in the face of his persistence, that, although I did want England to do well, my function was to report events exactly as I saw them without any patriotic embellishment. Strangely, Cork stuck doggedly to his initial argument, repeating the point that no matter how the team performed the English media had a duty to stand by them, glossing over their weaknesses if necessary. But the truth is what we see, not what they want it to be – an important fact of life Cork had missed. It did not apparently occur to him that the first requirement of a professional in any walk of life is to be honest with himself. Each individual player ought to be his own sternest critic, able to listen to and assess the views of others. On that basis, I recommend that any player with a grievance should approach me and press his case. A straightforward discussion would clear the air, give us both something to think about and should ultimately lead to some form of agreement. For my part, I would be happy to apologise and do my best to put the record straight if I found myself in the wrong, while the player might learn something to his advantage if he realised my remarks had some substance.

Sometimes a player takes his place on the field carrying a slight injury because the captain or the selectors realise that he is sufficiently important to justify the risk. Obviously they keep the potential weakness to themselves, so it is impossible for the commentators to be aware of the situation. In that case, because we are not mind readers, we might innocently be too critical, but such instances are rare. Some ex-players do try to ingratiate themselves with management and players in the hope of picking up inside information, but I think they compromise themselves by sacrificing their independence. Limited contact is fair enough, but it is not possible for a commentator to serve two masters –

the players and the public – and I do not go into any dressing room without a specific invitation from the captain. To me, the dressing room is a sanctuary for the players, a private place where they can let off steam and rid themselves of the tension which is part and parcel of any big match.

Nor do I proffer advice. I am often asked why I do not help the England batsmen by bringing my television comments to their notice. The answer is that I do not want to interfere. I always help whenever asked, no matter who the player is – I remember that when I was feeling my way in first-class cricket many established batsmen helped me, and I would never hesitate to return the favour – but that is a different business. I get genuine pleasure from seeing a batsman improve, but there is no way I would push in my nose where it is not wanted.

Reluctantly, I accept that I have crossed the divide between player and spectator, and that back seat is not always comfortable. But as I've said, I still sniff the air with a feeling of excitement and expectation on the first day of a Test match, and that stirring sense of occasion still reaches up from the ground to the commentary box. The carnival is not over just yet.

# CHAPTER TEN

# England's Supremos

When I began my county career Yorkshire had a cricket committee, but the playing side was run by the chairman, Brian Sellers, who ruled with a rod of iron and dominated the scene. The buck stopped with him, and everyone knew exactly where they stood. He, in turn, understood the need to get on with his captain, and the harmonious relationship between the administration and the dressing room provided a platform for success on the field, just as it should for England. The fact that it doesn't owes much to years of muddled management, which has failed to come to terms with the requirements of modern international competition.

Despite a lot of talk among committees about searching for real leadership, no one grasped the nettle and introduced the necessary structure to run the England team on really professional lines. A series of tentative steps over the last decade or so has indeed led nowhere, in fact reverting to the days of Micky Stewart's term of management (significantly, the former Surrey captain got the job only when Raymond Illingworth – the best captain I played under, but a man who has nevertheless done more to undermine the future of English cricket than any other – rejected it on the grounds that it did not carry enough authority). In many ways Stewart's appointment, confirmed at a TCCB meeting on 5 March 1987, represented an experiment. I have a lot of time for him and recognise that he worked very hard. He possessed the foresight to get people with the right credentials to help England's players to improve their game, and the strength of character to put personalities to one side. An unremarkable batsman himself, with just eight Test caps, he did not make the mistake of thinking that by using better players as coaches he in any way belittled himself. It takes a man who is comfortable with his own place in the scheme of things and who knows what he has to offer to call on the services of fellow professionals with more ability. He pioneered the idea of involving big-name players in the coaching of England, shrugging off the publicity that they received and willingly putting himself second.

I always got on well with Micky when he captained Surrey and subsequently, when I agreed to do whatever I could to improve the potential of the England batsmen. I still retain a great admiration for what he tried to achieve. In fact, it says much for Stewart's open-mindedness that I became associated with the England squad in the first place. Through my newspaper articles and comments on television, I was very critical of England's performances as they crashed 4–0 to Australia in 1989, pinpointing in detail the faults of the batsmen and constructively indicating what they should be doing to improve, and I suppose because of my track record my opinions made news themselves. England's lack of fight also gave me great concern. They surrendered so meekly to Australia, making a series of basic errors.

In the circumstances, my name cropped up regularly in the press, notably when I criticised Ted Dexter, the then chairman of selectors. He simply did not devote sufficient time to his important duties as the focal point of the whole set-up, often missing during Test matches. I regarded the way he went about his business as unacceptable. The chairman of selectors should be present at every Test, not only watching the play but also acting as the spokesman for England. Dexter preferred to play golf, and eventually managed the embarrassing trick of being 'unavailable' when Graham Gooch resigned as captain at Headingley in 1993. His detachment sent out all the wrong signals, and I suspect that he never really got to grips with the reality of the situation. The role of chairman of selectors demanded more of Ted than he was prepared to give. He invariably created the impression of being the part-time amateur, but England were not good enough to have anyone in charge part-time. Ted cared, but possibly he did not care enough. Cricket lovers felt that he was too ready to 'keep things in perspective', that he could not bring himself to fuss too much about the results, no matter how bad they became.

Gifted and wealthy, Dexter had little experience of what the rest of us call the real world. That is why I never nursed any animosity towards Ted, who was my first captain in Test cricket in 1964, and with whom I have never had a wrong word. He was, in fact, very kind to me as a newcomer to the international set-up, going out of his way to make me welcome. My first tour was to South Africa in 1964–65 under Mike Smith, and it could have proved a lonely and unhappy experience, even though we had a team table for dinner in the evenings. Dexter took his wife, Sue, on the trip with him, and on several occasions he invited me to join them for a meal, having noticed that, as a green youngster with a single-minded determination to do well, I was on my own while the rest of the squad went out and about on the town. I also played golf with him in Port Elizabeth, making up a foursome with John Woodcock of *The Times* and Michael Melford of the *Daily Telegraph*. Dexter was an outstanding amateur golfer, one of the best in the country, and I was a poor sixteen handicapper at the time, but he turned out to be marvellous company, helping me to play to something like ten as we won the match. It was one of the best golfing days of my life because Ted encouraged me to enjoy the game, showing me where to hit the ball and how to line up the putts without any hint of condescension. His instinctive ball sense enabled him to play with ease, and it also served him well as a batsman.

Importantly, he added courage to a masterly technique against the most ferocious fast bowling, yet he remained somehow distant. In one of the two Tests staged in Johannesburg on that tour I got out early and departed with the measured tread of someone coping with a serious disappointment. There must be at least ninety steps up to the pavilion at The Wanderers Stadium, and I certainly did not hurry through the excited ranks of South African supporters celebrating an early wicket; nevertheless, when I entered the dressing room Ted had not even risen from his seat to bat at number three. He sat absentmindedly, with his head in a book on hypnotism, oblivious to the excitement all around him.

It was typical of Ted that he indicated on his appointment as chairman of selectors that he wanted to involve me in the coaching of the batsmen, and he continued throughout the summer of 1989 to confirm that he intended to have a word with me. He recalled that Australia's Dean Jones had benefited enormously from my advice and insisted that England needed my expertise, but not once did I receive a call from him. I did come into contact with him two or three times, but he always wanted to talk about golf, so it was Micky Stewart who eventually approached me in the autumn to ask if I would be prepared to undertake some coaching.

In doing so, he took me into a situation which was all shadow and no substance. A number of articles appeared in newspapers linking me with England, as I was on record saying that I would never turn them away. Unfortunately, they all stressed that I would be obliged to give up my media work, which was clearly out of the question. I could see only too clearly all the danger signals. The authorities at Lord's as well as the England players were very unhappy about my public forum for criticising playing standards, and no doubt some people thought they could silence me while giving me a bit of a lackey's job on the fringe of things, calling me up once or twice when they felt I might be of some use. Stewart had spoken to me earlier in the campaign without going into any detail, and I took the trouble to discuss the possibilities with the captain, Graham Gooch, pointing out that seeing a player once or twice would not do much good, particularly if Stewart happened to hold different views. I did, however, promise Stewart at Headingley that I would consider any sensible proposals and give him a decision when I knew exactly what was expected of me. He expressed a fear that problems could arise if I coached certain players and then talked about them either in print or on television.

I understood that a lot of cricket followers were wondering where I stood, but I took great care not to rock the boat. I did not want to embarrass anyone by saying too much in public, but my own mind was crystal clear on the subject. I refused to queue up for a coaching job, nor would I throw away a media career which provided me with a good income for an unspecified role with England which carried no guarantees. Dexter's salary stood at around £20,000, Stewart's at £30,000, yet I could expect very little, and no practical offer was on the table. It did not make sense. To make matters worse, the fact that England, through Stewart, wanted my services appeared in the *Sunday Express* on 8 October 1989. Claiming an 'exclusive', Pat Gibson wrote:

> *Geoff Boycott, England's most outspoken critic during their disastrous Ashes summer, has been invited to put his knowledge where his mouth is. Boycott is one of several former Test stars who have been approached by England cricket manager Micky Stewart to help improve the players' technique. They include fast bowlers John Snow and Geoff Arnold and wicketkeepers Alan Knott and Bob Taylor – but Boycott is the most controversial choice. Now a Yorkshire committee man, newspaper columnist and television pundit, Boycott has made no secret of his belief that he should have Ted Dexter's job as chairman of the England committee.*

In addition, Gibson reported Stewart as saying:

> *I explained that I wanted to get Boycott involved with all the players from the fourteen-year-olds up to the senior side, and he expressed an interest in doing that. Since then I have talked to him again and pointed out that if he was going to be involved he would have to*

*make a choice between his media work and the team set-up because
everyone involved with the side has to be single-minded about it.
And he was still interested. I can understand that if he is going to be
employed by the media he has to say things that are going to make
an impact. At times I think that is sad, but I think it would be
much sadder if English cricket could not benefit from his great
knowledge and experience.*

Obviously Stewart had released the story and broken faith with me after
asking for confidentiality, and once more I found myself wondering just
how honest England were being in their dealings with me.

Pat Gibson's article represented the truth only up to a point, for I had
made it clear that I was not prepared to travel up and down the country
to suit the convenience of the England players. If they wanted me as a
specialist batting consultant, they would have to come to me; they
needed me, I did not need them. Nor had I waged any campaign to take
over from Dexter. I enjoyed the advantages of well-paid full-time
employment, which the England set-up was not offering. England
appeared ready to pick my brains at my expense, and some comments in
this respect by Robin Marlar in the *Sunday Times* on 10 December made
me smile. Referring to the opinions I expressed on television during the
Ashes series, he wrote:

*Boycott was precious close to going over the top as his laser tongue
tore strips off those in the driving seat, leaving no one in doubt that
he could have done better than Messrs Dexter and Stewart. It is,
therefore, a tribute to the forgiving natures of all concerned that
Boycott has now joined the panel of highly favoured coaches involved
in preparations for the forthcoming tours to the West Indies and
Zimbabwe.*

I did not see things that way at all. As someone doing a job like anyone
else, I begged no forgiveness. My criticism was fair and it was right,

which is exactly what the authorities did not like. In the final analysis, I was in a position to do England a favour.

When I did begin coaching in November, I pushed doubts about the details to one side and concentrated on the business in hand. My view was that I could identify technique, or the lack of it, quickly and show what had to be done to put things right. The onus then rested with the player, who had to put in the necessary hours of practice to make good habits instinctive. I appreciated only too clearly that playing correctly in the nets was one thing, doing the same in the heat of battle another. I could teach the correct way to practise, improve the shot selection process and advise on mental discipline, attitude and concentration, but the players had to respond positively.

Some of the notes I made as preparations got under way for the tour of the West Indies, starting in February 1990, illustrate the size of the task that faced me as a coach.

Mike Atherton: Good movement of feet, but he gets them in the wrong position. Right foot goes straight back and is, therefore, too far from ball. His guard is leg stump – feet outside leg stump – so when the ball is well up he has a long way to go across. He has a good stride, but he goes too much across the crease, so it does not benefit him and he is playing too much at forty-five degrees. Needs right foot back and across the stumps.

Graham Gooch: Played worse in nets than I have ever seen him play. Back foot goes back square and then swivels around so that both feet are pointing down the wicket with him full chest on. A dreadful position. He cannot get his feet out of the blockhole, so he is trying to bat on one leg.

Mark Nicholas (A team captain): Plays a little stood up when he goes forward and needs weight to come forward over ball. Plays the ball outside the line of his head when short outside off stump, and then moves back foot again.

Rob Bailey: Too far away from off stump, so he has too far to go against quick bowling. Off stump a bit of a problem. Left foot planted with toe pointing down pitch. Back foot not sideways enough.

Alec Stewart: Open stance with one foot back from the other which makes him a bit open-chested. Not quick enough on feet. Weight planted back when he plays back. When he ducks and drops hands, bat is left out towards slip.

James Whitaker: Too slow on his feet. Jumping and moving late. Never in position to play ball before it arrives. Biggest problem is always looking to be inside the line of the ball. Lots of courage, but no ability to adjust.

Those are just a sample of the technical points I began to deal with, but I knew that miracles would not happen overnight. Although we were dealing with the best of England's county cricketers, these flawed techniques had been ingrained for years.

Coaching is as much about thinking as anything, and I constantly underlined the value of patience in the West Indies, where slow over rates and a preponderance of short-pitched bowling combine to limit scoring opportunities. There is no merit whatsoever in trying to push along the scoring rate out there, where a lucky batsman might get a couple of half-volleys in a full session. The feedback proved very interesting. Bailey, for instance, admitted in the *Sunday Times*:

> *I feel that for the first time in my life the size of the challenge ahead has been made clear – thanks to Geoff Boycott. He has given me an insight into what lies ahead. And, as the old adage has it, forewarned is forearmed. When I saw myself on video and went through it all with Geoff I realised what a long way there is to go. Geoff has done an enormous amount of work in putting my mental attitude right. He has made it quite clear that if you survive for an hour in the West Indies you have probably faced only about forty deliveries. He's pointed out, too, that it preys on your mind when you're at the other end, and I quite accept his philosophy that you've got to put yourself in a cocoon.*

Nasser Hussain, another flat-footed player, added: 'Geoff had the bowlers sending down bouncers from seventeen yards to try to recreate the conditions we'll face out there. He did not encourage us to block, but he did tell us we'll need a sound defence.' Later, I received a postcard from Mark Nicholas, despatched from Zimbabwe, which read: 'It is good to see young players committed to playing for England. The batting so far appears to have benefited from your presence at Lilleshall.' Micky Stewart, on behalf of the Test and County Cricket Board, wrote: 'Not only have the players benefited from a technical point of view, but you have helped develop the right approach and attitude, which will prove invaluable. I intend making sure that the way we have worked over the past six weeks will be continued at every opportunity in the future, both at senior level and with the best youngsters.' More importantly, Gooch, as tour captain, sent me a letter in which he stressed: 'I trust you will continue to offer your services in the Caribbean as the tour moves forward. For myself, I would find that very reassuring.' Robin Smith went so far as to spend eleven hours on the train travelling between Southampton and Leeds to have a one-to-one session with me at Headingley in mid-January. He expressed no regrets at putting himself to such a great inconvenience, telling the local press: 'Geoff is so knowledgeable. Everything he says is meaningful. When he talks, you listen.'

On balance, then, it is fair to say that I gave England everything they might have expected in the winter of 1989–90, using video to spotlight points and moving back the nets to give a spread of four lanes so that the batsmen would not feel hemmed in when dealing with the short stuff. I stuck some hostile fast bowling up their noses, too, much of it from fewer than twenty yards. Stewart told me that during the first session most of the batsmen expressed outrage, with a good deal of cursing and swearing at the idea of travelling miles and giving up their otherwise free time to have their heads knocked off. Once I had talked them through my theories, though, and demonstrated the value of ducking and weaving and controlling their emotions to make a statement to the West Indies pacemen, they gradually relaxed and gained confidence against the short ball. They came to understand that they were not 'Aunt Sallies' and that preparing properly was the one way to make sure they did not take a physical pounding. They also began to appreciate that nothing would be gained from thrashing around the sort of half-volley that is as scarce as a snowball in the Caribbean.

I am proud of what I did in that period, because I was able to prove the point I had been making. With plenty of time at our disposal I was able to prepare the tourists mentally and, as far as possible, technically for a very tough series. Stewart gave me my head and I reported back to him quietly without much song and dance. At no time did I put him under any pressure as the man in charge of coaching, and we experienced no difficulties, agreeing readily that the attendance of players would be on a voluntary basis. If they wanted to come, fine. Certain batsmen did not need to worry too much, particularly Allan Lamb, who could handle pace well with his own methods.

I devoted time to the England cause for a total of nine days before leaving for the West Indies myself. It was only when I got back that I received a letter from Cliff Barker, the Test and County Cricket Board accountant, who forwarded a cheque for £802.40, made up of £700 in fees and £102.40 in travelling expenses. I returned the cheque and requested just my expenses; I did not want a payment which might compromise my position with the media. I was happy to help my country as much as I could, but I did not want to become a hostage to the TCCB. As a consequence I continued to work with players through the summer of 1990 in England, and during the build-up to the 1990–91 visit to Australia, the 1991–92 trip to New Zealand, and the 1992 World Cup staged by those two countries, always without payment. Thus in 1991, after being honoured by the media as Player of the Year, Gooch said: 'I don't think I have ever been so happy with my game, but I am always striving to improve my technique and that is where Geoff Boycott comes in. He's a good coach and a good friend, the first man I always turn to. I am not too proud to admit that I owe him a hell of a lot, particularly after the problems I had against the Aussies in 1989.'

The arrangement seemed to work very well, so I was stunned when Micky Stewart expressed doubts about my position so far as Graeme Hick was concerned. He was quoted in the *Today* newspaper on 18 December 1991 as saying he wanted to keep the struggling Worcestershire batsman away from the limelight and any connection with such a controversial figure as me. He said: 'Graeme's track record meant he had a very high profile against the West Indies last summer. That's why there have been no sessions with Boycott. We felt that if the stumps went over during any coaching there would be pictures all over the back pages next day and the high-profile process would start rolling again.' That was definitely a strange remark to make when Gooch, the top rated batsman in the world at the time, was still coming to me for advice occasionally without attracting unfavourable publicity.

The truth is that Hick has the problem: he finds it hard to cope with the publicity that goes with being an England player. What Hick and Stewart were essentially admitting, without really understanding it, was that the player couldn't handle the pressure at the highest level. Anyone who succeeds in Test cricket has to accept the harsh spotlight of centre-stage attention, and Hick ought to have been dismissing the possibility of his stumps being flattened as an irrelevance compared to the advantages to be derived from being coached. It doesn't matter if you make mistakes in the nets, for that's the right place to identify and iron out any weakness. Hick's main concern should have been with his performance out in the middle during a Test match, and I feel that the vulnerability which makes him a 'nearly man' to this day reflects poor thinking. His Test career has spluttered along because he lacks mental toughness.

During that period when I was helping the England players there were one or two other minor areas of disagreement. Allan Lamb complained in the newspapers that probably some of my comments did upset the odd individual, but Gooch stood very firmly behind me all the time. He remained convinced that well-founded, sensible criticism should be accepted and considered carefully. As he said, players who consistently do well don't get criticised. Those who make mistakes and don't want to hear or read about them should ignore the newspapers and turn off the television. As far as possible, I avoided any conflict of loyalty. Sometimes Gooch or Stewart asked my views on matters of selection, but I never interfered beyond that. I stuck to the principle that my thoughts on any aspect of English cricket were mine to do with what I liked, but I never used in print anything that I had been told in confidence. What Gooch or Stewart said to me behind closed doors remained a private matter. I also encouraged Gooch to back his own judgement. Whenever he raised a query with me, I offered my opinion, but I always added: 'But if you really think differently, go with it. You are taking the team on the field.' It is the captain's right to do what he thinks is best. You cannot have captaincy by remote control, so I was happy to act only as a sounding board for Gooch and did not take offence if he did not agree with me.

When Stewart finally went in the autumn of 1992, Keith Fletcher took over, an appointment inspired largely by the press. The major newspapers are based in London, where the majority of the senior cricket correspondents live. Cricket journalism involves a lot of travelling, with trips abroad in the winter, so, human nature being what it is, the leading writers usually trot off to a handy championship engagement near the capital whenever they get a break from Test duty. The most influential press people, therefore, enjoy a fairly close relationship with Essex, and they looked no further than Fletcher. As manager of the A team he stood out as the logical choice to the inner circle of pundits. A former county and England captain, he boasted all the right credentials, his claims emphasised by the success of Essex on the domestic front. The Essex president, Doug Insole, exerted considerable influence at Lord's, and Graham Gooch, another Essex man, was captain of England, so it all fitted neatly into place, giving one of the smallest counties on the circuit a massive boost in the process. No one else came into consideration. To compound this error, the hierarchy appointed Fletcher on a long-term basis without finding out whether he could do the job – he had, after all, been away from Test cricket since his last appearance for England in 1982 – although the odd voice was raised in opposition. Robin Marlar, in the *Sunday Times*, mentioned 'Fletcher's amazing overlong contract', and all the unseemly haste meant that his appointment came out of the blue without the cricket committee knowing much about anything.

I was convinced from the start that it was a bad decision made for the wrong reasons. I played with Fletcher and watched him as both captain and coach. He is a quiet, unremarkable individual with little presence, and to me his strengths lie in dealing with youngsters or players of limited ability who require encouragement. He understands their feelings and his natural environment is a homely club like Essex. The management of the national side stretched him too far. He found it too great a burden, and once Illingworth got rid of him he returned happily to the backwaters of county cricket and prospered. Nobody hears much about him these days and that is how he likes it, safely sheltered from the glare of the Test match spotlight. Essex is a marvellous little set-up and provides him with a comfort zone. Expectations are not all that high there, and Fletcher, a decent guy who likes a quiet life, is never given a task that is beyond him.

Running England is a different business altogether, and I could never see him meeting the demands. Every move at international level is put under the microscope. Every word is measured, so the person in the hot seat has to be very hard and assured, ready to face abuse and hostility from press and public alike without losing faith in himself. Fletcher probably thought he could run England in much the same way as he did Essex, but neither the media nor the England supporters would accept the consequences. His good qualities of kindness and decency were seen as a weakness on the international stage and he failed to stamp his authority on events. Once the traditional honeymoon period ran out, the knives appeared.

He had fallen behind the times. A good batsman, he never showed qualities of leadership as a player, settling in rather as a good team man.

There is at least one member of most dressing rooms who, whatever his official position, sets the standards and stands out as someone to whom the rest look up. As a batsman, Fletcher never made a mark in this direction, so it was a mistake to recall him from the wilderness after a five-year absence and elevate him to the England captaincy for the 1981–82 tour of India. At that time Essex were doing well, but that should not have been a decisive factor, and his failure as England captain came as no great surprise to me, particularly as he got off to the worst possible start.

In helping to select the touring party, he had pursued a misguided policy, pinning his faith on fast-medium seamers and relying on the evidence of earlier clashes with the Indians, which suggested their batsmen lacked courage. Sadly, the Indians' impressive improvement against pace passed him by, even though they had demonstrated it often enough. Opener Sunil Gavaskar stood out as a great batsman capable of dealing efficiently with the fastest bowlers, while Dilip Vengsarkar was one of the best players of short stuff in the world. The other batsmen were also capable of operating successfully on their own pitches, which offered precious little bounce anyway. Fletcher's seamers found that the ball did not swing either, and we lost the series 1–0, confirming that the captain's thinking was hopelessly out of date. I kept my own counsel at the time, but his shortcomings on what was my last tour were obvious.

Inevitably, then, the odds were heavily on the eleven-year gap between his farewell as a player and his return as manager proving too great a handicap. For over a decade Fletcher's relationship with Test cricket had been no more than sketchy, but, unabashed by his limited background, he quickly got off the mark by announcing that he would not be using me as 'an official coach'. Presumably he did not realise that I had never held an official position, and he offered a telling quote: 'It's not just a question of technique, it's what is between the ears that counts.' I agreed that it was essential to get people prepared mentally – I had spent many hours doing just that, to great effect – but was Fletcher really stating that technique didn't matter or that his thinking as a batsman was better than mine? I wondered briefly what might be going on between his ears, but trying to work out his motivation did not take up much of my time. It simply did not matter to me what Fletcher thought, although I cared very deeply about England's standing and regretted that petty jealousy appeared to be guiding his hand. Possibly he felt threatened by my success as a coach in the England camp and wanted me out of the way. If so, he was attaching greater importance to his own security than to England's prospects.

Gooch continued to rely heavily on me, and other players also sought some guidance, but I had no serious association with Fletcher, who blundered along in his own merry way. With England due to visit India in January 1993, Fletcher travelled to South Africa to assess the opposition in the first meeting between those two countries. I happened to be in South Africa too, and I could not believe his stupidity when he dismissed the Indians out of hand. They lost only one of the four Tests in South Africa, drawing the other three, but he cheerfully proclaimed: 'There is nothing for England to worry about in India.' Perhaps he would have made less of a fool of himself if he had done his homework and discovered that India rarely do well outside their own country. On their specially prepared pitches at home they are a different proposition entirely. I thought at the time that Fletcher was wrong to show contempt for the Indians, who were certain to react once news of his boasting reached them. The wise man waits until he has won before he congratulates himself, and the very wise man says nothing at all.

When England arrived in India, Fletcher's dismissive remarks inevitably lifted the Indians, who were indeed smarting at what they regarded as an insult, and history records that they went on to win all three Tests in the series. So much for Fletcher's judgement, which was found wanting as early as the first Test at Eden Gardens, Calcutta, starting on 29 January. Both squads were announced two days before the game, but later India sent for a third spinner, a move which clearly indicated the state of the pitch. Ignoring this obvious hint, England stuck with three seamers, were forced to follow on, and lost by eight wickets with the home team quietly laughing at them as their slow bowlers controlled the contest. Micky Stewart, on standing down as manager, had warned that the gulf between Test and county cricket had widened during his term of office, and it was a gulf that Fletcher, with his lack of vision, could not bridge.

When Ray Illingworth became chairman of selectors in the spring of 1994, Fletcher's days were numbered. Any comparison between the two was ridiculous, and you did not have to be a fortune teller to realise that Illingworth would not want to work alongside a man he regarded as a novice. I was one of the first to forecast Fletcher's demise, telling readers of the *Sun* that the Essex man would be axed within the year, which is exactly what happened. By turning to Illingworth – whose Chinese sign, interestingly, is the ninth, represented by the wise, clever and crafty monkey – the powers-that-be at Lord's gambled on being able to take advantage of his expertise while controlling his political manoeuvring. He had a reputation in the game for being difficult to handle and for wanting everything his own way, but England clearly felt they had nowhere else to turn.

Certainly, no one understood cricket better than Illingworth, who as a captain more often than not was one step ahead of the game. Calculating and careful, he was ready to listen to opinions he valued and then be decisive once he had weighed up all the pros and cons. The 1969 Lord's Test against New Zealand provided an instructive example of the Illingworth method working to perfection. One quick glance at the pitch on a grey, murky, overcast first morning was sufficient to convince me that batting would be a hazardous enterprise. The area around the famous ridge showed up ominously green and New Zealand included in their ranks one good paceman in Dick Motz. The Pavilion End appeared, in contrast, dry and cracked, suggesting that the ball would turn towards the end of the five days. Illingworth came to me as one of his senior players to see what I wanted to do, and I told him immediately that I certainly did not want to bat. 'That's fine,' he replied, 'but what would you do if you were captain?' I turned away, trying to avoid giving an answer. 'Don't ask me that,' I replied. He persisted, so I had to admit that I would run the risk of taking the first innings and relying later on Derek Underwood, unplayable as a brisk left-arm spinner on wearing strips, to win the match. Illingworth was lucky with the toss and he did decide to bat, but before play got under way he explained his thinking to the team. 'I know it's going to be difficult batting in these conditions,' he acknowledged, 'but if we work hard and get a reasonable score on the board we'll win the match when it turns square later on.' I got out in the opening over for a duck, caught off the shoulder of the bat by a delivery from Motz which reared wickedly from not much short of a length, but Underwood, taking 7 for 32 in New Zealand's second innings for match figures of 11 for 70, did indeed carry England to a comfortable victory.

Throughout, Illingworth and I were very much on the same wavelength and he regularly talked things over with me on the field. Indeed, on occasions I could instinctively answer his question before he posed it, because I understood his thinking. I filled other roles for Illingworth, notably by standing at mid-off to liven up Sussex fast bowler John Snow, who had a bit of a lazy streak. Our exchanges developed along increasingly angry lines.

Me: 'Do you think you're going to get anyone out bowling that rubbish?'

Snow: 'Mind your own business.'

Me: 'Well, I wish I was batting. I'm not surprised he walloped that, you're only bowling half pace.'

As he got more irritated, Snow would complain to Illingworth, but without much response, and he always raised his pace and his game, if only to keep me quiet.

Illingworth, in fact, never left anything to chance. When we went to Australia in 1970–71 he took three openers with him – John Edrich, Brian Luckhurst and me – on the grounds that the new-ball spells would be crucial. The problem was that only two of us could go in first, so one would have to drop down to number three. Illingworth made up his mind that I had to open, but still went to the trouble of discussing things with all three of us. It did not matter much to me who was at the other end, so, with Luckhurst desperately wanting to avoid waiting in the pavilion with his pads on, Edrich volunteered to move down the order. Crucially, we were all happy at being consulted and the arrangement worked well. Such detailed planning ahead is one aspect of cricket to which Illingworth always paid serious attention, and he could also think clearly on his feet. No matter how good the preparation, a captain must forever be aware of changing situations and be able to respond as a game evolves.

Adaptable though he was, however, Illingworth stood by a number of basic principles, always insisting, for instance, that players must attempt to complete any possible catch, no matter how difficult. He did not blame an individual for missing a chance, but he came down pretty hard on anyone who did not make every effort, an approach which ensured that teams under his leadership generally caught a lot of good catches and saved a lot of runs in the field. Equally, his first thoughts invariably centred on winning. He had no interest in building a safe position before pushing for victory. Without getting overexcited, Illingworth wanted to win by the most straightforward method possible, and to that end he preferred five bowlers so that if it proved difficult to bowl out the opposition he had the necessary options at his disposal to retain control.

On top of that, Illingworth was a good player himself. In the nicest possible sense, he was a mean offspinner, begrudging every single, and in county cricket he usually delivered the goods on any pitch which allowed turn. Although finding wickets more difficult to come by in Test cricket, he played his part and contributed importantly, never upset by the sense of occasion. If anything, he underbowled himself, especially on flat pitches, but he appreciated the value of good quick bowling and used it whenever possible. His batting added valuable strength to the late middle order, and he completed a very respectable two centuries and five half-centuries in his sixty-one Tests, which yielded 1,836 runs at an average of 23.24.

When attempting to make an accurate assessment of the whole man, however, the most difficult question to answer is how such a good captain could become such a bad manager. Even his critics could not have envisaged how poorly he would perform in this latter capacity. Given the advantages of unrestricted authority, which he wielded after getting rid of Fletcher to add the responsibility for coaching to his workload, Illingworth still fulfilled all my worst fears. Drawing from my experience of his term in sole charge at Yorkshire from 1979 to 1983, when he effectively attempted to operate like a dictator, I expressed my doubts about this dual role from day one.

After Illingworth had made a move to oust me from the Yorkshire committee and misread the feelings of the Yorkshire members in the process, and after the new committee, elected after the revolution of 1984, had chosen to dispense with his services instead, he and I had gone our separate ways, but in 1990 the BBC took me in as part of its commentary team, broadcasting alongside Illingworth. As professionals, we kept what happened in Yorkshire firmly in the past and talked freely about cricket without sharing any secrets or pursuing discussions too far. So I was stunned when, out of the blue, Illingworth revealed in 1993 that he rated me as the 'perfect choice to lead a new era of hope'. As England played a distant second fiddle to the rampant Australians and Gooch prepared his resignation speech, Illingworth wrote in the *Daily Express* of 26 July:

> *The game needs a real supremo, a Mr Cricket, and who better than Geoffrey Boycott? There are too many jobs at the top – Ted Dexter, chairman of selectors, team manager Keith Fletcher and Ossie Wheatley, chairman of the England cricket committee. That creates more problems than it solves, and I would merge all three roles. The job needs 100 per cent dedication and commitment from a man who has played the game at the top level himself. Boycott is perfectly suited.*

That article inspired a whole host of imitators. Colin Price suggested in the *Daily Mirror* of 11 August: 'Boycott is undoubtedly the People's Choice, a man with the bottle to put pride and fight back into our shambling game.' On the same day, Matt Driscoll revealed that 'over 90 per cent of *Daily Star* readers want Geoffrey Boycott to become the saviour of English cricket'. Even Tony Greig added his voice to the clamour: 'I would appoint Boycott straight away if he is big enough and serious enough about helping English cricket.' The media simply went crazy, although I neither sought the job nor mentioned it. Still finding my feet in television, I had enough on my plate, but when I thought about the sequence of events an interesting question arose: Had Illingworth been serious in his advertisement of my qualifications, or had he been wily enough just to set the hare running because he wanted the position for himself? After all, virtually everything he wrote about me could have applied to him.

Pondering the possibility, I recalled something that Price had also written in the midst of the furore: 'Boycott already knows that his outspoken views have made him as popular with the Oxbridge set as under-arm bowling.' Illingworth also knew that my standing at Lord's remained low, and the fact that he had been approached before Stewart to become the first manager confirmed the presence of supporters in the right place. Machiavelli advised: 'Disguise your true inclination and play the hypocrite well.' Maybe I am giving Illingworth too much credit, but it is not fanciful to imagine, with hindsight, that he put my name in the spotlight merely to get the ball rolling in his own direction. It is certainly a fact that a mere eight or so months after penning the *Daily Express* article, in the spring of 1994, he took over from Dexter, even if the rest is supposition.

Coincidentally, in January of that year Alan Smith, the secretary of the TCCB, had contacted me. The counties had been asked to put forward names of potential candidates as chairman of selectors, and I figured among the nominations. Tony Greig, proposed by Sussex, showed no enthusiasm, and Smith's approach hardly encouraged me to regard myself as more than a rank outsider. 'Geoffrey,' he said, 'your name has been suggested, but I don't think you would really be interested because of your lucrative newspaper and television work. The job pays £25,000 and I don't think the committee will be prepared to go above that figure.' He stressed that I would be expected to attend all the Test matches and, for reasons of protocol, to visit each county at least once every season, all the time emphasising the possible drawbacks while fulfilling his obligation to put me in the picture. I told him that I was not interested in being put on a shortlist, adding that the TCCB should headhunt the man who fulfilled their requirements and talk about money afterwards. By putting a ceiling on the financial side of the equation they were limiting their scope. Presumably Illingworth emerged as first choice without much effort on the part of the TCCB.

He came into power against a confused background, although, initially at least, all was sweetness and light with his captain, Michael Atherton. Two things he said publicly at the time were interesting. In the *Mail on Sunday*, he claimed: 'I am only one member of the selection panel, but I do have the clout if I have to use it.' I certainly recognised the Illingworth I knew in that remark, and noted that nothing was changing. Turning to the captaincy, he added: 'By and large Michael is pretty aware of what is what on the field. He is not too far off the mark.' At that stage, therefore, Atherton enjoyed his confidence, but at the end of the season the cracks had started to appear and the press were aware of all that was happening behind the scenes.

The collapse gathered the momentum of an avalanche on 23 November 1994 as England limbered up for the opening shots in the Ashes battle. Illingworth, speaking from his home in Pudsey, lashed out in the *Daily Express*, reprimanding Atherton for 'undermining England's fast bowlers' after being defeated during the selection process over Angus Fraser. The Middlesex bowler did not get the vote, despite a strong plea from Atherton, who made his disappointment only too clear. Illingworth showed more of his true colours by complaining that Atherton had not telephoned him from Australia to seek his advice. He clearly resented finding himself on the outside, although with tour manager Mike Smith and team manager Fletcher on hand, Atherton presumably saw little reason to call on someone 12,000 miles away in England.

Recognising the dangers, Illingworth suggested that the roles of tour manager and team manager could be filled by one man – maybe another case of sowing the seeds in the hope of reaping his own rich harvest. Official policy reasonably enough called for Illingworth and Atherton to present a united front, but their relationship deteriorated when Illingworth flew out to Australia for the two Tests over the Christmas holidays. England stumbled to humiliating defeat at Melbourne, losing six wickets for thirteen runs in a miserable total of 92, and the *Sunday Times* reported that at the all-embracing post-match depression, 'Illingworth was busy sniping at Keith Fletcher, the amiable but increasingly lost tour manager, and M.J.K. Smith, the millionaire and press-shy tour manager.' Illingworth, true to form, searched eagerly for scapegoats, moaning: 'It's amazing to me in two or three months how things have drifted.' Pointing the finger at Fletcher and Smith, he insisted: 'It's their jobs on the line, not mine.'

As the tour lurched on its sorry way, Illingworth and Atherton, representatives of generations worlds apart, gradually gave up the pretence of a relationship. The two could not get on, the war of words developing in public and private to such an extent that Christopher Martin-Jenkins reported in the *Daily Telegraph* on 10 January 1995: 'They have to some extent been point-scoring off each other, using the press as a convenient way of saying "I told you so".' There may well have been some truth in Illingworth's conviction that the advances made under his hands-on management in England during the summer's Tests against South Africa and New Zealand had been dissipated, and undoubtedly Fletcher was living on borrowed time, but he could not escape censure. Management is about getting the best out of people, and Illingworth was clearly not doing that.

He spoke to me at the Sydney Test to grumble about Fletcher and to seek help in bringing down the axe. Not wanting to become involved in any cloak-and-dagger activities, I advised him simply to go to his main backers, the two men who had proposed him as chairman: Worcestershire's Duncan Fearnley and Yorkshire's Sir Lawrence Byford. What means he finally used to dispose of Fletcher I don't know, but Illingworth achieved his ambition to become the most powerful man in English cricket by the spring, and one of his first moves was to telephone me. The call reached me at the Sandy Lane Hotel, Barbados, where I was staying while working for Trans World International covering the West Indies series against Australia. He wanted me to resume my coaching activities with England and, without hesitation, I agreed, although, having been taken by surprise, I played for time. Illingworth suggested two half-days prior to each Test in 1995 with a fee of £500 each session. I repeated the sentiments I had expressed so many times before, insisting that nothing would be gained from a handful of clinics. I suggested that I should put my ideas down on paper so that we could jointly agree an arrangement.

I wrote to Illingworth on 21 March outlining a series of proposals aimed at supplementing the two half-day meetings by putting them within the framework of a more substantial set-up. I advocated coaching get-togethers as early as possible in the season before the Texaco Trophy matches, during the Texaco Trophy, on occasional days during the season when the first-class programme allowed, and at various convenient centres during the periods set aside for Benson and Hedges Cup and NatWest quarter-final matches, when some players would not be involved. Looking further ahead, I proposed preparation days before the winter tour to South Africa, two half-day sessions before each Test in South Africa, coaching at net sessions before the one-day internationals in South Africa, and during the World Cup in India and Pakistan. I also queried the position of players on the verge of the England scene, pointing out that they probably needed most help, and advised that greater attention should be paid to the Under-19s so that faults could be eliminated before they became ingrained. I told Illingworth that 'helping

England's current and future batsmen should be seen as a vital role with a set programme tackled professionally. It should not be on a piecemeal basis. I would be happy to be part of such a programme under your chairmanship and would consider discussing a package deal with the TCCB over a one-year period. I would expect to be paid a professional rate and I regard the money on offer as insufficient.'

My work in the West Indies caused an inevitable delay in the negotiation process, but, to accommodate England, I obtained permission to miss the last two Tests, returning home early in the hope of reaching an agreement with Illingworth along the lines I suggested. He expressed satisfaction with my programme, promising to sort out a realistic salary scale with Alan Smith. Only too well aware of TCCB thinking, I offered a few guidelines on the subject. For some strange reason, coaching, the key factor in the development of talent, languishes a long way down the list of financial priorities at Lord's, where staff spring up like weeds for all manner of administrative posts. To my mind, with an important principle at stake, this was the right time to put down a sensible benchmark, not only from my point of view, but also for anyone following in my footsteps. I explained to Illingworth that my fee would be £1,000 for each full day. I could pick up more than twice that for a speaking engagement, while in the commercial world consultancy rates went a lot higher. To sweeten the pill, I agreed to give my time freely when asked for help by players at other convenient times, such as before the start, during or at the close of play at Tests. The TCCB always demands top rates for tickets as well as broadcasting and advertising rights, so, I reasoned, they ought to be content to pay out similarly at the other end.

The outcome was a meeting with Smith and his assistant, Tim Lamb, at Lord's, where I talked them carefully through my plans, and we reached the stage of agreeing that the whole twelve-month process would take in some seventy days, plus the possible off-the-cuff sessions for which I would not charge. I watched Smith and Lamb doing their sums and noted the concern in their eyes as they contemplated putting a bill totalling £70,000 before their executive. This was more than Smith received and more than Illingworth's salary, which had swollen to £40,000 when he made running England a one-man show. Smith went into his usual secretarial shell, saying that he would have to get back to me, which he did, with the news that the TCCB were scaling down the operation and moving forward cautiously one step at a time. He informed me that they wished to go ahead with Illingworth's original idea of two half-days before each Test, paying £8,000 for the whole summer. According to Smith, David Acfield, the then chairman of the TCCB cricket committee, refused to sanction a more ambitious approach, which just about summed it all up. A third-rate county spinner, who happened to be a Cambridge University graduate and international fencer, wielded sufficient power to block a proposal put forward by a batsman with masses of international experience and an outstanding playing record.

So, after all that effort, we found ourselves back at square one, and the whole sorry episode saddened me. The powers-that-be at Lord's were haggling like misers over the future of the game when they should have been making every effort to sustain it. They cheerfully accepted the many hours I put in for nothing to help Micky Stewart, but as soon as the question of serious money cropped up they began counting the cost in minutes. True to type, they were trying to use me on the cheap, failing to accept that part-time measures were no cure for the sickness in the England ranks.

Part-time coaching in the build-up to a Test match is likely to be counter-productive in the sense that a batsman does not want to be going into a big game with some new idea on his mind. Even a small adjustment can genuinely cloud the thinking, and it is also a handy excuse for failure, making it too easy for a low score to be explained away with a casual, 'Oh well, I was trying to do what the coach told me.' No player, however talented, can bat well in a match while trying to solve a technical problem. The work has to be done, preferably over a lengthy period, in practice away from the pressures of competition so that when a player gets into a Test match situation he is not struggling with some fresh concept. Try telling one of the world's top golfers to change his swing during his practice rounds for one of the major tournaments and he would laugh at you, but those running English cricket pretended to believe that somehow cricketers could perform miracles and cure faults virtually in the blink of an eye. Nothing made sense. Smith and the TCCB could hardly argue that they were holding back to see how I fared. There was nothing left for me to prove so far as coaching was concerned, as Gooch, among many, would have told them. It all smacked of nothing more than a public relations exercise, a sop to the England supporters who might easily be impressed by the fact that the TCCB had called up someone like me. They could then say: Well, we asked him, but he refused.

Wearily, I explained to Smith that the official policy was not the way forward, stressing that to be effective I needed to be in touch with the A team players coming through as well as the senior squad to create a smooth ongoing process tailored to make the transition from county to Test cricket less complicated. My words fell on deaf ears, although Illingworth persisted in trying to persuade me to accept the TCCB offer, promising meanwhile to sort out something more permanent and reasonable for the winter. I refused to be sucked into a set-up in which I had no confidence, realising only too well that without a magic wand I would be left to shoulder all the blame when the imagined transformation did not take place. Illingworth understands golf, and I reminded him that it took Nick Faldo two years to perfect a new swing, working on the project nearly every day.

In the circumstances, I was angry at the way in which I was led up the garden path and annoyed by the steady drip of unfavourable publicity in the newspapers. Illingworth and the TCCB were aware before they entered into lengthy discussions with me that I was working for the *Sun*, and had been for five and a half years since October 1989, and that I had been employed by Sky and the BBC for four and a half years. It was very old ground, trodden often enough in the past, so much of the argument about my media connections was rubbish, but that did not stop Christopher Martin-Jenkins writing in the *Daily Telegraph* on 26 April: 'Both Illingworth and the board officials are concerned that Boycott should not be seen and heard criticising batsmen under his charge. If he accepts the additional role he will have to bite his tongue sometimes, which will not come naturally. Nor, however, would he have a free hand to speak and write as frankly as he might wish. There, no doubt, lies the rub.' Peter Johnson, in the *Daily Mail*, informed his readers on 8 May:

*Boycott is the obvious choice as batting adviser. His appointment was expected last week, but has been complicated by his work as television commentator and newspaper columnist, which is far more lucrative than the £400 per day part-time work Lord's are offering. There could also be a conflict of interests. The fear is that Boycott, wearing his media hat, would be publicly critical of the men he was being paid to help. In an unguarded moment he might even reveal team strategy or an individual player's flaws. Illingworth is obviously aware of this, but respects Boycott's ability so highly that he is prepared to compromise.*

The heated newspaper debate over my position largely missed the professional point. Certainly money was important to me in that I was determined to defend my right to demand an acceptable rate for the job, but the whole structure of the coaching system was much more important, and my conscience would not let me undertake the sort of half-baked patching-up exercise that Lord's seemed to think would be enough. That was the real sticking point for me, and I think that more recently the England team has paid a high price for the niggardly vision of those at Lord's.

My situation was not the only thing exercising Illingworth's mind, for when I visited his house to talk about coaching he steered the conversation round to Atherton's captaincy, confessing that he had grave reservations about his leadership. 'Why, then, pick him as captain?' I asked. To my amazement, Illingworth muttered unconvincingly about possible press reaction to the sacking of the England captain. The press had never worried him before and he had used newspapers to suit his own purpose more than once, so this hesitancy was uncharacteristic. 'Don't reach the end of your term in charge regretting that you didn't do something you thought was right,' I warned him. 'You are there to make decisions.' When it came to the crunch, though, Illingworth compromised, naming Atherton as the captain for only the first three Tests against the West Indies in 1995, a step which highlighted a lack of faith in the Lancashire opener and put the chairman himself in the firing line. Patrick Collins, in the *Mail on Sunday*, claimed: 'One more calculated insult, one more piece of gratuitous humiliation from the chairman of selectors is all it would take for Atherton to decide that the game is no longer worth the candle. And, given Raymond Illingworth's track record, the insults and humiliation may not be long delayed.' Collins revealed that Atherton had received no advance warning of the Headingley press conference at which Illingworth showed his hand, and reported:

> One source close to Atherton confirmed the captain was close to quitting. 'Everyone knows what Illy's up to,' he said. 'He wanted to show that he was in charge, that he was the man the press should be speaking to. But it was essential for him to pick Mike because if he played some other captain and England got beaten out of sight then the public might turn on Illy. This way he thinks he can't lose. If things go well in the first three Tests then Illy will seize the credit as the man who straightened out Atherton. If they get stuffed, you can guess who'll take the blame.'

That accurately reflected the picture of Illingworth manipulating the odds in his own favour. Personally, I did not think Atherton was the best man to captain England either, but I would not have messed him about, and I felt I might easily find myself in the same boat as a part-time coach, acting as a stooge for Illingworth, whose insecurity grew in step with poor results: a draw with the West Indies was followed by a 1–0 defeat at the capable hands of South Africa (who also administered a morale-sapping 6–1 drubbing in the one-dayers) in the 1995–96 series. In April 1996 he complained in the *Daily Mail*:

*One or two people have been involved in a bit of back-stabbing. It has really annoyed me. People seem to forget I have been in cricket for forty-five years and I have friends in every county. I don't have to ask. The information is volunteered. I think I might know who is manoeuvring anywhere at any time in English cricket. I do know the identity of the people who have been trying to stuff me. I tend to be a bit like an elephant – I don't forget.*

Illingworth's thinly veiled threats must have been aimed at the players, and it was pure vindictiveness. His reputation for never forgetting or forgiving is well deserved. He obviously operated on the basis that, as the boss, he could say what he liked in the press without according his players the same privilege, an attitude which is not conducive to good team spirit. If he desired loyalty, he should have reserved his outbursts for the dressing room. It was noticeable, too, that he rarely used the unlimited power at his disposal, his actions almost entirely governed by a desire to hedge his bets, leaving a hole in which he could bury a handy scapegoat. The only occasion on which he really stood up to be counted arose at Lord's against West Indies in 1995, when Steve Rhodes was due to keep wicket. After inspecting the pitch, Illingworth omitted the Worcestershire keeper and included Alec Stewart in a dual role, even though Atherton insisted that Stewart preferred to play solely as a batsman. Illingworth was right, and England won the game.

If he had made more cricket decisions as manager and gone with his gut reaction more often, stamping his authority on events, he must surely have done a better job. Certainly if he had publicly supported his captain and players, whatever he said in private, he would have provided an atmosphere in which essential harmony could have flourished. Invariably his excursions into politics betrayed cricket's best interests, and he could not stop himself muddying the waters in my case, giving *Daily Mail* reporter Alan Fraser the clear impression that 'Boycott had a somewhat inflated view of his value, and turned down a coaching job for financial reasons' – no mention of the TCCB's refusal to take coaching seriously, or of his own part in unsuccessfully supporting my scheme. Just another brick in Illingworth's protective wall.

Every twist in the tale convinced me that I was well out of it, and in my absence England continued to blunder about. By the spring of 1996 they were a shambles, not because they had lost a series in South Africa and gone out at the quarter-final stage of the World Cup, but because they did not have a reasonable idea of which players should be in which teams in terms of Tests and one-day internationals. Too much chopping and changing confused everyone. The chairman and captain remained at loggerheads, existing at arm's length behind a smokescreen of unity which fooled no one. Any remaining sense of purpose was an illusion, as Jack Russell, the Gloucestershire wicketkeeper, acknowledged in his book, *Jack Russell Unleashed*:

> *By the end of the last World Cup Illingworth had lost our respect*
> *and was a lame duck. His relationship with captain Mike Atherton*
> *became so difficult that the players lined up in Atherton's corner,*
> *leading to the feeling that we weren't pulling in the same direction. I*
> *also heard criticism of Atherton's field placing and tactics in front of*
> *other players. It amazed me that so many influential people kept*
> *peddling the line that the two got on. A better working relationship*
> *between Atherton and Illingworth would have surely brought a*
> *clearer strategy and improved performances in the World Cup. We*
> *were clearly behind the times tactically, lacking in form and listless,*
> *with the captain unable to raise the game of the players. In my*
> *opinion Atherton was treated like a schoolboy at times, and when*

*things went wrong Illingworth was quick to place the blame
elsewhere – even though he said the buck stopped with him when he
was appointed supremo in the spring of 1995.*

As all around him crumbled, Illingworth also stood accused of
finishing off the career of Robin Smith, a tremendous player of fast
bowling, too early and of destroying Devon Malcolm, who did not
receive the thoughtful handling his exceptional pace merited. In every
conceivable way Illingworth wasted the chance of imposing real values
on English cricket, because, despite his success as a captain with
England, Leicestershire and Yorkshire, he dithered as a manager. With
his background as a tough, up-front leader, he possessed exactly the right
references, so his inability to fulfil expectations has made cricket's top
legislators wary of ever again putting all their eggs in one basket.
Although we undoubtedly need some sort of forward-thinking dictator,
the England and Wales Cricket Board now flinches at the thought of
creating another potential monster.

Towards the end of Illingworth's reign, David Lloyd arrived on the scene
and was appointed England coach in March 1996. The Lancashire left-
hander had always been a good friend of mine, and in the 1970s, when
I led the way as England's premier batsman and he was making progress
up the ladder, he spent many hours talking to me about the game. His
thirst for knowledge impressed me, as did his well-developed sense of
humour. I recall in 1967 Lloyd dismissing me at Sheffield as a Roses
clash drifted towards an inevitable draw. Yorkshire were batting in the
second innings, the only real interest centring on whether I could reach
a half-century before the close. Lloyd came on with his gentle, lollipop
left-arm lobs with my score on 49. I went to cut him and nicked it to
slip, where Geoff Pullar, not normally accustomed to the position, was
enjoying a rest. He missed the ball, but it stuck between his thighs, and
I departed without adding to my score. Later, at Old Trafford in 1980, I
was in full flow and well beyond the century mark when Lloyd entered

the attack, again tossing up his innocent so-called spinners, the sort of stuff against which no self-respecting batsman would expect the slightest difficulty. I mistimed my stroke and chipped him the easiest of return catches, and he often recounted these incidents at great length to anyone prepared to listen – embellishing the tale, of course, if I happened to be in the vicinity, because that was the sort of relationship we enjoyed.

After I opted out of Test cricket in 1974, Lloyd took my place in the England side, and he often said that I did him an enormous favour, for he went down to Edgbaston and compiled an unbeaten 214 against India. When I was asked to commentate for BBC television in the 1990s, Lloyd was already established on the radio, and sometimes we worked in adjoining boxes, laughing together and sharing our views on various developments. All in all, therefore, we got on very well – until Lloyd became the Lancashire head coach in 1994. In that same summer Lancashire's John Crawley was making his debut for England against the South Africans, and I suggested that, as he played too much across the line for comfort, some hard work was called for with his county coach. My observation contained nothing too heavy in terms of criticism, and I honestly thought I was giving Lloyd a plug, but when I came off air I received a phone message, via Peter Baxter, the head of BBC radio, from Lloyd. Calling from Old Trafford, Lloyd had told Baxter in pretty strong language to tell me to mind my own business and to keep my opinions about Lancashire cricket to myself.

Totally bemused, I rang him back as soon as I had gathered together my thoughts, hoping to discover what had prompted such an outburst. He was in an agitated state, and I discovered that he and the Lancashire players had thought I was having a go at them, but, as someone working in the media, Lloyd ought to have understood my position. In the course of his angry flow, Lloyd actually agreed with my assessment of Crawley, admitting they were attempting to correct his technique, but he furiously insisted that I should have ignored the evidence of my own eyes. It was clear that, with such a bee in his bonnet, he was not going to listen to reason, and as he ranted I gained my first insight into how paranoid Lloyd can be about 'his lads', meaning any bunch of players with whom he happens to be working. In more ways than one he allows emotion to play too big a part in his professional life.

Following his England appointment, I interviewed him for the *Sun* at Trent Bridge, where he was watching players as part of his selectorial duties. We went through a question-and-answer session which the *Sun* published virtually without any editorial interference, and I certainly exerted no influence, accepting that how Lloyd went about his job was his business. I reserved the right, however, to make it clear that I did not think much about the introduction of various initiatives which were supposed to boost morale. Lloyd encouraged what he apparently called the Churchill spirit using recorded speeches and patriotic music in the dressing room, but this razzmatazz left me cold. Bonding became the next gimmick, with a trip to La Manga thrown in for good measure. As far as I could see the only benefit to be derived from a ten-day holiday jaunt was an improvement in physical fitness, which would have been fine had the players been taking a break from intensive work in the nets at home. Sadly this was not the case, although the players naturally jumped at the chance to top up their tans, swim in the open air and sharpen their skills at golf and tennis. Perhaps I am old-fashioned, but I follow the theory that the way to improve at cricket is to practise, and, in common with most former players, I shook my head in wonderment.

Lloyd, eagerly promoting his 'brave new world', provided the newspapers with pages of lively copy, but most senior cricket journalists privately nursed doubts too. Behind the glitz and glamour, all the old weaknesses flourished, with no one paying attention to fundamental details. The dangers of ignoring grass-root principles became apparent when Michael Atherton came to see me during the 1996 NatWest final, having been dismissed in the early stages of Lancashire's 129-run triumph over Essex. He raised two topics, one relating to the composition of the winter touring party to Zimbabwe and New Zealand, and one concerning his batting. I willingly gave him my opinions on the potential tourists he mentioned and also agreed to look at his technique before the tour, after ensuring that my intervention would not bring the wrath of Lloyd down upon my head. Atherton explained that the England players had permission to approach anyone they respected, and added that he would pay me privately.

Reading between the lines, everything Atherton said meant that the England and Wales Cricket Board, as it had become, retained a skinflint's grasp on the purse strings. The absence of an officially arranged coaching scheme left the players to fend for themselves, with the England captain, a key batsman in an often shaky line-up, coming to me cap in hand and at his own expense. What a disgrace. In no circumstances would I take money from any England player seeking to improve his own and the country's prospects, so I swallowed the fact that the ECB were effectively getting me for nothing yet again and compared dates with Atherton. His holiday plans took in a trip abroad with his girlfriend, while my television commitments required me to be in India for most of the time between the end of the English season and departure day for Zimbabwe in November. Our free days simply did not match up, but really it was Atherton's responsibility to make the greater effort if his batting worried him so much.

When I got back from India, I picked up a message from Michael on my answerphone, so I called him a few days before the team departed. I offered a couple of sessions immediately and, as I was going to Zimbabwe anyway, promised to see him out there whenever I could. But he decided his busy schedule prevented a pre-tour get-together after all and made it clear that Lloyd did not want any ex-players involved in Zimbabwe. So much for Lloyd's dedication. I could, of course, afford to shrug my shoulders. Atherton's decision made life easier for me, but I noted with interest that Ian Botham had already been asked to attend nets as a bowling coach and motivator during the tour. The inference, therefore, was that Lloyd simply did not want me about, so I stepped back and let them get on with it.

England's ill-conceived preparations affected their performances in Zimbabwe, where they were unable to win a match of any significance.

On England's first visit to cricket's ninth-ranked Test country, Lloyd set a dreadful example. His exhibition of petulance scarred the Bulawayo Test, the first to end in a draw with the scores level. England suffered some bad luck and were denied victory by a combination of negative tactics and a generous interpretation of the law relating to the bowling of wides during England's second-innings run-chase, but nothing could justify Lloyd's childish tantrum at the close. He not only refused a proffered handshake by a Zimbabwean official, but was rude and offensive, giving a V sign to the crowd. He raged: 'We flippin' murdered them.' That stupid exaggeration returned to haunt him as England drew a rain-ruined second Test at the Harare Sports Club just after Christmas, before losing the one-day series 3–0. With match referee Hanumant Singh reprimanding England for 'the manner of their appealing', Lloyd would have been wise to keep his thoughts to himself, for he had been in the game long enough to accept that in cricket the swings and roundabouts spin regularly. To Lloyd's shame, ECB chairman Lord MacLaurin felt it necessary to lecture him on his general conduct and remind him of the spirit of the game.

Needless to say, the Zimbabweans were quick to throw Lloyd's words back in his face as England's humiliation continued until they reached the calmer waters of New Zealand. The trouble with Lloyd is that he cannot shake off the image of the typical old flat-capped Lancashire comedian, so the man in the street finds it difficult to take him seriously. His antics in Zimbabwe made him even more a figure of fun, and, despite a 2–0 Test triumph in New Zealand, his reputation remained in tatters as England faced up to the 1997 Australian tourists.

Having followed England's fortunes closely at home and abroad since 1990, I came to the conclusion that Atherton no longer justified his place in the limited-overs side, basing my opinion on his form and wide-ranging changes in the one-day game. The question of personalities never arose. Simply, his record from the lead-up to the 1996 World Cup through to the end of the New Zealand tour told the story clearly enough: 25 innings, 541 runs, and an average of 21. Of course I recognised that the game had moved on from my days as an opening batsman. We played carefully and sensibly against the new ball, expecting to pick up the tempo with wickets in hand in the closing stages of our innings. Modern legislation, however, required two fielders in catching positions for the first fifteen overs of an innings and permitted only two outside the thirty-yard circle for the same period, so it was no longer practical to push the ball around for singles. Success depended on having at least one opener capable of hitting over the top to collect a string of boundaries before the fielding side was allowed to adopt defensive measures. England, for example, promoted Phil DeFreitas in the World Cup in a bid to achieve the desired rate of around five or six an over, and Sri Lanka won that 1996 World Cup on the back of some impressive enterprise. They gave wicketkeeper Romesh Kaluwitharana instructions to throw the bat as a makeshift opener, and Sanath Jayasuriya moved up the order from six to play a wide range of strokes which unsettled bowlers and put fielding teams on the back foot. The rapid scoring required in the first fifteen overs of one-day internationals did not suit Atherton's style, and I argued in the *Sun* that England could find better-equipped batsmen to do that particular job.

In the event Atherton did play in the one-day series against Australia and, after falling for just 4 at Headingley, played beautifully at the Oval for an unbeaten 113 off 149 balls. He followed that up with only a single run at Lord's, but England won all three games by six wickets. Using that one innings at the Oval as the peg on which to hang his prejudices, Lloyd wrote sneeringly in the *Daily Telegraph* on 27 May:

*One former England opening batsman had his customary pop at the team, and in particular the captain, Michael Atherton, saying his play was too slow for one-day cricket. Well, it takes one to know one. I say this because the management, coaching staff and players have no control over anyone's opinions and views, and the only way to influence people's perception of the team is for the team to perform and perform well. The bottom line is to win.*

By using the word 'customary' Lloyd implied that I was against his players as a matter of course, and he mixed his defence of them with a vigorous attack on me, referring to my past record as a batsman. In doing so he displayed a sad lack of maturity. Instead of considering my article logically, Lloyd allowed his passions to take over. I had stressed that the changing circumstances of limited-overs cricket dictated a different approach. I made no comparison between myself and Atherton, and I also admitted that only at my best in the 1970s could I have expected to be chosen regularly for England's one-day line-up under the reshaped structure. Lloyd's cheap jibe said a lot more about him than it did about me, because the manner in which I played under different regulations was irrelevant. Was he actually claiming that anyone who could not bat better and score more quickly than Atherton had no right to express an opinion? In the forlorn hope of creating some common ground, I delivered the facts and figures to the England dressing room at Edgbaston before the first Test with a covering note, but I did not receive a word in reply.

When it comes to rushing in with mouth open and brain in neutral, even Lloyd cannot equal Ian Botham, who could hardly wait to advertise his own inability to mark, read and inwardly digest anything. He let fly with both barrels in the *Daily Mirror* on 28 May, writing: 'Let's nail these jibes that Mike Atherton isn't worth his place in England's one-day side. I didn't hear too many complaints that Atherton was ill-suited to one-dayers when he made 127 against the West Indies at Lord's two years ago.' Botham fell into the same trap as Lloyd, failing to grasp that the rules had been changed since then. He continued: 'Boycott, of all people, had the nerve to label Atherton a "slowcoach". Talk about the pot calling the kettle black.' Here, too, he echoed the mistakes made by Lloyd, and further demonstrated to me his ignorance by insisting that if I did not apologise to Atherton I was more bigoted than he thought. I imagine that his ghost writer, Chris Lander, introduced the word because I doubt if Botham understood its meaning. For his education, the Oxford dictionary states that a bigot is someone with 'intolerant adherence to a creed or view', while the Collins dictionary defines a bigot as a 'narrow-minded person who is intolerant of other opinions'. Far from being bigoted, I merely gave my opinion, for which I had been asked by the *Sun*, and let everyone else think what they liked.

What Botham did not know is that as far back as the winter of 1989 I had been helping Atherton with his batting. Additionally, throughout his early years as captain and during the dirt-in-the-pocket furore, I had talked to him face to face and on the telephone, offering support and advice. A little research would have shown Botham that I always spoke highly of Atherton's Test match batting and, while I did not rate his captaincy all that highly, I have always liked him as a person. The real bigot is Botham, who sees things as he wants them to be with the result, in my view, that he dodges the truth. He regards himself as a good friend of Atherton, but he would be a better friend if he told him the truth, however unpalatable it might be. One good innings – and Atherton did bat very well at the Oval – hardly proved anything, so Botham, close to the England team through working with them in the nets, was parroting the Lloyd line and throwing his considerable weight behind the England coach.

Botham also warned me: 'You had better start getting used to writing nice things about England because we might just have turned the page and begun a bright new chapter.' More wishful thinking, for I am still waiting for England to write this bright new chapter, despite Botham's guidance as a bowling coach and presence as a motivator. All his comments on television and in the newspapers seem to reflect his friendly relations with the players, encouraging him to make the kinds of noises the dressing room likes to hear. His desire to be popular appears sometimes to undermine his objectivity. All those high hopes he encouraged disappeared as England lost the 1997 Ashes series 4–1 and lost three Tests the following winter to a weak West Indies team. Lloyd and Botham could point to success against the South Africans in 1998, although England were not all that convincing, but it was business as usual as they went on to crash once more, by three Tests to one, in Australia on the 1998–99 tour, casting further doubts about Botham's judgement. It is sad that such a brilliant cricketer should be so sour about me. It takes more courage to be realistic and run the gauntlet of unpopularity than it does to dance to a popular tune.

Botham certainly did not do Atherton any favours, for just four months after his *Daily Mirror* outburst, at the end of the 1997 season, the selectors left him out of the one-day set-up, announcing two separate captains for the Test and one-day squads. The parties for Sharjah in November 1997 and for the limited-overs internationals against West Indies in 1998 were led by Surrey's Adam Hollioake. Trying to smooth things over, the chairman of selectors, David Graveney, hid behind a smokescreen. He explained that Atherton needed a rest and would not go to Sharjah, but that if he found his best form he might still play in the one-day games in the West Indies. He fooled no one, least of all me, for his actions fully justified my article the previous spring. Everything I wrote came true. Botham should have been big enough to apologise to me.

In the overall scheme of things, Botham does not matter all that much, but David, in his official capacity as England coach, has to conduct himself carefully. Unfortunately, Lloyd further demonstrated his damaging siege mentality and lack of realism when England lost to Sri Lanka by a margin of ten wickets in the one-off Test at the Oval in August 1998. Offspinner Muttiah Muralitharan contributed massively to the visitors' ten-wicket triumph with a match haul of 16 for 220, and, as England's hopes crumbled, Lloyd reacted badly by expressing doubts about the legality of Muralitharan's action. National newspaper writers revealed later that they were so surprised they checked three times with Lloyd about his suspicions, giving him the chance to retract. As Peter Johnson wrote in the *Daily Mail*: 'Lloyd must have known that his unsolicited comment would cause controversy and offence. He still went ahead and made it. It was a calculated attempt to excuse England's inadequacy.' Even if Lloyd seriously thought he was speaking off the record, it was a dangerous thing to do because the International Cricket Council had already cleared Muralitharan's action, after the December

1995 Melbourne Test during which Darrell Hair no-balled the Sri Lankan on seven separate occasions.

I have no reason to attend press conferences so I know nothing first-hand about the circumstances of Lloyd's comments, but his view was all over the papers on the Monday. A very upset Lloyd claimed that he had been 'done over' by the press, who, however, maintained their version of events. The president of the Sri Lankan board, Thilauga Sumathipala, was present at the Oval and he issued a statement, part of which read: 'Sri Lanka have had a wonderful tour, the public have warmed to us and the way we have played. What Lloyd said was his own opinion and it is up to the England and Wales Cricket Board to deal with it. We are disappointed at the way he handled the whole issue as there is a set procedure, and we have made our views known to the ECB.' Once the president became involved, Lloyd was in deep trouble, with another major incident developing.

The president's intervention also gave Lloyd's comments added significance from a television point of view, particularly with Muralitharan steadily working his way through the England second innings. Simon Hughes did a bit on the incident to camera before David Gower interviewed Richie Benaud and me during the tea interval on the Monday. Like a huge snowball rolling downhill, the situation blew up out of control as England headed for defeat. For me, it was a case of telling the truth, and I said on air: 'Perhaps it would help if England got a coach who could keep his mouth shut. He is casting inferences and aspersions that always seem worse when you are losing.' Surprisingly, in view of their ongoing claim that members of the England dressing room never listen to our television comments, Lloyd heard my words and exploded. I took the full force of his anger, although I said my bit quickly and did not go on about Lloyd at any length.

Gower, Benaud and I had also discussed the possible make-up of the England squad for the trip to Australia for two or three minutes as the Sri Lankans returned to the field after the break. Before we had finished, Lloyd appeared at the entrance to the studio, bristling with indignation and almost bursting into flames. I was the first member of the commentary team on duty after tea, so I hurried to leave the studio and return to the box. Lloyd stood his ground and would not let me get through. 'What have I done to you?' he asked. 'Why are you always having a go at me? If you have anything to say you should say it to my face.' I pointed out to him that he had not spoken to me since I wrote about Michael Atherton not being a good one-day player, and, actually, there was no reason for me to speak to him. I was employed as a television commentator, not by the ECB or Lloyd, and it would be a farce if I had to go around discussing any thoughts I might be intending to put forward with every individual they concerned. I reminded him that he had thought it fit to attack me in the *Daily Telegraph* over the Atherton disagreement, at which point he became very vague and uneasily denied writing the article. I possessed a copy of the paper, however, and repeated that what he had said about Muralitharan did not sound good against the background of a Sri Lankan victory. I also mentioned the many hours I had spent, as the leading player in the 1970s, talking to him long after the close of play, helping him with his own career. I did not think it was my fault we had drifted apart. He asked why I did not telephone him, and I told him that I didn't have his number. He gave it to me and suggested: 'Let's shake hands.' We did so, but immediately he let fly with a flood of obscenity. 'Wait a minute,' I said, 'we've just shaken hands and then you give me more abuse.' He mumbled a bit, and then muttered, without a hint of an apology: 'Let's shake hands again.'

I went home after the match, but next day the papers were full of the story of our confrontation, so I telephoned his home. The answerphone was on and I left a message to assure Lloyd that nothing had come from me. Although I had received a lot of media enquiries, I refused to comment. I could have made things worse for him, but I kept my own counsel. A lot of people did hear Lloyd though, so I also contacted Lord's to inform them that I had said nothing. Later, Lloyd was reported as saying: 'Geoff and I had a good laugh together and we shook hands after our chat. It is not unusual that two people have a difference of opinion. We used to be good pals but we drifted apart for various reasons.' I would hardly have gone so far as to say we were good pals again, and I did not remember laughing much, but I wait to see what happens in the future.

My main grievance against Lloyd was that he was damning Muralitharan by innuendo, and I know from my own bitter experience that you cannot fight this type of slur. You can refute an inaccurate statement, but hinting and whispering are much more of a problem. Lloyd displayed a mean spirit, and it was fairly predictable that Illingworth would follow up with his four-penn'orth. Writing in the *Yorkshire Evening Post*, Illingworth indicated that he felt Lloyd was 'right to question Muralitharan's action', adding: 'I would want to see it filmed from numerous angles and have the authorities give another view on it, because to me it is a highly unusual action and can look somewhat suspicious.' Turning to my comments, Illingworth claimed: 'Coming from Boycs, who, let's face it, opens his mouth more than anyone, it is quite incredible, and is perhaps the greatest case of the pot calling the kettle black I have ever come across.' Illingworth completely missed the point. It is my job to make comments, but as England coach Lloyd is governed by regulations which prevent him offering personal opinions. These should be saved until after he has retired. Illingworth certainly could not have got away with questioning Muralitharan's action while manager of England, but now he is no longer employed by the ECB he, like me, is free to say what he likes. It was crass of him to fail to grasp the difference between the two roles.

Failing to learn any lessons himself, Lloyd also went looking for Dean Jones in the commentary box during England's 1998–99 tour of Australia. Jones, who had been critical of England's fielding, happened to be unavailable, which was fortunate for Lloyd; the coach might easily have found himself in trouble again. I realise that patriotism governs Lloyd's approach to life, but he should appreciate that it is impossible to stop criticism of England until they start winning. A certain diplomacy is required in Lloyd's job, so he should use his brains more often and look to his priorities, which are avoiding controversy and improving England's record. There are times when the pampered senior squad deserves a kick up the backside, but he continues to mollycoddle them.

Cricket is a tough game and a firm hand is essential at times. Lloyd's supporters point out that his heart is in the right place. I do not dispute this, and I know that he is not a bad man, but that sort of comment is in itself an admission that the man is not up to the job. Other aspects of his make-up matter far more. As a former specialist batsman good enough to play Test cricket, he is in charge of the batting, which lets down England so regularly that it has become a joke. Either the players are not listening or Lloyd is giving them bad advice. Whichever way you look at it, he loses out. He no longer speaks to me, although he disparages me behind my back, which is a pity, but it is his loss. Simply, Lloyd spends too much time defending himself and the England team, forever popping up with a quote or two to deflect criticism.

The contrast with Australia could hardly be greater. Their coach, Rodney Marsh, is virtually anonymous. The captain is left to do the talking, and it's the captain's personality which comes through. Before his recent retirement, Mark Taylor was frank and sensible, win or lose, and always appeared to be in charge. Similarly, in South Africa, Hansie Cronje leads from the front, with coach Bob Woolmer staying in the background. The Australian and South African players fight their own battles, and are more often than not successful at it. England would benefit from following their example.

# Titans of
# the Willow

B atting, particularly at the highest level, is not merely a matter of technique. The correct mental approach is also vital, with concentration and self-discipline key factors in the make-up of any truly great player. Attention to detail is important too, and no natural talent continues to flourish without constant fine-tuning. Ability has to be stretched over a lengthy period of reliable consistency rather than displayed with a brief, flashy brilliance. That is why I believe that Sachin Tendulkar, the little Indian maestro, is currently the world's best batsman.

There are those who regularly advance the claims of West Indian Brian Lara, but when I compare the two in every conceivable way I invariably find myself giving the edge to Tendulkar. The West Indies have produced some wonderful batsmen, and I rank Garfield Sobers and Viv Richards as the two best run-makers in my time, both quite outstanding in their individual ways. Throughout a golden spell in 1993, 1994 and 1995, I elevated Lara to third place in my personal list of great batsmen, setting him alongside Graeme Pollock, the brilliant South African left-hander who is so difficult to pigeonhole because of his enforced absence from the international scene. Political considerations restricted Pollock to playing his twenty-three Tests in England, Australia and New Zealand in addition to his home country, so he cannot be judged under all conditions. Quite a bit has to be taken on trust, but from what I saw of him I suspect that he would have coped with just about anything, and I bracket him with Lara at his best.

On first sight, Lara's natural skills simply took my breath away. He picked up the length so quickly, building his game around great reflexes allied to perfect eyesight. *Daily Mail* columnist Ian Wooldridge wrote of his amazement when playing golf with Lara, who could identify the markings on the ball when it appeared no more than a speck in the distance to him. Lara also derived great benefit from superb footwork, gliding into position with graceful ease to unfold his wide range of strokes. He didn't hook, but then he didn't need to, sensibly content to let the really short ball go by. His trademark was the pull off one leg, helping the ball on its way from his back foot with the right foot in the air. His selectivity of stroke was flawless, providing the basis of his scoring ability. When any batsman gets the length wrong he is in trouble, but Lara rarely erred in that direction. His timing was impeccable and he operated with an easy fluency which enabled him to rocket along without taking the slightest risk. He was, in fact, poetry in motion, using his bat with a rapier-like precision to direct the ball effortlessly into gaps in the field.

In that sense he was very different to Viv Richards, who more often resorted to brute force to satisfy his desire to dictate to the bowler. Richards, whose macho swagger on his way to the middle gave due warning of his intentions, sought always to impose himself on the bowlers. Lara, without a matching physical presence, was neatly clean and clinical, impressively orthodox, yet with an elegance of stroke play which carried the textbook approach into another dimension. His greatest asset was that by seeing the ball early he could get into position quickly, gaining that crucial extra split-second when dealing with a delivery. A batsman seeking merely to defend does not need quite so much time, but in no more than the blink of an eye Lara gave himself the opportunity to do more than preserve his wicket. He created the means to pick up runs and leave the fieldsmen and bowlers helpless in the knowledge that their best was not good enough.

In every way Lara, taking the cricket world by storm, earned a privileged position in life. He did not, perhaps, become rich by the standards of the outstanding personalities of some other sports, but his earnings were substantial from a cricket point of view. Certainly, measured against the benchmark of the West Indian economy he enjoyed huge wealth. Although there is very little sponsorship in the West Indies, where the shortage of major companies imposes restrictions, Lara received due reward for his efforts. One perk linked to his wonderful world record Test score of 375, compiled against England at St John's, Antigua, in the winter of 1994, virtually guarantees him free first-class air travel for life. British West Indies Airways offered him 1,000 miles for every run, a generous gesture which leaves Lara with the scope for endless journeys whenever the mood takes him. The government of Trinidad and Tobago, Lara's native land, also weighed in with the gift of a prime plot of building land, enabling Lara to set up home in a superb setting above an area of grassland the West Indians call the 'savannah', where they hold annual carnivals.

At that time, Lara simply could not put a foot wrong, and his achievement in scoring 501 not out for Warwickshire against Durham at Edgbaston in 1994 is so great that it is almost impossible to put it into perspective. Some attempt must be made, though, and when I discussed Lara with my good friend Sunil Gavaskar, I asked the brilliant Indian opener about his own biggest innings. He told me that he had reached 340 for Bombay against Bengal during the 1981–82 season. My most productive innings amounted to an unbeaten 261 off the President's XI attack in Barbados in 1974. We could both modestly claim to being able to play the game well, but neither of us got within shouting distance of Lara's monumental effort, and I must admit that I never even so much as contemplated climbing so high a mountain. That Lara innings was the stuff of legends, an unbelievable amalgamation of sheer ability, concentration and stamina far beyond the capabilities of the ordinary mortal. People can query the quality of the Durham attack, which was no more than moderate and no doubt became hopelessly ragged, but no one else has taken such massive advantage of the opposition and many weak bowling sides have soldiered on in county cricket.

At the age of only twenty-five, then, Lara held two world records of such mind-boggling proportions that they might never be beaten. His future appeared to be as secure as the Bank of England vaults, a succession of years filled with runs and stirring deeds. Unexpectedly, however, from that remarkable high point there followed a rapid descent to the foothills of failure. Where did it all go wrong? Fame and fortune can easily go to any young man's head, and Lara found himself with an abundance of both very quickly. Perhaps it was a case of too much too soon, and Lara may have been slightly unnerved by the glittering lifestyle which suddenly presented itself. One record would have put him on a pretty imposing pedestal; two brought him the sort of adulation which must have been difficult to handle. Perhaps he began to believe his own publicity too readily, to let the endless stream of admirers blind him to the realities, for in Trinidad the world was his oyster. No one denied him anything; nothing was beyond his reach. Lara, in fact, reached such celebrity status that British West Indies Airways delayed flights to accommodate his schedule, normal passengers forced to wait for the great man's arrival. I could never imagine British Airways treating any English cricketer with similar exaggerated consideration, not the great Jack Hobbs, not Sir Leonard Hutton, not Peter May. It couldn't happen in this country, but it did in the West Indies for Lara on a number of occasions.

In the circumstances, I suspect that Lara lost touch with his roots. To maintain his incredibly high standards he had to work at his game and continue to be highly motivated. The moment he allowed distractions to creep in he became careless about his technique and plunged down a slippery slope. All the runs in the record books are no help to a player without dedication and self-discipline. Top sportsmen must constantly be driven by the need to succeed. That is why the multi-millionaire golfers such as Greg Norman, Nick Price and others can be seen relentlessly pursuing excellence on the practice ground at every major tournament. Money no longer matters to them; the winner's cheque is incidental to the satisfaction of proving their ability at the highest level.

My theory is that Lara lost a sense of purpose with his batting, and that an element of boredom set in as he looked for new fields to conquer. Importantly, he obviously expected to get the captaincy of the West Indies as a matter of course. A cascade of runs during the series in England in 1995 – 145 at Old Trafford, 152 at Trent Bridge, 179 at the Oval – confirmed his pre-eminence, and Lara probably felt that the premier position for the series against New Zealand was his by right. He could see himself following easily in the footsteps of his heroes, Sobers and Richards, who stepped up to lead their country on the back of dazzling feats of batsmanship. The West Indies selectors thought otherwise, giving the captaincy to the more experienced Courtney Walsh.

This decision related to a number of incidents in Lara's life which gave the West Indies board cause for concern. Nothing all that serious scarred his background, but some minor episodes combined to create doubts, and behind the scenes all was not exactly running smoothly. Lara's ambition apparently brought him into conflict with the captain, Richie Richardson, and he temporarily walked out on the team during the summer of 1995. Presumably Lara wanted to replace Richardson, but he bowed to the persuasion of Peter Short, the then chairman of the West Indies board, returning to play superbly. An uneasy truce collapsed when the party returned home, with Wes Hall, the tour manager, submitting an unflattering report. The board, after allowing Lara a personal hearing, fined him. Lara reacted by withdrawing from the party which flew out to Australia to take part in the Benson and Hedges limited-overs series. Various reasons for this decision were put forward, and his friends made much of the fact that he was tired, but generally the feeling grew that Lara had acted in a fit of pique.

Evidence of the increasingly strained relationships in the West Indies camp resurfaced when the World Cup came around in February and March 1996, Lara falling foul of officialdom once more. Kenya surprisingly beat the West Indies in the early rounds of the competition, the result proving a source of acute embarrassment for most of the team. Lara, though, chose the moment to raise the race issue, going into the Kenyan dressing room and making a thoughtless comment. The gist of his remarks was that if West Indies were to suffer defeat he would much prefer it to be at the hands of black Africans than white South Africans. Lara initially tried to deny that he had said anything along those lines, but a journalist had been present at the Kenyan celebrations and his tape recorder faithfully recorded Lara's exact words. His subsequent apology did little to ease West Indian distress, and on the flight home he committed another blunder. Boasting that he had got rid of Richardson as captain and removed former world-class fast bowler Andy Roberts as coach, he turned his attentions to Dennis Waite, the long-serving physiotherapist, saying: 'You are next.' The outburst clearly did Lara no good, for Waite is widely respected by all the great West Indians of recent times. Michael Holding, Viv Richards, Joel Garner, Malcolm Marshall, Desmond Haynes and Gordon Greenidge number themselves among a host of stars who admire the Australian's skill and knowledge. Such foolishness could not be tolerated. Following a written complaint by Waite to the board, Lara was called up to say he was sorry.

Under those circumstances, Courtney Walsh represented a much safer option in the eyes of the West Indies board, for he has always been a solid, reliable professional about whom no one has ever said a bad word. In taking that logical step, however, the West Indian authorities upset Lara, who, as far as I could see, stopped working on his game. Part of him must have been miffed, because for the first time everything was not going his way. Although during my playing career I wanted to be captain of both Yorkshire and England, batting represented an end in itself for me. I did not mix up the two facets of the game. Batting was not enough for Lara, who desired more. Mixed emotions crowded in on him, because if he did well and the West Indies did well as a consequence, he would be propping up Walsh as captain and pushing his personal Holy Grail further away. I would never insult Lara by saying that he didn't try, but the impression grew that his heart was no longer in his batting. I watched him play some very rash shots during this unhappy period, and, while some may have thought he was resting on his laurels, I felt that the incentive had gone, that he lacked the stimulus of a challenge. The captaincy had become his only target, so his mental attitude was wrong.

In happier eras for West Indian cricket, the selectors, with real strength in depth at their disposal, could have taken a tougher line with Lara, but politics are an integral part of Caribbean cricket and weaknesses all along the line made the Trinidadian indispensable to the team. Wrestling with the demands of public unrest, the selectors went so far as to ignore Lara's poor form and nominate him as captain for the tour to Pakistan in the autumn of 1997. Still hesitant and uncertain, the West Indies board turned down the recommendation, just as the MCC did in 1967 when the England selectors wanted to give the job to Brian Close for the trip to the West Indies. Hamstrung by inadequacies all around him, Walsh took the side to Pakistan for the Test series. The West Indies were crushed 3–0.

Lara suffered along with his team-mates, showing few signs of his brilliance, but the whitewash forced the hand of the selectors and the board, who turned to Lara for the visit of England to the Caribbean in the early spring of 1998. The long-awaited promotion inspired Lara. His enthusiasm revived and he began to work hard again on his batting, but he quickly learned the hard lesson that the art of batsmanship is very complicated. Once a player loses that subtle quality which makes him stand out from the crowd it is very difficult, if not impossible, to get it back. Even the most gifted player cannot just turn his talent on and off. With serious application a good player striving to revive a faltering career might salvage 90 per cent of his ability, but there will always be a little bit missing. The gulf between very good and truly great is enormous.

I think Lara will bat well again at times and there will be tantalising glimpses of his genius, but the truly golden days are gone for ever. By neglecting his skills and assuming that he could turn back the clock whenever he felt like it, Lara betrayed a precious gift which deserved to be polished, nurtured and honed endlessly. Too many loose shots now creep insidiously into his game, and too much playing and missing highlights his insecurity. Simple mistakes confirm to me that his judgement of length has all but deserted him. He now stays on the back foot to balls of fullish length. Against fast bowling his feet are finishing up in the wrong place, so he cannot get his body into the correct position. As the bowler gets into the delivery stride, Lara jumps back and plants his feet firmly. Forced to move again when the ball is delivered, he lets his head dip and he jumps back even further. All this erratic movement puts him dangerously close to the stumps, and it came as no surprise to me recently when Allan Donald went around the wicket to him in South Africa and Lara, for the first time in his career, actually trod on his stumps. Top-class pacemen like Donald and Australia's Glenn McGrath, who miss very few tricks, now go around the wicket to Lara almost immediately because when the ball gets a bit big on him he finds it difficult to get out of the way. The ball follows his clumsy foot movement, threatening his chest. Tucked up and with his arms virtually pinned, Lara becomes a static target; he can do no more than hopefully fend the ball away. His most effective strokes, square on the offside, are out of the question, which is why McGrath has dismissed him several times from around the wicket.

The art of bowling is to make a batsman play in a way that either frustrates or worries him. The successful bowlers aim to cut off the batsman's favourite shots and force him as much as possible to play in areas he doesn't like. It is a battle of wits that Lara is losing, as he attempts to pick up runs by throwing the bat at the ball with his feet planted nowhere near where the ball pitches. In this way he relies far too much on chance, as he does by trying to fetch the ball from outside the off stump to pull and hook. The danger is that he often arrives late, with the result that the ball goes up in the air. Conrad Hunte, a distinguished

West Indian batsman himself, believes that Lara's eyesight is no longer quite perfect and has advised a trip to the optician. 'I don't think he is seeing the ball as early as he used to,' insists Hunte. Lara's most impressive strokes are no longer in evidence, and, although his concentration is still good, he has lacked patience. The West Indies board reacted to a disastrous tour of South Africa by effectively putting Lara on probation, making him captain initially for only the first two tests against Australia. This move, coupled with intense media and public critism, appeared to jolt him back to reality, for in the second test at Kingston in March this year he made a superb 213.

The question is how to make the most of the ability that remains. Despite his decline, Lara is still potentially a destructive force, and I think that he should go in first for West Indies in limited-overs internationals. Most one-day games are staged on good batting pitches, and with only fifty overs available it makes sense to give your best stroke-player as many deliveries to face as possible. It is counter-productive for any team to leave their most prolific run-maker kicking his heels in the dressing room while lesser batsmen struggle out in the middle. When that happens, the bowlers often get a stranglehold on the proceedings which is difficult to break, and the current regulations offer enormous scope in the early stages of an innings. The occasions on which Lara might get out to the new ball could be accepted as a reasonable price to pay for this increased opportunity, for then his less gifted colleagues would be given scope to prove their worth. West Indies are currently handicapped by a fragile batting line-up in which Lara, with all his problems, easily looks the best, so they would get most value out of him as an opener. The point is that when he gets established, he has the range of strokes to really punish the opposition attack. With no bouncers allowed in one-day cricket Lara would not be under the same pressure as he is in a Test match, and with the bowlers forced to pitch further up it is just possible that he might start getting his feet gliding into position. The psychological possibilities are worth considering, too, for the responsibility of going in first could persuade Lara to knuckle down and make the best of things.

Whichever way you look at the situation, though, Lara faces a huge task to reorganise himself. West Indian cricket was in disarray when he took over from Walsh as captain and the blame attaches to no one set of shoulders. The thumping administered by Pakistan was nothing to do with Walsh's leadership; the team framework threatened to collapse entirely at any moment. I wrote at the time that the captaincy would either make or break Lara and that his career hung in the balance. He desperately wanted the honour of leading his country, but, like me and one or two other senior figures, he soon discovered that by fulfilling his ambition he had pinned himself to a bed of nails.

Lara inherited a poor squad by standards much lower than those normally associated with West Indian cricket. The lack of a reasonable opening batsman exposed the deficiencies in a patchy middle order, and the pace attack relied too heavily on the ageing legs of Curtly Ambrose and Walsh himself, both of whom were already susceptible to the aches and pains of advancing years. Although wonderful competitors, Ambrose and Walsh required careful handling and did not represent quite the match-winning combination West Indies required. Their possible replacements were no more than promising. Equally, the spin bowling department was threadbare with only the occasional offbreaks of Carl Hooper on hand. The future looked bleak when Lara became captain and, as a consequence of the general decline in West Indian cricket, nothing much has changed, despite victory in the 1998 series over England. From personal experience I know that leading a moderate side is difficult and mentally demanding, so leading a bunch of demoralised, ordinary cricketers must be a nightmare for Lara, forcing him to put so much of himself into running the rest of the team.

Turning up on time for meetings and nets has never been a strong point among the West Indians, and Lara instinctively marches to the sound of his own drum. This tends to make him a loner, and it is noticeable that off the field Lara is spending more and more time away from his colleagues. He likes nothing better than to be on the golf course, which is fine within reason, but he should realise that he will never be capable of earning a living at the game. His lack of self-discipline is evident in the way he persistently fails to keep appointments – his favourite expression is 'I will come along later.' The South Africans organised a visit to Robben Island when the West Indian party was in Cape Town for the 1998–99 tour. Robben Island, of course, is where the authorities imprisoned Nelson Mandela during the angry years of apartheid, and it is like a shrine to many of the country's blacks. Indeed, people of all races and creeds visit the place to see where this great man spent so much of his incredible life. As the coach prepared to depart, Lara indicated that he was not ready and said he would make his own way to the launch departure point. Unfortunately, he took his time and kept everyone else in the party waiting for nearly twenty minutes. It seems to escape him that it is up to him to set the tone, especially for the younger players.

Setting a bad example socially is one thing, but Lara is also guilty of being too casual about the team's preparations. In South Africa, the senior players complained that they were being overtrained and, despite the appalling string of defeats, Lara agreed, so net and training sessions were scaled down. His authority seems to surpass anyone else's, and whether or not he believes the crisis in West Indian cricket is his fault, Lara is the man who will be held to account at the end of the day.

To balance the picture, the board cannot escape censure, for they handled a players' revolution before the South African tour very badly. Matters came to a head as the West Indies reassembled following an ICC Trophy tournament in Bangladesh in October 1998. Lara and Hooper joined several others in London, while team manager Clive Lloyd turned up in South Africa with another contingent. After three days of uncertainty most of those in South Africa flew to London, where confusion reigned. Doubts about the tour taking place increased by the minute and, as captain, Lara was seen to be part of the rebellion – possibly the instigator. The West Indian players did have genuine grievances, claiming that they did not always fly club class, that insurance cover had not kept pace with inflation and that promised retainer contracts had not materialised. For their part, the board argued that their hands were tied by economic factors as they had lost their major sponsor. To make matters worse, they were let down by several island governments, which failed to deliver promised additional funds. Only four honoured their commitments, so the board's finances did not stretch to contracts. Other areas of concern involved the two-squad system for Tests and one-day internationals which meant that some leading players would be asked to rest for the March and April 1999 series against Australia without adequate compensation for the loss of earnings in South Africa.

The whole complicated business sadly sent out the clear message that the players had held the board to ransom and won, an outcome which put a lot of power into a few hands. By ending the stand-off in London, the board members presumably thought they were doing the right thing in terms of fulfilling their obligation to the South Africans, but their actions left Lloyd, as manager, and Malcolm Marshall, as coach, impotent. In the long term the board must regain complete control over the West Indian team, Lara and all, at whatever cost. Their responsibilities are clear enough, while Lara ought to acknowledge that without cricket he will soon be forgotten. His records are there for ever, but cricket followers want to see some flesh on the bare bones of statistics.

While the golden promise of Brian Lara's youth has been tarnished by events off the field and a loss of fluency on it, Sachin Tendulkar's star shines more brightly than ever. The twenty-six-year-old Indian batsman does not hold any first-class world records and the odds are against his exceeding Lara's two huge totals, but his love of cricket and his desire to score runs burn undiminished. Tendulkar is a very wealthy young man, with sponsorships and contracts guaranteeing him at least $700,000 a year, and with vastly improved television coverage of cricket in India the sponsors literally queue up to get in on the act. The two big interests for the man in the street in India are the cinema and cricket, both avenues for escapism for the poor as well as the rich, and all the Indian players profit from the abundant advertisements and sponsorship.

Tendulkar finds himself in the happy position of being able to supplement his earnings almost at will, but every time he strides out to bat, bowl or field, his enthusiasm for cricket illuminates the scene. When Tendulkar arrived in Yorkshire in 1992 as the county's first overseas recruit, his obvious talent marked him out as one of the most promising batsmen in the world. Two years earlier, at the tender age of seventeen, he had startled the England team and their supporters by scoring a superbly crafted and unbeaten 119 in the second Test at Old Trafford, and from then on he was firmly established in his homeland as something very special indeed. We in Yorkshire, however, are guarded in our opinions about cricket, and an unrivalled tradition makes spectators demanding judges. Not everyone agreed with the committee's decision to break with the convention of selecting only those cricketers lucky enough to be born within the boundaries of the Broad Acres, so Tendulkar's welcome was polite but reserved. As the second choice behind Australian pace bowler Craig McDermott, he had a lot to prove, and some of the more disgruntled supporters waited in the wings ready to pounce on any shortcomings.

By changing the course of the club's history, Yorkshire understood well enough that they were gambling with limited resources. Their finances were distinctly rocky, and if Tendulkar had failed with the bat or behaved carelessly by being seen out drinking or nightclubbing on the eve of a match, the outcome would almost certainly have been disastrous. Happily, we picked a winner. The more critical observers insist that Tendulkar did not make all that much of a mark at Yorkshire, but with 1,070 first-class runs under his belt at an average of 46.52, I disagree. Unfailingly well-mannered and charming, with a shy smile on his lips, he settled quickly into the dressing room, and the Yorkshire public, shrugging off their reservations, took him to their collective heart. They recognised quality and they liked what they saw, so it is fair to say that no one could have done a better job of breaking the ice on behalf of the imports.

Tendulkar's presence also enabled Yorkshire to disprove once and for all the persistent but ill-founded rumour that their selection policy discriminated against ethnic minorities. Much nonsense appeared in newspapers and on radio and television about the wealth of talent being denied opportunity by the county club, all of it emanating from sources lacking serious contact with cricket. The simple truth was that no black or Asian player in the many local leagues reached the required standards, but the accusation received regular and embarrassing exposure until Tendulkar's appearance on the scene. I am delighted to have been a prime mover in Yorkshire's decision to broaden their recruiting base, and I am especially proud of the fact that our first signing turned out to be such a genius. There are some with the benefit of hindsight who boast that they knew from the start that Tendulkar would go on to perform great deeds, but few can read into the depths of the crystal ball, and in a mediocre Yorkshire side he was still some way short of being the finished article. All the same, he sparkled occasionally, created a lot of interest and left behind a wealth of goodwill, so I would not have swapped him for any other player.

That season with Yorkshire helped to accelerate Tendulkar's progress along the learning curve of development, and he returned home to India better equipped to embellish his reputation. Before long, his credentials as a batsman stood up to the closest examination, but his progress was hampered by his hasty elevation to the captaincy of India. In stark contrast to Lara, who impatiently promoted his claims in that direction, Tendulkar found the extra burden thrust upon his shoulders while he was still emerging as both a cricketer and a person. His shrewd cricket brain and sturdy character stood him in good stead in a testing role and he desperately wanted his team to succeed, but the huge demands on him meant that he had to sacrifice some personal glory. Circumstances prevented Tendulkar from concentrating on the thing he did best, so the team suffered too. He did score steadily enough while in charge, but I believe his true destiny was to pile up mountains of runs.

In one sense, therefore, the Indian selectors acted sensibly when they sent him back to the ranks. I remember discussing Tendulkar with Sunil Gavaskar during the Sharjah tournament in December 1997, and in the course of our conversation I indicated that I intended to write an article advocating that very move. I stressed that my motive was to protect Tendulkar, not to undermine him. 'His batting is being affected, and as he is such a polite, friendly character, he is not really the man to give the Indian side the kick up the backside they should get,' I said, adding, 'His value to the team is too great as a batsman to allow him to expend his mental energies on looking after others.' Gavaskar, who is something of a father figure to Tendulkar, warned, however, that such a suggestion would stir up a hornets' nest. 'Sachin is like a god to Indian supporters,' he said, implying that India could not afford to lose face by overturning their original decision. For once, Gavaskar had misjudged the situation, for shortly afterwards the Indian selectors followed my view and gave Tendulkar free reign to put his own form first.

The result has been a procession of wonderful innings in both Test matches and one-day internationals, India, of course, prospering at the same time. The avalanche of runs spoke volumes about Tendulkar's personality. Whatever the pros and cons of his spell as captain, he must have suffered some hurt and humiliation when the axe fell, for the news dominated the Indian headlines. Common sense and a considered appraisal of the situation could not disguise the fact that this national hero had been marked down as a failure in his challenging dual role. What disappointment Tendulkar felt he kept to himself. He made no comment and he did not sulk. Relying on deeds and not words, he calmly got on with life and batted with such sublime assurance that the politics of Indian cricket lost all their significance. To a population numbering over nine hundred million, the great majority passionately devoted to the game, Tendulkar's fantastic stroke-play was all that mattered. The way in which he reacted at a time of great stress illustrates the difference between Tendulkar, who did not cause a moment's fuss or trouble, and the petulant Lara. The product of a careful upbringing in India, Tendulkar, despite his superstar status, simply refused to waste his time in altercations with the Indian board and selectors and settled happily into the framework of team discipline. The most exciting thought is that there is so much of Tendulkar still to come. His wicket is the biggest prize for bowlers all over the world, but I am confident that he can handle the challenge.

As his career unfolds, it is inevitable that comparisons with Gavaskar, 'The Little Master', will arise. It is the bar-room game that cricket followers around the world like to play, and the debate is certain to be fierce in India, but there is no definitive way in which players of different generations can be measured accurately against each other. Gavaskar, like me, played under regulations which permitted unlimited amounts of short stuff, with the umpires standing back and allowing the fast bowlers to do their worst. Legislation eventually brought a restriction of one bouncer per over, and now bowlers can have two bites at the cherry, although today there are only a handful of really dangerous pacemen to test a batsman's courage. Gavaskar unflinchingly took on the might of the West Indies and won his share of battles against the constant battery of speed. A classic opener, Gavaskar played comparatively few limited-overs matches, but Tendulkar has grown up with the constantly changing version of the game in which new tactics are regularly forced on the sides. Nothing can detract from Gavaskar's contribution to Indian cricket, so, instead of making almost meaningless comparisons, people should enjoy Tendulkar in his own right while they can.

Similarly, there is the temptation, especially in India, to set Tendulkar's record alongside that of Don Bradman, just as in England even sober, respectable cricket correspondents fell into the trap of mistakenly describing Graeme Hick as the 'new Bradman' when the Zimbabwean was sweeping majestically across the county scene in the mid-1980s. There can hardly be a more pointless exercise than trying to associate any player with the legendary Australian, who sits alone on the highest pinnacle of achievement. In the broad sweep of history, even Tendulkar is one of the crowd, albeit as a member of the front rank. Bradman is something else. He retired with a Test average of 99.94 –

forty better than Graeme Pollock (60.97), George Headley (60.83) and Herbert Sutcliffe (60.73), who follow at a respectful distance. To take the point a stage further, Wally Hammond averaged 58.45 and Len Hutton 56.67 – two superb English batsmen who are statistically little more than half as good as Bradman. Additionally, Bradman made his runs at a rate which is beyond comprehension, so the public would be doing Tendulkar a service if they just accepted him for what he is – a modern polished gem.

The only worthwhile way to assess batsmen of different eras is to study the records of the individual set against those of his contemporaries. In rating Tendulkar as currently the best batsman in the world, I base that opinion on his technique and overall approach rather than his statistics – although his Test average of better than fifty provides useful confirmation – for only a handful of runs separate him from a number of others with proven ability at the highest level. Technically, it is impossible to fault him, for his footwork and judgement of length are exquisite against all forms of bowling. I can only see one slight weakness, and that is an occasional touch of overconfidence which prevents his going on to complete the big double and treble hundreds. In forward defence he gets in a good stride for a small man, keeping bat and pad close together and bending his knee sufficiently to get his weight over the ball. When playing back defensively he lets the ball come to him, playing it late. Like Lara, Tendulkar relies on one shot which is his trademark: whipping the ball just short of a length through the onside with his bottom hand to destroy the illusion in the bowler's mind that he has produced a good delivery. This ability to despatch the ball with a straightish bat through mid-wicket is an important weapon in his armoury, for it stops the bowler tying him down. His balance is excellent when facing seamers, as he stays on the balls of his feet to give himself the chance to move positively in either direction. This nimble footwork permits him to take the ball early or late around the line of the off stump, steering it in front of square with the full face of the bat or just behind square. He employs a very heavy bat for a small, chunky man, but with his flawless timing he whistles the ball away almost effortlessly.

The steady encroachment of one-day cricket into the first-class programme is often blamed for the decline in standards in England, but Tendulkar encounters no difficulty switching between the two formats. Already he holds the record for the number of centuries in limited-overs internationals at nineteen, yet he required seventy-nine games to collect his first. His nineteenth arrived in his one hundred and ninety-sixth match, and he now averages a century every six one-day innings. This is a sensational achievement which underlines the fact that it is possible to score quickly in an orthodox manner. Tendulkar relies on his timing and placement rather than on slogging, his performances improving significantly since he started to go in first. Rare failures can be tolerated, because if Tendulkar gets set he dominates the bowlers and puts India on top. His success is one reason why I advocate Lara moving up the order. With Tendulkar in full cry, all his partners have to do is give him the strike as often as possible by pushing the singles in the initial stages of each over. His colleagues are smart enough to realise that there is nothing to be gained from trying to compete with Tendulkar, good players though they may be.

With the roundabout of one-day cricket gaining momentum worldwide, the top personalities are more and more in demand and there is the danger that eventually Tendulkar will become jaded. The body is more resilient than many think, but mental pressure is silently debilitating, and the Indian selectors should pay careful attention to Tendulkar's schedule in order to stop him burning himself out before he becomes aware of the risks. By resisting the temptation to include him in every game they can extend his career for many productive years to the benefit of all concerned.

It might seem that there is little left to motivate Tendulkar, but he has yet to complete a first-class double hundred, and while I don't attach all that much importance to this feat, it could be something that niggles at the back of his mind, spurring him on. Unquestionably he will set all sorts of records in the one-day games because he is so far ahead of anyone else, and because India and Pakistan fulfil more fixtures than other countries. There is also the captaincy of India. Some time in the future India will reappoint him and he will be better prepared the second time around. I hope his promotion does not come for a little while yet, but I am convinced that when the time is right he will do extremely well. Usually he can be seen in deep conversation with Mohammad Azharuddin, who is in his second term of office, and with extra maturity Tendulkar will be ideally suited to the job.

Perhaps by then he will have learned that it is necessary to get tough now and again, even when the hard word is foreign to your nature. A few sharp words in the right direction can work wonders, and the feeling persists that India, by tending to let things drift, fail to play to their full potential. An older, more assertive Tendulkar will not let his team treat decency as a weakness, and there is no doubt that his excellent memory will enable him to guide his bowlers effectively. All that, of course, is in the future. For now, Tendulkar's claim to eternal fame rests on the glittering batsmanship which makes him the world's number one.

# CHAPTER TWELVE

# The 1999 World Cup

E nglish cricket is desperately looking for the massive lift that success in the 1999 World Cup would give our domestic game, but history is against an England win, and I regard South Africa as the likely winners. In the aftermath of a depressing Ashes tour of Australia, England's more enthusiastic supporters have put their faith in home advantage, which, particularly in May and June, could cause problems for the visitors, but it is important to note that the host country has not emerged triumphant from any of the previous six World Cups. West Indies captured the trophy on the first two occasions at Lord's in 1975 and 1979, while India beat all the odds to snatch the crown out of Caribbean hands at the same venue in 1983. Australia's turn came at Calcutta in 1987, when the competition moved outside England for the first time, Pakistan swept the board in Melbourne five years later, and finally Sri Lanka confirmed their arrival on the scene as a major force at Lahore in 1996.

An abundance of high-class pace bowlers made the West Indies an all-conquering force under Clive Lloyd, and they were favourites to win just about every game they played, so their early World Cup achievements were fairly predictable, although Australia ran them very close in a magnificent first final, which kept a full house enthralled until just before a quarter to nine at night. That remarkable game in June produced 565 runs and a final margin of seventeen amid a great deal of excitement as Australia lost five batsmen to run-outs. Interestingly, 26,000 spectators paid a total of £66,950 for the privilege, which sounded good money in 1975.

More recently, the element of uncertainty has added to the glamour of each World Cup occasion, and this year it is reasonable to expect that English weather and English pitches will increase the problems of predicting the outcome of matches involving the leading nations. Another crucial element is the fact that matches are scheduled to start at 10.45, when the pitches will probably be fresh, giving the bowlers something to work on as the ball moves about. As a sequence of NatWest Trophy finals has shown, winning the toss can be vital in England at certain times of the year. At least in the early rounds, captains in the World Cup will be tempted to field first and wait for the pitches to dry out a bit later in the day to offer better batting conditions. The added advantage to this is that by dismissing their opponents cheaply a side can ensure against having to score quickly themselves.

The question has been raised as to why the competition is being staged so early on in the English season, and as I understand it the answer is that in August and September players from all countries except England would have been short of match practice. Virtually everybody plays during the winter, so the players are in the same state of readiness in May, giving all concerned an equal chance.

The World Cup has been expanded this year, with more teams taking part, and the eventual winners will have battled their way through ten matches, so countries may increase their squads from fourteen to fifteen, which gives them more room for manoeuvre in terms of selection. I will also be looking for new ideas; the sides which show most imagination can expect to catch their opponents by surprise. One thing which sticks in my mind from the 1992 World Cup was the way in which New Zealand used their offspinner Dipak Patel as an opening bowler with the new ball. Nobody had tried that ploy before and it upset calculations all round. New Zealand reached the semi-finals, and only a fantastic innings by Pakistan's Inzamam-ul-Haq, during which he plundered the short boundary at Auckland and scored at almost two runs per ball, halted their progress. Patel's accuracy at a gentle pace confused a lot of opening batsmen, who were accustomed to facing seamers from the start. Openers are geared up to handle speed, and they usually have a few runs under their belts by the time the spinners appear, so Patel presented an unexpected challenge which often proved unsettling.

England share with the West Indies and Australia the distinction of appearing in most finals – three. Sadly, they have found themselves cast in the role of bridesmaid each time. Having played in the 1979 final myself, I recognise that the West Indies, arguably the best one-day side ever, were simply too good for us that day. Chasing a total of 286, Mike Brearley and I put on 129 for the first wicket, but no matter how hard we tried we simply could not score quickly enough to keep up with the required rate. Four West Indian fast bowlers made it so difficult that England lost by ninety-two runs. England, however, had only themselves to blame in 1987 when Australia pipped them by seven runs in Calcutta, for they were going along nicely in pursuit of Australia's 253 for 5 when Mike Gatting missed that now infamous reverse sweep, and a collapse left them on 246 for 8 after their fifty overs. England let themselves down again in 1992 when they lost to Pakistan in Melbourne, Graham Gooch dropping Imran Khan, who went on to score 72, the decisive innings of the match. England have had their chances but failed to grasp them, and there were only occasional signs during the recent one-day triangular series in Australia that the present squad is better equipped to cope with the pressures of big matches.

England's team plans will be built around bowlers who can maintain a disciplined line, little seamers who just 'kiss' the surface of the pitch and force the batsmen to put pace on to the ball with their strokes. The attack looks a bit ordinary, but it could be all right in the conditions. England's biggest problem is the absence of a really outstanding all-rounder. The county scene is crowded with players who bat and bowl a bit, but that is not the same thing. Vince Wells, Mark Ealham, Adam Hollioake, Ian Austin and Andy Flintoff hardly amount to a formidable combination, although they are all capable of nagging away with occasional movement through the air or off the seam. I feel they might do quite well in the opening rounds, but there are serious doubts about their ability to be effective on better pitches in June, especially if the weather is dry and sunny.

Darren Gough is the key bowler without any doubt. He is capable of snatching early wickets to put the opposition under pressure and, although people think that the one-day game is all about keeping the runs down, I am convinced that the best way to succeed is to dismiss the top batsmen on the other side. The fielding side gains an advantage every time a new batsman has to play himself in. Gough can do serious damage with the new ball, and his control of the inswinging yorker is a devastating weapon in the hectic closing overs of an innings. A determined and gifted competitor who thrives on the centre stage and possesses a charisma which grabs attention and demands support from the crowd, he will be the focal point for England. By hitting form he could inspire the rest of the team, but Gough cannot do it all on his own. England need another strike bowler, another paceman who might cause major problems. Alan Mullally, who did a sound job in Australia, is likely to be Gough's new-ball partner, but he has not displayed the same ability to break through. England must regret that Chris Lewis, who has all the attributes of a match-winning all-rounder, cannot get his act together. Lewis can be quite sharp with the ball, can hit powerfully in the lower half of the order, and can save countless runs with his athleticism in the field. At times he displays all the qualities that England require, but his track record is disappointing and he rarely lives up to expectations.

Alec Stewart will shoulder a tremendous responsibility by tackling three jobs: captain, wicketkeeper and leading batsman. To me, the tour of Australia took a lot out of him, because he played in virtually every fixture. Before the England party was selected I wrote that he should not be captain if he intended to continue keeping wicket, and everything that happened during the trip confirmed that I was right. As a result of his exertions, Stewart failed to maintain his best form with the bat, playing little cameo innings without going on to dominate. Being so tired, he lost it mentally and continually got out slogging. Fortunately, he will get periods of rest before and during the World Cup, and in our cooler climate he should remain much fresher. Stewart is good enough to control an innings and steer England to a huge total. He scores quickly and instinctively, so it is not a big step for him to channel his aggression more productively.

It is important for England to lay the foundations of their innings and they have recalled Mike Atherton who has not played in a one-day international since May 1997. His selection is due to the fact that English pitches in early summer are often seamer friendly and in these circumstances it would be important to combat early movement. Keeping wickets in hand could be crucial.

Atherton is ideally equipped to go in first with either Stewart or Nick Knight, who is a cross between an orthodox batsman and a pinch-hitter. Knight mixes textbook strokes with unexpected bursts of improvisation, responding sensibly to whatever situation arises. Like Stewart, he naturally gets on with things but, also like Stewart, he really ought to guard against giving away his wicket by attempting to do too much too soon.

Given the right platform, Graeme Hick could be the player to help England seize the initiative with the bat. His Test match form is erratic and he is never going to be the massive run-maker that many thought he would be, but he seems to come alive in the limited-overs matches. Regulations prevent the faster bowlers using short deliveries to force him onto the back foot, so Hick can plant his left foot down the pitch with confidence and swing his bat through the ball. A situation in which the openers have already pushed the field back by putting together a decent partnership is ideal for Hick, who appreciates the value of working the ball into the gaps without neglecting to punish errors in length and line. On those occasions he looks a class act and, together with Graham Thorpe, he is equipped to give England a powerful engine room in the middle order. Thorpe's long-standing back trouble, which caused his premature return from Australia for treatment, is a worry for the England selectors because they know that having a good left-hander about is very valuable. Many bowlers don't like left-handers, and Thorpe is adept at nudging the ones and twos which keep the scoreboard ticking over. For that reason he is a better one-day prospect than Nasser Hussain, and he also handles wrist spinners well.

As a competent rather than athletic fielding side, England should reach the semi-finals, but only a real patriot would put money on them getting much further, and the same applies to the holders. Sri Lanka have been a breath of fresh air with their uncomplicated, entertaining approach. Since winning the World Cup, they have given the public wonderful entertainment with their uncomplicated and exuberant batting, especially the pinch-hitter *par excellence* Sanath Jayasuriya and the old campaigner Aravinda de Silva, but I suspect that in the last twelve months they have gone past their peak. Their best years are behind them and their top players are beginning to show the signs of wear and tear. The controversy over the action of their outstanding bowler, offspinner Muttiah Muralitharan, is another cause for concern for them, and they still rely on the nucleus of the team which prospered so splendidly three years ago. The selectors have failed to inject new blood into the side, and it is too late now so far as the World Cup is concerned. The chance to gradually blend the new generation with the old passed them by a little while ago. Among the emerging prospects is batsman Mahela Jayawardene, and Gamini Perera and Nuwan Zoysa are highly rated among the bowlers, but they are only just finding their feet and the World Cup is no place for players still learning their trade.

Sri Lanka's poor performances of late underline their weaknesses, although they are still a dangerous side when they click. Importantly, they are no longer feared. Following their World Cup triumph many people regarded their expressive and exciting talent with awe, but their air of invincibility has disappeared, giving way to self-doubt. Sri Lanka suffer from the fact that too many of their one-day games have been played in Asia, as they fulfilled a hectic schedule. Pitches in that part of the world, with stump-high bounce and little or no movement from the new ball, are perfect for stroke-play. Batsmen on the subcontinent find it much easier to hit through the line or go over the top, especially with the fielders close in for the first fifteen overs. These circumstances are tailor-made for Jayasuriya, whose incredible power has enabled him to despatch the bowling to every part of many grounds. When on song, he makes the field placing irrelevant. He is a very destructive player, and he and his partner, Romesh Kaluwitharana, who is very much a cutter and a slogger, pioneered the fashion for using a pinch-hitter to ensure free-scoring opening partnerships. This pair regularly creates scope for their colleagues to push the ball around, with de Silva, a superb touch player, taking full advantage.

The Sri Lankan attack is also suited to Asian conditions with a proliferation of slow bowling. Muralitharan, as a truly great offspinner, spear-heads their attack, supported by Kumara Dharmasena and the two best batsmen: Jayasuriya, with his slow left-arm, and de Silva, who bowls very tidy offspin. On dry pitches, captain Arjuna Ranatunga, enjoying the luxury of varied bowling options, has not worried too much about seam. The only quality seamer is Chaminda Vaas, who is likely to find himself ploughing a lone furrow in England, where it will not be possible to rely so heavily on spinners. With coolish weather in May, the slow bowlers can expect to struggle to grip the ball, but the seamers will get appreciable movement, so, as he tries to compensate for an obvious weakness, Ranatunga's acknowledged leadership skills face a tremendous test. He will not find it easy to keep control of things in the field, and because of this Sri Lanka are likely to lose out.

None of the doubts that trouble England and Sri Lanka apply to the favourites, South Africa, who are on a winning streak with their confidence justifiably sky high. Successful in ten out of fifteen one-day competitions since just before the last World Cup in 1996, their battle-hardened squad responds magnificently to pressure under a tough, resourceful captain in Hansie Cronje. Their ranks are packed with top-class all-rounders and they can make runs all the way down the order, with agile wicketkeeper Mark Boucher and pugnacious spinner Pat Symcox possibly as low as eight and nine. One certainty is that South Africa are the best fielding side in the world, and they will have an edge in that sense over all their rivals.

A superb team spirit flourishes under Cronje, who is a splendid captain. He handles all aspects of his job with a calm efficiency, keeping a firm grip on matters behind the scenes while dealing with the media politely and thoughtfully. He does not allow defeat to get to him, and is always quick to praise the opposition without in any way diminishing his own players. He keeps the balance exactly right and hardly misses a trick. Cronje sets the tone throughout, maintaining an impressive fitness, and underneath his pleasant exterior he knows what he wants and makes sure that he gets it. He listens to advice from his team-mates and coach Bob Woolmer, but he runs things his own way and makes the cricket decisions. Cronje is also a better batsman than he looks. Perhaps he does not always get behind the line of the ball, staying a shade on the leg side, but this is not a handicap in one-day cricket, and he can crucify spinners, employing the sweep slog to devastating effect. He and Jonty Rhodes in the middle of the order, batting at four and five, have the ability and cricket know-how to assess each situation and do whatever is necessary. Following the loss of early wickets they can minimise the risks and score sensibly or, given the benefit of runs on the board, they can increase the tempo.

Rhodes is an excellent placer of the ball and can run any fielding side ragged by taking a stream of singles. Jonty, of course, is in the spotlight whenever South Africa are in the field, for he is unique – a genuine jack-in-the-box. I have never seen any player who dives so much and gets up so quickly; he reminds me of the 'Kelly men' I used to have as a child, models with a weight in the base which sprang back immediately no matter how often you knocked them over. Rhodes operates just backward of point, where the ball comes at the most awkward heights and at different paces. The bounce is unpredictable in that position because some balls fly off the edge and some are deliberately steered in that direction, but he is usually equal to the task. At one time he did not hit the stumps with his throws very often, but he has worked on that, and now only the very foolish take the slightest chance when he is around. Rhodes's greatest strength is his obvious enjoyment of the game, for he is always smiling, and there is no doubt that he consistently sets the standards for the rest of the South African team, all of whom throw themselves around brilliantly. Opener Herschelle Gibbs is another superb athlete in the field, and a lot more will be heard of Dale Benkenstein. In fact, while other sides rely on posting one or two good fielders in important positions, South Africa don't really carry a passenger. There isn't room for one. Even Symcox, the slowest mover at the age of thirty-nine, possesses a great arm which stands him in good stead in the outfield.

And if they aren't enough attributes to have as a team, in terms of wicket-taking no bowler in the tournament is more dangerous than Allan Donald, one of the all-time greats. He does not hold back to concentrate on length and line, but rather gives it all he has got – and he is extremely fast. Cronje cleverly uses Donald as first change, partly to allow his most explosive strike force more control once the shine has worn off the ball. This is also a good tactic, because the opposition openers know they are not going to get much respite for long as they try to establish their side's innings. As they go about their demanding business they are aware that Donald is waiting in the wings, and his lurking presence preys on their minds.

In support are Shaun Pollock and Lance Klusener, two totally different all-rounders. Pollock operates at a lively pace so close to the stumps that he occasionally knocks off the bails at the non-striker's end in his follow-through. He is very straight and accurate, giving little away. His record reflects impressive economy, but he is capable of picking up wickets as well. I don't think he really appreciates just how good he can become. Pollock also strikes the ball impressively and has demonstrated his ability to put together a proper innings. Klusener, an aggressive cricketer, is quicker than Pollock, deceiving batsmen for pace as he skids through. Less accurate than Pollock, he is more likely to run through the opposition from wide of the crease. Again in contrast to Pollock, he is more of a big hitter. A powerful left-hander deploying a heavy bat, Klusener is used in a variety of roles, sometimes going in as high as number three, which underlines the point that he is not a slogger. His power is invariably harnessed in the right way.

Additionally, Jacques Kallis, the best batsman in the side, is improving all the time as a seamer. No one plays straighter than Kallis, whom I recommended to Yorkshire two years ago. Although very orthodox, he increasingly sweeps the spinners efficiently. Kallis is a likely opening bowler and, at six foot two inches and with broad shoulders, he too is much nippier than people think. Pushing the ball through, he also swings it away from the right-hander, and he could well be one of the top performers in the World Cup because he thrives on responsibility. On English pitches, Cronje might be very effective with his little seamers, too. He cuts the ball around with a good change of pace and he swings it enough to make himself another realistic bowling option.

Strength in depth all round is South Africa's trump card, particularly with those not regularly in the first eleven pushing hard for recognition, and they have enough variety to handle whatever comes their way. They will be more fiercely committed than any squad following all those years when South Africa were banned from international competition. The present players realise how lucky they are to be able to parade their skills on the world stage, and their aim is to give a perfect performance every time. The next World Cup, in 2003, is in South Africa, which gives Cronje and his men another incentive – if they needed one!

Australia, of course, stand out as the main challengers to South Africa in my book, because their selectors have done such a good job. The Australian administrators were the first men to be brave enough and sufficiently far-sighted to nominate two captains – one for Tests and another for one-day internationals – despite taking quite a bit of criticism from those who argued that the national team should have only one captain, the more so as Mark Taylor was leading the Test team so skilfully. The selectors refused to be deflected from their purpose, however. They acknowledged that Taylor was a brilliant catcher at first slip and a good, solid opening batsman, but pointed out that these rightly valued Test match qualities did not rank all that highly on the limited-overs scene. The other contentious decision involved the dropping of Ian Healy, a wicketkeeper with a marvellous record in Test cricket. At first glance this looked foolish, as Healy dealt with the prodigious variations of Shane Warne so well, having developed a close understanding with the bowler over the years. Healy had served Australia faithfully as a batsman too, making crucial runs to ease them out of tight corners on many occasions. Despite all this, the selectors took the view that, much as they admired Taylor and Healy, Steve Waugh was a better bet as one-day captain and Adam Gilchrist had exactly the credentials they wanted from an opener-wicketkeeper.

Gilchrist, virtually unknown outside his own country, had to overcome some initial hostility, for Healy is a national hero in Australia and the public did not take kindly to the change. It took nerve for the selectors to stick to their guns, but they remained steadfast and let results prove their point. Gilchrist turned out to be an inspired choice. He is a strong left-hander prepared to go for his shots from the start, ready to take chances in order to dominate the bowling. Despite his bold approach, he is also capable of compiling big centuries, his overall attitude marking him down as an ideal World Cup competitor. Mark Waugh complements him splendidly, relying more on his skills as a touch player after being promoted from number four to play his natural game as an opener. When things go well for Australia, Waugh provides the backbone of the innings, holding it all together by working the ball either side of the pitch and staying in for a long time. He is able to rotate the strike by using his 'soft' hands to drop the ball short of the fielders and pick up singles, and this opening partnership is probably as good as any in the World Cup. Regularly, Gilchrist and Waugh give Australia a good head of steam, and if either gets near to batting through the innings there are always a lot of runs on the board.

Two of Yorkshire's prolific overseas recruits, Darren Lehmann and Michael Bevan, are also important figures for Australia. Lehmann was very annoyed when overlooked for the 1999 trip to the West Indies, and his disappointment could well prove the fuel for some impressive World Cup performances. Lehmann rarely looks to be scoring quickly, but he misses few chances and advances with a neat efficiency. By opening the face of the bat he gives himself a lot of angles for cutting and late cutting, and improvisation is the cornerstone of his game. He eagerly plunders anything even fractionally wide of the off stump, and when bowlers straighten up to deny him room he produces a characteristic stroke involving a lot of bottom hand which literally shovels the ball over mid-wicket. Lehmann has also perfected a controlled slog on the leg side and sweeps effectively against the spinners, even from outside the off stump. His temperament is rock-solid – nothing appears to worry him – and I think he is a very fine player at number four.

Bevan, batting at six, has a special talent for organising the tail-enders towards the end of an innings when the side which stays calm can win a match. To make the most of this ability, Australia keep him permanently at six, no matter who else is in the team. The normal routine of the one-day game means that Bevan is usually called upon to raise the run rate, and he can do this without throwing caution to the wind by attempting to hit too many boundaries. He puts away the bad balls, but he also prods the good ones into the gaps, and there is no faster man between the wickets in the world. Bevan gets from one end to the other in a flash, turning many easy singles into hard-run twos. His personal rate is around a run per ball, although he never appears to be straining or hitting with all his power. For Bevan it is more a matter of timing and placement. He regularly finishes not out to make sure that Australia use up the full allocation of overs, and in this way his batting serves an important purpose.

With Steve Waugh consistently piling up the runs in his own solid way, Australia can claim to be the most accomplished batting side in the world, and this undoubted strength is supplemented by two of the world's top three wicket-taking bowlers in Glenn McGrath and Shane Warne. Imran Khan stressed the value of getting out batsmen whenever possible to prevent a side building partnerships, and this pair is deadly. No side will find it easy to play them. As recently as February 1999 McGrath and Warne demonstrated against England in the first final of the Carlton and United one-day series in Australia that they are capable of turning a match on its head. England were apparently strolling towards victory before the dynamic duo combined to bring about a collapse. McGrath is extremely accurate for a bowler of his pace, keeping the ball around the line of the off stump, and he experiences no trouble when going around the wicket to the left-hander, invariably dropping right on the spot immediately. Some bowlers who go around the wicket because they know it is a good ploy take time to adjust and thus lose a lot of the advantage. Not McGrath, who can also bowl well at the death. It is a huge bonus for Australia to include a bowler like McGrath, who is effective no matter how his captain employs him.

Warne, as England know to their cost, spins the ball immensely and adds great variety and control, so he is difficult to get after. He rarely offers a bad ball, and very few batsmen 'read' him with confidence. Even those that do are not sure just how much the ball is going to turn because he varies the amount of spin he imparts, causing some deliveries to turn a little and some to turn viciously. Shrewdly, Warne exploits the nagging fear in most batsmen's minds by playing up to his image in interviews. A great manipulator on the psychological side of match play, he talks expansively about deliveries which exist only in his own mind, claiming that he can do all manner of wonderful things which logically are beyond even his range. But he is justifiably a legend in his own lifetime.

As is the case with South Africa, Australia have deep reserves of strength, as they proved against England, and those in favour at any one time are well aware that the selectors do not hesitate to drop players who fall even marginally below the desired standards. Despite a cascade of runs, Greg Blewett cannot get into the limited-overs line-up, and Lehmann's exclusion from the touring party to the West Indies was all the illustration you could possibly need of the ruthless nature of Aussie cricket. While players who fail for England retain their places, their Australian counterparts are on trial in every game. They must perform well or accept the consequences, which is why Australia will fight like tigers throughout the World Cup and why even South Africa will worry about them.

The qualities which South Africa and Australia bring to the international arena are comparatively easy to assess, but Pakistan represent the great unknown quantity. They have the ability to be brilliant, but they match this with an unequalled capacity for self-destruction. In many ways they are ruled by the moon. A match for anyone on their day, they can so quickly disintegrate into a rabble. The Pakistanis are perpetually vulnerable to internal squabbling, and what is not clear is how much the publicity and rumours surrounding the infamous match-fixing allegations have affected them. Some of the players were called as witnesses to the court of inquiry and some were accused by their colleagues of being involved in betting. Such a troubled background does not exactly augur well for good team spirit, and the judge at the latest court of inquiry made it crystal clear that he thought some players were lying. A number of leading Pakistani cricketers were obviously anxious about the possible outcome of the judicial hearing and could not give sufficient attention to their matches with Australia. We are still awaiting the official findings, but Pakistan continue to operate under a cloud of suspicion.

But there have always been factions in Pakistani cricket, notably the Lahore and Karachi cliques. Little groups from various centres pull for each other, so life in the dressing room can become difficult if one member of a favoured few is omitted. For example, when Wasim Akram lost his position as Pakistan captain, his best friend, Waqar Younis, had led the delegation to the board which brought about his demise.

Nothing is straightforward in Pakistan, and when a player is dropped he usually rushes into print in the newspapers to tell tales of either real or imagined misdeeds. Often a local politician is dragged into the argument, and interference with the selection process is rife. Everything becomes so personal, and a lack of trust and collective confidence is going to undermine the Pakistani cause in the World Cup.

From the outside it is impossible to assess accurately what is going on in Pakistan at the moment, but the key to their prospects lies in leadership. Imran Khan carried a natural authority which enabled him to pull together all the strings, and under his benevolent dictatorship Pakistan became a major power. A great all-round cricketer and a strong man in every sense, he knocked a few heads together and made it clear that anyone who crossed him would not play again. He ruled with a rod of iron, but he also continually told the players how good they were, employing the stick and the carrot in equal measure. When Imran moved on to other things, Pakistan had no one to replace him, so he left a power vacuum. Currently coach Javed Miandad is cast in an important role. Wasim could do a good job as captain with the right support, but the leadership has changed hands too often for comfort. The impression is that the selectors shuffle the names like a pack of cards and pick out one at random. It is a ridiculous system, for Pakistan cannot hope to get a united team when no one is sure from one year to the next who is going to be in charge. Pakistani players can be very headstrong and each one wants to do his own thing, so it is difficult to instil collective discipline.

Imran enjoyed the advantage of knowing that his position was unassailable, but Wasim is not so fortunate and he cannot be guaranteed unqualified backing from the top. Nor is Wasim so forceful a personality as Imran, so he will be looking to Javed for some assistance. How much help is forthcoming remains to be seen, for the relationship between the two is not special. To complicate the plot, many people feel that Javed instigated the coup in which Waqar and other players got rid of Wasim as captain. There is also a school of thought that Javed is angling to return as a player. He is the only cricketer to have taken part in all six previous World Cups and he has been hinting at the possibility of a comeback if Pakistan don't improve. There is no doubt that Javed was a fine batsman, but he spends too much time criticising the current crop of batsmen and does not offer enough encouragement.

In the World Cup, the major question mark hangs over the batting, for Pakistan have some excellent bowlers in Wasim, Waqar, offspinner Saqlain Mushtaq and legspinner Mushtaq Ahmed. Saqlain is one of the best slow bowlers about, while Mushtaq, despite a tendency to be expensive, gets people out. Waqar and Wasim require no introduction in England and are very much at home in our conditions, while Azhar Mahmood is a good batsman and a useful medium pacer. Among the batsmen, Shahid Afridi stands out as one of the most explosive strikers of the ball I have seen. He might struggle a bit in England, where the ball does not come on to the bat, but he might also put one or two bowlers to the sword. Opener Saeed Anwar's style is very reminiscent of David Gower, and he is an effortless timer of the ball, although his form has become a bit patchy. Looks can deceive so far as Ijaz Ahmed is concerned, for he shuffles around in the crease a lot before getting established and, as he stays back, he is a prime candidate for lbw, but if he gets in he is a dynamic stroke-player. Inzamam has his critics, who claim he is lazy and overweight – and there might well be some truth in these accusations – but he is a truly gifted batsman with an extensive repertoire of shots. And as he demonstrated in the recent series against India, when Pakistan's batting looked brittle, Moin Khan, the wicketkeeper, is a gritty fighter, and I expect him to show up well.

Like a slow-burning firework, Pakistan might splutter into brief, dazzling life at any moment, but the West Indies appear to be burned out. Muddled thinking has created total confusion in their ranks, with fierce arguments raging about the captaincy and the composition of their squad. With trouble off the field and on it, nothing in the last year has suggested that they will be much of a threat this summer. Following the humiliation of a 5–0 Test whitewash – the first in their history – and a

6–1 thrashing in the one-day internationals in South Africa, confidence and team spirit are at an all-time low in their camp and it will be a miracle if they pull themselves together sufficiently to make a decent show. Defeat quickly becomes a bad habit, and the selectors, confusing themselves with all their chopping and changing, have no idea about the composition of their best one-day squad. If it all comes together for the World Cup it will be a miracle.

Their biggest problem centres on the inter-island rivalry which permeates the entire hierarchy. West Indies cannot hope to turn the tide without a more thoughtful selection policy in which manager Clive Lloyd and coach Malcolm Marshall should be involved. Equally, those in charge must demand greater dedication. Some players are simply not fit enough to play international cricket and many are merely going through the motions, untroubled by a general lack of discipline. In the great days of West Indian cricket, Lloyd enjoyed unchallenged authority in the dressing room and demanded a high level of professionalism. I think that he should once more be given overall power, with Marshall as his second in command. Players who cannot or will not accept discipline should be sent home, no matter how high their standing. I firmly believe that the captain should run the cricket side of things, but these are very trying times for the West Indies and events in South Africa emphasise that the time has come for drastic measures. The embarrassing results sparked a lot of public disquiet in the Caribbean and the West Indian supporters deserve better.

There are three basic elements to cricket – batting, bowling and fielding – and the West Indies are struggling in all departments. The present players seem to be ready to give up at the first sign of difficulty, and that is not good enough. From what I saw in South Africa the fielding is careless, but this is something that is very easy to improve by hard work. There is no excuse for players juggling the ball on the floor or going to make a stop one-handed. Opportunities for run-outs crop up often in one-day cricket and it is important to keep up the pressure on the batting side, yet time and again in South Africa West Indian bowlers went to take returns from fielders in front of the stumps. That is an elementary mistake for which schoolboys would be scolded; precious moments are wasted in the act of turning to break the wicket. Worse still, the bowler occasionally dislodged a bail or a stump with part of his body before the ball arrived. The only fielders displaying the necessary athleticism in South Africa were Keith Arthurton and Shivnarine Chanderpaul, so that is one aspect of the Caribbean operation to which special attention should be paid.

The bowling is another. I have seen enough to know that it is not all that bad – given some reasonable organisation. Like Sri Lanka, in the past year or so the West Indies have missed chances to inject some youth and enthusiasm into their team; consequently they have a lot of ground to make up. Franklyn Rose, the Jamaican fast-medium seamer, has hardly played since Brian Lara took over the captaincy, although he did get injured towards the end of the South African tour. He should be in the side all the time. He cuts the ball around and swings it a little at a reasonable pace, so he is ideal for the end the faster men don't want. Mervyn Dillon, from Trinidad, is a young, strong lad with a bit of extra pace. In the ICC one-day tournament in Bangladesh in October he picked up the Man of the Match award in the final, yet the West Indies sent him home from South Africa before the limited-overs series got under way. This was a ridiculous decision because Dillon is definitely the sort of bowler the West Indies ought to be encouraging. Nixon McLean is another in the same category, and he should be persuaded to bend his back and try to bowl quicker. He has the potential to be very fast and he makes some deliveries nip back sharply. Learning to move the ball away is the next step, but McLean could become more than just useful. The West Indies cannot continue to rely on Curtly Ambrose, who is almost at the end of his career, and it is crucial for them to transform their pace potential into an effective unit, because their slow bowling looks thin.

Carl Hooper has improved as an offspinner and, operating around the wicket, he raises some doubts in the minds of batsmen who are not sure how much he is turning the ball. Hooper is the nearest West Indies have to an all-rounder, for he is a very accomplished one-day batsman, able to play off the front or back foot with ease. His timing is so instinctive that he makes batting look both graceful and easy, and it is a mystery why he has not carved out a much better record in Tests. Unfortunately, he is so inconsistent that he cannot be relied upon to make a big impact regularly, and he was among the disappointments in South Africa, where the batting was pathetic. Again, bizarre decisions made matters worse. West Indies sent home Stuart Williams, who failed in the Tests as an opener, yet the chancy approach which brought his downfall would have been perfect in the limited-overs series. Williams has a good one-day record and times the ball well, but his weakness is that, being too flashy, he edges the ball too often. In a Test match he tends to get caught at slip, but in the limited-overs games an edge regularly flies for four. Definitely, Williams is a much better bet than Philo Wallace, who endured a terrible time in South Africa. Williams and Chanderpaul could form an effective opening partnership. Chanderpaul has steadily improved his technique, particularly on the offside, and is a determined competitor, although he might just be found wanting against the new ball in English conditions.

No one has yet had the courage to write off Lara, even though his best days appear to be firmly set in the past. The cricket world keeps watching, waiting and hoping for a glimpse of the Lara of old, but nothing happens. Despite a few fleeting hints of something more substantial, Lara manages nothing more than brief, rather frantic innings which contain some fine strokes but nothing of his greatness. Without Lara at his best, I suspect the West Indies will always be short of runs and will find themselves struggling among the also-rans.

India, on the other hand, expect to score heavily, with Sachin Tendulkar leading the way. The doubts surrounding their prospects concern the fact that they invariably play their best cricket at home and do not travel well. Although that World Cup triumph in 1983 is a reminder that they can deliver the goods in English conditions, their game is more suited to the pitches of low bounce which abound in the subcontinent and on which spinners prosper. Back in 1983, India were driven on by the all-round efforts of Kapil Dev, by a considerable distance their highest Test wicket-taker with 434, to which he added 5,248 runs. With Kapil Dev at the height of his powers in their ranks, India might well be favourites this time, but he retired in 1993.

Much is now expected of legspinner Anil Kumble following his ten-wicket haul in Pakistan's second innings of the Delhi Test in February 1999. He thrives on turning pitches and will not find much assistance over here in May, but he took 105 first-class wickets for Northamptonshire in 1995 to underline his ability to adapt. Usually Kumble looks to attack, but he will have to curb his instincts at least in the opening stages of the World Cup if the weather is cool and the atmosphere damp. His flatter, quicker pace will allow him to skid the ball through a bit, but in his case patience is likely to be a virtue. Kumble's best plan should be to frustrate batsmen into errors.

Javagal Srinath is the major Indian strike bowler. As a tall man, Srinath achieves useful bounce which is allied to well-directed aggression, and he hits the pitch hard. As a result, he occasionally drops a yard too short in England, despite his experience with Gloucestershire. This tendency means that he can be expensive at the death; a fuller length would serve him well in the World Cup. Undoubtedly, though, he is at the heart of India's bowling plans and a lot depends on him. Venkatesh Prasad, his new-ball partner, will be encouraged by memories of some splendid performances on the India tour of England in 1996. He pitches the ball well up, bowls outswing and nip-backers, and uses his exceptionally big fingers to produce both leg and off cutters. India left him out for a year when he lost confidence, but Prasad is back in the side now and bowling really well. The other important factor is that India are still searching for an international-class third seamer. Unless they conjure one out of thin air, their three leading bowlers face a long, hard grind, because the support spinners are likely to be very expensive. Orthodox spinners can get away with tossing the ball up in India, but the same tactics will not be successful over here.

A lot of India's one-day victories have been based on a good start with the bat under the guidance of Tendulkar or Saurav Ganguly. All eyes will be on Tendulkar, who carries the hopes of a nation on his back in circumstances which make talk of pressure in English cricket meaningless. Over nine hundred million Indians will be hanging on his every innings! Every time he gets into his stride, Tendulkar will make runs because the bowlers will find it impossible to tie him down and his colleagues will guarantee him most of the strike. If he stretches his innings across a lot of overs, India will finish with the sort of massive total that even a moderate attack will be able to defend. Ganguly, the left-hander who bats at six in Tests, has become a great opening partner for Tendulkar and, as a punishing offside player, he can contribute significantly. He is not afraid to hit the ball in the air and his legside play is improving steadily. I christened him the Prince of Calcutta because he is such a stylish batsman, and the nickname stuck, much to his delight. His little seamers cannot be discounted either. He is one of those niggling little bowlers with the knack of picking up a wicket here and there.

Of the other batsmen, Ajay Jadeja, the best fielder in the side, does a similar job to Bevan for Australia, adapting his innings to suit the circumstances in which he finds himself. He is adept at manoeuvring things to keep the bowling and can also attack briskly. Mohammad Azharuddin has nothing to learn as either captain or batsman. He has been everywhere and done everything, experiencing all the ups and downs of professional sport along the way. Nothing is new to him and he just goes on in his own calm and efficient way, getting the best out of his team. A very wristy batsman, he can score quickly by orthodox means, deflecting the ball with untroubled elegance. It does not seem to worry him whether he is captain or not, because there is no political intrigue in the Indian dressing room.

Instead, a genuine bond among the players has led to complete harmony. Jadeja, as vice-captain, and Tendulkar willingly contribute from a tactical point of view, directing their energies towards improving the side's prospects. In fact, Tendulkar can be seen regularly in discussion with Azharuddin on the field, the outcome often being a few overs from Sachin, who bowls what I describe as liquorice allsorts – a variety of little 'dart' balls, turning his lack of height to his own advantage. He can produce a little in- or outswing, occasionally dropping in a leg-break or offspinner, and his bowling, which has no pace, is difficult to force. Tendulkar gets his wickets by out-thinking batsmen rather than by dint of any great bowling skill. His very presence, coupled with a quiet self-assurance, enables him almost to hypnotise the opposition, and he responds to pressure by using his astute cricket brain. India are one side who prefer to bat first, but either way I suspect that their lack of strength in depth will count against them.

New Zealand have produced few truly great cricketers and their weakness remains this shortage of exceptional talent, but they combine effectively as a unit and can invariably be relied upon to make the most of what they do possess. They demonstrated during their recent visit to South Africa that they are capable of upsetting the odds, but their limitations are likely to prevent them getting past the quarter-finals. They will be more accustomed to English conditions than any of the other visiting teams, because of the climatic similarities between their two islands and this country. They are used to all the weather variations, from cold and damp days to hot and sunny ones, and they, too, play on pitches freshened by rain as well as strips that are slow and low. They will feel comfortable about whatever is offered up to them in the World Cup.

Their best batsman is Stephen Fleming, the captain, a tall left-hander with a preference for the front foot who bats at number three. This means that he usually has the chance to play a long innings in most matches, and New Zealand often build around him. Another sturdy competitor is Nathan Astle, whose power belies his smallish frame. He is very strong and, in full flow, can be hard to stop because he gets on with things by taking the attack to the bowlers. Probably New Zealand's best-known cricketer is Chris Cairns, a sound all-rounder, who has been troubled by a series of injuries, the most recent of which has kept him inactive in the lead-up to the World Cup. Because of these problems

Cairns has dropped his pace to a brisk medium, but he is a tall man with a high action who can make the ball bounce sharply. A robust batsman with experience on the championship circuit with Nottinghamshire, Cairns is the vital member of the middle order. As a solid striker he occasionally takes an attack apart, and he can be particularly severe on spinners, so it will be up to him to boost the New Zealand run rate in the majority of their matches. Chris Harris, the best fielder among the Kiwis, is the typical bits-and-pieces cricketer who flourishes in the one-day game. A decent left-hander who does not panic when things get difficult, he bowls a mixture of gentle seamers which are a shade more demanding than they appear from the boundary edge. Gavin Larsen will also be important to the New Zealanders. He has been around for a long time and his experience should stand him and his team in good stead. Nothing in his bowling catches the eye, but he nags away and frustrates batsmen, particularly if there is anything in the pitch to help him.

Zimbabwe are still on the fringe of the 'big league', but they did achieve a staggering triumph over England in the 1992 World Cup in Australia and whitewashed them 3–0 in the limited-overs series in their own country during the winter of 1996–97. They are a joy to watch with their uninhibited style, but a distinct shortage of quality players leaves their selectors with few choices. This is not necessarily a short-term handicap, for the team has stayed much the same for the past three years, developing a good spirit. Importantly, virtually everyone does a bit of everything in the Zimbabwean side. All the players get totally involved in everything, a little like the old days in the school playground, where every boy wanted to bat or bowl all the time. Their captain, Alistair Campbell, will not be short of options, and while none of his players is out of the top drawer, each and every one is an enthusiastic cricketer.

Heath Streak and Eddo Brandes, the opening bowlers, are among the better-known personalities. Even at thirty-six, Brandes can be a handful. His 4 for 21 wrecked England on that famous 1992 occasion, while he picked up 5 for 28, including a hat-trick, at Harare in January 1997. (To underline the value of Brandes's effort, his victims were Nick Knight,

Alec Stewart, John Crawley, Nasser Hussain and Mike Atherton – the first five in the England order.) Operating at a brisk pace, he hits the deck hard, making the ball go away from the bat off the seam and through the air. Streak compensates for a lack of real pace with good control, and his association with Hampshire will stand him in good stead. Zimbabwean cricket owes a lot to the Flower brothers, the better of whom is wicketkeeper Andy. A well-organised left-handed batsman, Andy held the captaincy for a spell, but he found the three jobs too demanding and stood down from the leadership to concentrate on his batting and wicketkeeping. Zimbabwe will also rely heavily on wrist spinner Paul Strang, who had a season with Kent in 1997 and Nottinghamshire in 1998 as an all-rounder. Without being really penetrative, he has enough variation to be testing, and I expect him to make his presence felt with both bat and ball.

The three 'minnows' – Kenya, Bangladesh and Scotland – might easily be steamrollered, but for them the World Cup is part of the learning curve and, while seeking ways to improve, they should concentrate on enjoying themselves. A number of games might be tight for a while, as has been the case in our domestic knockout competitions, but generally the top sides will pull themselves together and find an extra gear. However, this should not stop Kenya, Bangladesh and Scotland adopting a positive attitude and looking for the plusses throughout their brief moments of glory on the world stage – and there is always the possibility of an upset, as Kenya proved against the West Indies in the last World Cup. It should be a stirring tournament.

# INDEX